Finance and Development in Thailand

**PRAEGER SPECIAL STUDIES IN
INTERNATIONAL ECONOMICS AND DEVELOPMENT**

Finance and Development in Thailand

Alek A. Rozental

PRAEGER PUBLISHERS
New York • Washington • London

The purpose of Praeger Special Studies is to make specialized research in U.S. and international economics and politics available to the academic, business, and government communities. For further information, write to the Special Projects Division, Praeger Publishers, Inc., 111 Fourth Avenue, New York, N.Y. 10003.

PRAEGER PUBLISHERS
111 Fourth Avenue, New York, N.Y. 10003, U.S.A.
5, Cromwell Place, London S.W.7, England

Published in the United States of America in 1970
by Praeger Publishers, Inc.

Library of Congress Catalog Card Number: 72-108755

Printed in the United States of America

For Gail and Lynn
who need not read beyond this page

PREFACE

This book is based on field research conducted under the auspices of the National Planning Association (NPA) under contract to the Agency for International Development. The research extended from 1965 through 1967 and a "Draft of Final Report on Finance and Development in Thailand" was submitted to AID in 1968. The draft was revised and updated for this publication but the bulk of the material in the text refers to the period ending December 1967.

The purpose of the study was threefold. In the first place an attempt was made to contribute to the theory of economic growth. In spite of the work of Gurley, Shaw, Patrick, and others, the role of financial intermediaries in the growth process has never been made quite explicit. In particular, the relevant literature has little to say on the ways and means of structuring financial institutions and instruments in order to speed up the rate of growth of real output over time. Yet, as recent empirical work of Adelman and Morris has demonstrated, improvement in the performance of financial markets is perhaps the single most important variable in accounting for differential performance among developing countries.

Secondly, the study was to provide the students of South East Asia in general, and of Thailand in particular, with a comprehensive description and analysis of the financial markets in a open, dualistic economy of which Thailand is a prime example. The book contains material not ordinarily available in published form and, in addition, presents data hitherto not available at all. While the information on life insurance or provident funds may have its applicability limited to Thailand, that on the structure of unorganized financial markets in urban areas should be of broader interest.

Last, but not least, the study endeavors to provide the development planner in the field with specific and pragmatic suggestions for the improvement of the performance of financial intermediaries in Thailand. Some of these suggested reforms and modifications have begun to be implemented since the first draft of this study was made available to the Thai planning authorities.

Grateful acknowledgments are due to my former associates at the Center for Development Planning of the NPA for many valuable comments and to the officials of the United States Operations Mission to Thailand for their logistic support. Above all, however, this book owes its existence to the Thais, official and private, whose cooperation, insights, and knowledge were of the very essence for the success of this study. These Thais are too numerous to list individually, but two names must be mentioned. Dr. Puey Ungphakorn, in the dual capacity as Governor of the Bank of Thailand and Dean of the Faculty of Economics at Thammasat University, was the one individual whose cooperation was the sine qua non of the entire enterprise. Thammasat University provided physical and research facilities and the even more precious atmosphere of scholarly inquiry. The Bank of Thailand lent its prestige, funds, and skills to many aspects of the research effort. Dame Suparb Yossundara, assistant to the Governor of the Bank, not only made sure that Dr. Puey's wishes and instructions were carried out promptly and efficiently, but provided wise counsel herself.

I wish to thank all these persons for their contributions to this study. They are responsible for much of its content, except for the errors which remain my responsibility alone.

CONTENTS

ix

LIST OF TABLES

xviii

LIST OF FIGURES

Finance and Development in Thailand

CHAPTER **1** FINANCIAL MARKETS AND
DEVELOPMENT PLANNING--
A CONCEPTUAL FRAMEWORK

The significance of financial markets (that is,
the complex of institutions and instruments which
bring together lenders and borrowers) to a country's
economic development derives from three widely held
beliefs. In the first place, it is believed that
these markets can play an important role in mobilizing voluntary saving and directing these savings into
development outlets. In the second place, it is
frequently asserted that such a role is not played
to the full in the less developed countries or else
is discharged ineffectively. Finally, it is contended that in a country such as Thailand, with its
export-oriented, largely agricultural economy, there
exist distortions in the structure of financial markets which impede progress toward industrialization
and diversification--the economic course the country
has apparently set for itself.

In this chapter these beliefs and assertions will
be examined, although not all of them will be fully
studied, since certain of the issues raised can best
be examined in the light of empirical findings re-
served for later chapters. More particularly, this
chapter will focus its discussion on the nature of
the connection between financial markets and development planning and will endeavor, in the light of this
discussion, to develop an outline of a conceptual
framework for development planning strategy, in the
area of finance, designed to facilitate and to speed
up the rate of economic growth.

3

RELEVANCE OF FINANCIAL MARKETS

It would seem rather obvious that there is some relationship between a country's financial structure and its stage of economic growth. Any definition, whether formal or operational, of a stage in the development of a country's economy includes some mention of the money and capital markets and of financial institutions. In general, more complex and, hence, more "developed" financial markets are associated with "higher" stages of growth. But such an association is by no means either clear or unambiguous. It begs the rigorous definition of both financial structures and stages of economic growth which is capable of furnishing even a weak ordering relation.

At its extremes such an ordering does not present much difficulty. Very poor countries will usually have very simple financial structures, however measured. Very rich countries will show a converse relation. For example, one of the simplest ways of measuring the complexity (or the degree of development) of a financial structure is to look at the proportion of demand deposits to the gross national product (GNP). While this index pertains only to the spread of the "commercial banking habit" in a country, commercial banks have been found, historically, to be the precursors of all other institutions operating in the money and capital markets.[1] This index will be low for countries with low per capita incomes and high for the rich and hence presumably more developed countries. But for a number of countries this index will give surprising results. Even a cursory scrutiny of these deviations from the expected trend will suggest that the relationship is strongly affected by the political organization in a country. To cite one example: the Soviet Union may have a lower index than India not because the former country is less developed, but because it chooses to limit severely the role of demand deposits in its economy.[2]

Similar irregularities will appear no matter how sophisticated the indices of financial structures are being devised. Indeed, such a sophisticated index has recently been developed by Raymond Goldsmith, and

its value is severely affected by circumstances having little to do with the stage of economic growth
as commonly understood.[3]

Even if there were an observable correlation between, for example, the ratio of financial assets to
GNP and per capita income, it is still not clear
whether the accumulation of these assets is merely a
reflection of higher levels of income or whether the
process of asset accumulation, by itself, in some yet
to be explained fashion, has helped to bring about
these higher per capita incomes.

For example, in most of the "mixed" economies en-
joying high levels of income and consumption, a large
proportion of the population hold claims on financial
intermediaries, saving and loan accounts, pension
funds, and shares in mutual investment companies.[4]
In what way did these holdings act as catalysts in
the development process and in what fashion did the
acquisition of these claims help to raise the level
of per capita income?

The question is a crucial one. If, indeed, financial structure is simply a fortuitous reflection
of a level of economic development already reached by
a country, then the study of this structure, while of
academic interest, is of little value to those concerned with developmental planning. If, however, it
is true that financial institutions and instruments
can serve as catalysts, if not outright determinants,
of economic growth, then such a study acquires operational significance. This is so because if one un-
derstands the ways and means by which a financial
structure accelerates or impedes economic growth, one
can, in principle, devise a structure which enhances
the acceleration of growth while minimizing the impediments.[5]

Statistical evidence which bears on the issue,
while not conclusive, is highly suggestive. Two empirical studies are particularly relevant.

The first of these studies analyzes the results
of savings surveys in a number of countries of the
Economic Commission for Asia and the Far East (ECAFE)

conducted in the second half of the 1950's. This
study shows a clear relationship between the percentage of household saving to personal disposable income
and the ratio of saving in financial assets to tangible assets.[6] (See Figure 1.1.)

    Even more suggestive is a recent study by Irma
Adelman and Cynthia Taft Morris which attempts to
provide a set of objective criteria to determine a
country's development potential, and, by implication,
to indicate the kind of indicators which are associated with rapid economic growth.[7] Seventy-three developing countries were divided into three categories,
based on past performance, of high, moderate, and low
growth countries. Using the technique of discriminant
analysis, twenty nine complex indicators were used to
determine the factors (groups of indicators) which
best explain the differences between these groups of
countries. It was found that a single discriminant
function of only four variables accounted for 97 per
cent of the discriminable variance between groups.
Of these four variables, the degree of improvement in
financial institutions was the most important.[8] One
possible implication of the study is that an improvement in the performance of financial institutions
would have the effect of placing a given country in
a higher growth category (see Chapter 9 for further
development of this point).

FINANCIAL MARKETS IN THE SAVING-INVESTMENT PROCESS

    Both statistical evidence and intuitive under-
standing of the growth process have to be fitted into
the analytical framework of economics if the role of
financial structures in planned development is to be
fully understood. In economic theory growth is closely associated with capital formation. The accumulation of capital assets over time is a necessary,
if not a sufficient, condition for raising the levels
of income and consumption. To a large extent, even
in countries with a substantial influx of foreign
capital, the rate of capital accumulation will depend
on the volume and disposition of domestic savings.
Savings can be mobilized in a number of ways. They

FIGURE I.I

Rate and Form of Household Saving in Four ECAFE Countries
1954-1959

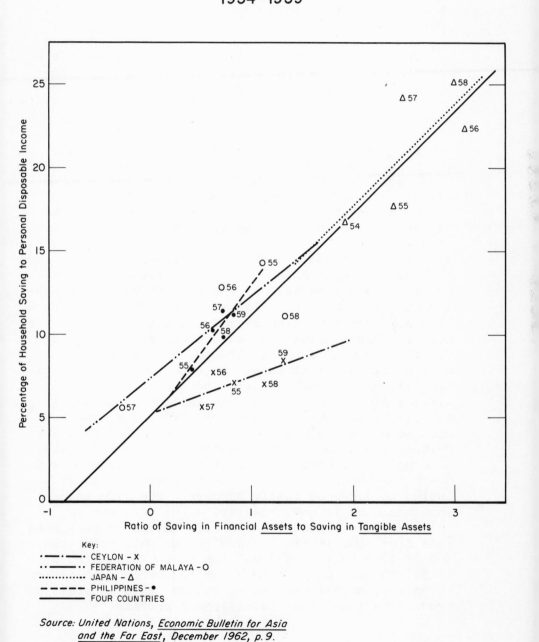

Source: United Nations, *Economic Bulletin for Asia and the Far East*, December 1962, p.9.

can be extracted from national output forcibly and
compulsorily by taxation, inflation, and confiscation,
or they can be diverted from consumption to investment voluntarily by offering various inducements to
consumers to part with current control over resources
in exchange for a claim over a greater volume of resources in the future.

The literature on development planning abounds in
discussions of the reasons for low levels of voluntary saving in less developed economies. While the
most important explanation lies in low levels of real
income, a multitude of social, psychological, and at-
titudinal obstacles have been adduced, and doubts are
expressed whether these obstacles can be removed by
the mere improvement in economic organization.[9] One
tends to be somewhat skeptical of these noneconomic
impediments, if only because countries which have
achieved impressive rates of capital formation were
at one time or another said to operate within a similar set of constraints to voluntary saving. This is
not to say, of course, that it suffices to change some
financial instrument or to create a financial institution in order to augment the flow of voluntary saving, but rather that social mores and attitudes do
change, sometimes quite rapidly, and that in this process of change, financial strucutres and their adap-
tations can play a part. Indeed, to the extent that
a given financial structure is accepted in a society,
it will, of necessity, influence the beliefs and attitudes of the population. An insurance company is
a social institution as well as a financial one. It
used to be maintained by some, for example, that the
Chinese would not tolerate soliciting for life insurance policies, both because of their attitude toward
death and because of the role of surviving kin in relation to deceased family members. The life insurance business is now, however, a thriving one in
Taiwan. Total assets of all life insurance companies
rose from some 16 million New Taiwan dollars at the
end of 1959 to over 600 million at the beginning of
1965. Moslems have found a way to overcome objections
to collection of interest by calling such interest on
productive loans "participation in profits."[10]

A major problem in development finance is that
such savings as do exist tend to go to less productive uses. Traditional theory has never dealt very
satisfactorily with the concept of "productive" versus "nonproductive" investment, but if the aim of
development planning is to maximize the rate of accumulation of capital assets over time, then one
should distinguish between such investments as luxury
dwellings, which do not generate further capital assets, and machine tools, which do.[11] While both initial outlays may be classed as investment, it clearly
matters which type predominates. Thus posed, the
task of creating an appropriate financial structure
for rapid development is not only to augment the flow
of voluntary saving but also to channel it into a
more productive investment mix.

Intermediation in the saving-investment process
appears to be a necessary concomitant of economic
development because of the nature of the supply of
investible funds and the mechanics of growth which
takes place in the less developed countries, at least
in those of the "mixed" variety. The very useful distinction between "surplus" units and "deficit" units
or economic sectors* applies with special cogency to
the less developed countries, where the bulk of saving originates in households but where most of the
investing is done by other sectors.[12] The process of
economic growth is associated with industrialization.
This, in turn, suggests the growing requirement for
outside funds, both because of the increasing needs
for fixed capital and because of the spread of the
corporate form of business organization. Thus the
importance of an efficient mechanism to transfer funds
from the surplus to the deficit units becomes apparent.

---

*Deficit units are those which at the end of the
accounting period reveal an increment in debt exceeding the increment in financial assets. The opposite
is true for surplus units.

In principle, the increasing need of corporations and government could be satisfied not only by financial intermediation but also by instrumentalities of direct finance, whereby claims against business and government are sold directly to households. But the thinness of capital markets in the less developed countries, together with the whole complex of social forces militating against this type of finance, make this extremely unlikely. It is only at a very advanced stage of development that direct financing via stocks and bonds becomes truly significant.[13]

That more efficient financial institutions facilitate the channeling of investible funds into a more productive mix has long been recognized in the literature on economic growth.[14] In commenting on their findings, Adelman and Morris have this to say:

> The importance in D_1 [the discriminant function] of the variables representing the degree of improvement in financial institutions (F) is perhaps not surprising. It will be recalled that this indicator is an overall measure of the success of the economy in increasing the flow of domestic resources through financial institutions and the extent to which these financial organizations provide medium and long-term credit for investment in the major sectors of the economy. The degree of improvement in financial institutions, therefore, describes one fundamental aspect of successful economic performance in a developing country, the loosening of the saving-investment constraint through domestic effort. It is interesting to note that this general indicator of the effectiveness of institutions for saving and lending was chosen by the discriminant analysis in preference to the more specialized index offered by the rate of investment itself.[15]

It would thus seem that financial markets can, and should, play a positive role in development planning.

Far from being merely mirror images of a given stage
of economic growth, they can contribute significantly
both to the level of voluntary saving and to the more
efficient allocation of savings. From this position
it is but a step to seeing whether principles and
techniques can be evolved whereby the structure of
financial markets is better adapted to that dual task.
On a purely pragmatic level this has, of course, long
been recognized. The record is replete with proposals
for the establishment of financial institutions which
are designed to improve the allocation of investment,
augment the flow of voluntary saving, and accelerate
capital formation. But these proposals are usually
not rooted in any clear-cut concept of the way in
which financial markets should be structure so as to
achieve a higher rate of growth.[16]

A CONCEPTUAL FRAMEWORK

A conceptual framework capable of supporting a
structure of financial markets designed to speed up
the rate of economic growth can be constructed in
three layers. The first of these layers is composed
of those criteria of economic efficiency which have
to do with optimum allocation of resources, full utilization of these resources, and reduction of constraints to competition. Classical economic theory
enables one to detect deviations from economic efficiency, if not necessarily to eliminate them. But to
the developmental planner bent on accelerating the
rate of growth, improvements in the efficiency of existing institutions and instruments of the financial
markets may not be of overriding importance. In fact,
such improvements may actually be counterproductive
in those cases where the market arrangements facilitate the flow of funds into channels which have very
low priority from the standpoint of developmental
strategy. Hence, the second layer of the conceptual
framework should include an implicit or explicit set
of developmental goals and priorities against which
the performance of the existing markets can be tested
and toward which it can be structured. Finally, and
this is particularly true in the developing countries,
only a portion of the financial markets is actually or
potentially amenable to developmental guidance. Many

of the financial flows take place outside the purview
and the scrutiny of developmental authorities, who,
even when armed with the knowledge required to reform the financial markets and the power to do so,
may still not be able to influence the vast volume of
financing which flows through the so-called unorganized markets.

Each one of these conceptual layers is discussed
below.

Economic Efficiency

Those criteria which deal with resource allocation and the relation of the market structure to allocation efficiency are an integral part of the
economist's intellectual baggage and need not be discussed here. Certainly the financial markets in the
less developed countries have their share and more of
the inefficiencies brought about by monopolistic practices, by underutilization of resources, by lack of
knowledge and skills, and by all the other circumstances which cause institutions to operate below the
optimum.

One convenient index of the extent of these market inefficiencies is the discrepancy between the
rewards offered to the savers and the costs to be
borne by investors. While these rewards and costs
need not be confined to the purely financial, they
tend to be reflected in the rates of return, on the
one hand, the cost of capital, on the other.[17] This
is illustrated in Figure 1.2. Given the demand and
supply for lendable funds, it is seen that the market clears at S because the extra return R_IR_S does
not accrue to the savers. Thus, not only is the flow
of saving less than it would be in the absence of
the "gap," but also the cost of investment is greater
than it would be otherwise. A gap measured by the
distance R_IR_S probably exists in all countries but
is said to be particularly great in the less developed
countries. This follows from the contention that in
these countries not only are financial markets imperfect, but, in addition, nonpecuniary factors affect both the costs and the rewards.[18]

FIGURE 1.2

"Costs" and "Rewards"
Expressed as a Rate of Interest

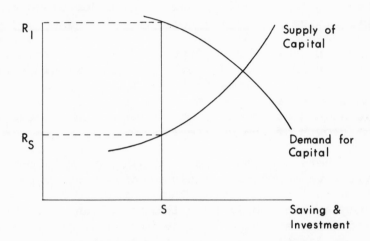

Moreover, in the underdeveloped countries, the
variance in the distribution of interest rates is
larger than in the advanced countries. In many countries, the rates of interest prevailing in the monay
market for certain limited purposes compare favorably
with those obtaining in much more advanced countries.
On the other hand, capital for other purposes, particularly those connected with the acquisition of dur-
able assets, is either completely unavailable or available only on prohibitive terms. Furthermore, the
interest rates announced by the existing institutions
obscure the existence of much higher rates prevailing
outside the orthodox banking and financial institutions.[19]

One possible strategy, then, which pertains both
to the efficiency of the market structure and to developmental objectives, would be to reduce the spread
between the reward to the saver and the cost to the
investor, particularly if the investor is one anxious
to obtain long-term assets.

Developmental Goals and Priorities

The developmental bias toward the accumulation
of capital assets and, hence, toward long-term finance is, as stated previously, firmly established
in the literature and often finds expression in the
dictum that capital formation is a necessary, if not
a sufficient, condition of economic growth.[20] This
helps but little in devising an order of goals and
priorities. It tells nothing about which segment of
the economy should have first claim on resources--
whether public infrastructure, agriculture, or indus-
try--or what should be the emphasis within each of
the segments. More importantly, it tells nothing
about the requisite shift in priorities, both sec-
toral and structural, which correspond to the stages
of growth of the entire economy.

There are, at best, certain hunches whose quantitative expression lacks precision but whose direction is clear enough. These directional hunches
suggest that Thailand's former reliance on exports
and trade as the primary vehicles of growth will have
to be decreased in favor of greater emphasis on manufacturing capacity, particularly manufacturing for
exports, if the country is to continue to grow in the
future.

During the past several years, the ratio of total
investment to GNP approximated 20 per cent annually
in Thailand, but less than one-fourth of capital formation could be attributed to "manufacturing." In
1965, for example, of the Gross Domestic Product of
81 billion baht, capital formation accounted for 18.5
billion. Of this amount, only 4.2 billion could con-
ceivably be attributed to manufacturing, and even
this figure is grossly inflated by the inclusion of
construction equipment in the subtotal for "machinery
imports" and of automobile assembly in that of "value
added to transportation equipment."

While the rate of growth of value added in manufacturing has, in recent years, been in excess of the
growth rate of the GNP, much of this growth appears to
have been either of the "packaging" variety--imported

manufacturing components assembled and labeled in
Thailand--or else devoted to the production of building materials and components which fed the construction boom in urban areas. Both types of manufacturing activity add relatively little to the expansion
of the productive base of the economy and do little
to enhance its ability to increase the production of
goods and services over time.

Those concerned with the country's development
strategy think that increased emphasis on manufacturing, which relies more on local entrepreneurship and
local resources and less on imported skills and equipment, describes the best path for Thailand's development to follow. Thus, the Minister of National
Development said in 1966:

> First, while the proportion of total
> investment to Gross National Product
> has reached a highly respectable level
> of 21 per cent, only a small portion
> of this investment is being channeled
> into the manufacturing industries.
> During the past five years, real manu-
> facturing output increased at the an-
> nual rate of only 7.6 per cent. If we
> are to fulfill the annual target of a
> 10 per cent increase in manufacturing
> products in our next Five-Year Plan,
> and if we are to reach the industrial
> take-off stage in the foreseeable
> future, inducement must be provided
> to shift the emphasis from investment
> for short-term commercial gain to the
> so-called growth investment. That is
> to say, the government will encourage
> only the type of capital outlay which
> is based on long-term profits involv-
> ing the establishment of permanent un-
> dertaking with an eye toward future
> expansion.[21]

In the second five-year plan (1967-1971) the target
for the manufacturing sector is an annual growth rate
of about 11 per cent (compared with the GNP target

of some 9 per cent). In the words of the authors of
the plan, "Accelerated industrial development is an
objective of the Second Plan which has been adopted
in order to realize a structural change in the economy, with the manufacturing sector growing, creating
employment opportunities, and utilizing greater supplies of indigenous raw materials."[22]

These statements are little more than value judgments. Even so, they do not appear unreasonable. In
any event, in the absence of a generally accepted,
rigorous growth theory for a country such as Thailand,
these judgments must orient the development strategy.[23]

Organized and Unorganized Financial Markets

Armed with a set of developmental priorities
which, in the case of Thailand, emphasize the formation of small-scale and medium-scale manufacturing
plants which produce for export those goods and services in which the country has a comparative cost advantage, the planning authorities can begin to improve
the efficiency of the financial markets and to attempt
reforms and modifications of these markets so as to
make them more responsive to those developmental needs.
But the effectiveness of these modifications and reforms is restricted by the fact that in most of the
developing countries a large number of financial
transactions are conducted outside the formally organized markets. In many sectors of the economy the
financing of enterprises is outside the purview and
scrutiny of developmental authorities. In fact, it
may be convenient to consider those markets over which
the authorities do not exercise supervision to be
coterminous with the unorganized ones.[24] Inasmuch as
the unorganized markets tend to be amorphous, informal, and unofficial, there is little legislation and
regulation which covers their operation; hence, not
much is known about the institutions and instruments
making up the unorganized markets beyond the widespread conviction that their scope and importance is
indeed wide (see Chapter 7).

To term these markets "unorganized" is a mistake.
Such markets as those for moneylending, the rotating

credit societies, and trade credit or mortgage credit
are often highly organized, if frequently in a somewhat clandestine fashion. To the extent that these
markets account for a substantial proportion of the
total value of transactions in an economy, they tend
to deflect one individual's savings into another's
consumption or into those investments which have a
low priority, given the societal desire to accelerate
capital formation. This is one reason why the participants in these markets are anxious to remain outside the "organized" orbit and why the activities in
these markets are often shrouded in secrecy. The
lenders find the outlets for their surplus funds attractive in terms of the return offered and the timing
of the pay off. The borrowers find themselves compelled to resort to this market for a variety of reasons, of which one of the most important is that,
given the purpose of the loan and the character of the
available collateral, the unorganized market is the
only place where they can obtain funds. No doubt
other considerations also play a part. For example,
in the organized money markets the degree of disclosure required, the danger of tax or other liability
resulting therefrom, and the sheer administrative
cumbersomeness of indirect transfers operate as powerful constraints on would-be borrowers and lenders who
choose to operate outside them.

But it should not be thought that the unorganized
market is entirely composed of shady lenders and des-
titute or furtive borrowers plus a generous sprinkling
of tax dodgers, smugglers, and gamblers. Many of the
transactions taking place in the unorganized markets
are among kin, close friends, and business associates.
Such transactions will occur in any society, however
well organized. Yet other types of transactions are
simply not amenable to the discipline of the organized
money market, or amenable only at a heavy administrative cost. Many forms of trade credit, for example,
can hardly be institutionalized through the traditional mechanisms of the money and capital markets.

Such things as discounts for prompt payment, for
instance, are a form of financing which falls into
this category. Much of agricultural credit will

probably always remain outside the orbit of formal
organizations inasmuch as the lender-borrower relation
in the countryside frequently involves the lender
acting as a shopkeeper, extension agent, crop buyer,
and miller at one and the same time, while the borrower acts simultaneously as a consumer, entrepreneuer,
and laborer.

It remains true, however, that unorganized markets in most of the less developed countries act as
a brake on economic growth in a number of important
respects. They hold down the rate of capital formation by diverting a portion of saving to consumption.
They lead to an investment mix that tends to be less
productive over time than would be the case if allocation of saving to investment were determined by responsible and specialized institutions concerned with
expanding the productive base of the economy.[25] They
insulate a large portion of the economy from public
control and policy. They deprive the fisc of some
revenue and, hence, of control over real resources.
They create a pattern of interest rates which weigh
heavily on those least able to bear the explicit or
imputed costs of borrowing. Finally, they perpetuate
forms of behavior not conducive to social discipline
and responsibility.

On the other hand, it should be recognized that
unorganized markets fulfill many needs which are not
being satisfied elsewhere. Some of the practices in
these markets have evolved from deeply held custom
and have roots in primal organization and mores. In
some cases, furthermore, a segment of the unorganized
money market has developed practices and forms which
turn out to be remarkably efficient in relation to
their purposes.

Nevertheless, it would seem that one way in which
financial markets can enhance development would be by
enlarging the scope of the organized money and capital markets and correspondingly reducing the size and
the scope of the unorganized markets. To the extent
that this is done by adapting the institutions and
instruments in the organized money markets to the
functions hitherto performed outside them, it must
be concluded that real progress has been achieved.

It should be emphasized at this juncture that the mere prohibition or elimination of some of the activities performed in the unorganized markets is not likely to do much good. The very existence of such activities under the common handicaps attached to them demonstrates their vigor and their acceptance. To remove them by decree or policy action would either not be effective or, if effective, would merely leave unattended a deeply felt economic need. The latter can be justified only in those relatively rare cases where it can be shown that such activities are detrimental to important social goals and values. Rather, the task of the organized financial markets is to take over and absorb those activities which, for one reason or another, thrive in the unorganized markets.

Such a task, while difficult, is clearly not impossible of achievement, as the historical experience of many of the developed and developing countries testifies.

The task may be facilitated by the fact that transactions in the unorganized markets are subject to a number of handicaps. On the one hand, these handicaps cause the interest rates and other costs of borrowing to be high, but, on the other hand, the risks, administrative costs, and lack of legal redress may make the real return to the lender much less attractive than would appear on the surface. By the same token, organized transactions could, under certain circumstances, become more attractive to lenders and borrowers hitherto reluctant to handle them for a variety of reasons. One possible situation in which functions of the unorganized market could be taken over, at least in part, by the organized institutions is agricultural credit; it has been pointed out that "in most ECAFE countries the organized capital market is only a part of the capital market--the larger segment being the unorganized market. The unorganized market is centered in the rural areas."[26] (See Chapter 3 for a detailed discussion of the existing pattern of financing of rural households in Thailand and for specific suggestions for reducing the scope of unorganized markets in financing these households.)

It is thus possible to consider the organized
market as the medium through which financial structure can be brought to bear on the development process, provided such an extension is related to the
size of the unorganized market, and provided also
that the relative shrinkage of the latter does not
lead to elimination of services with detrimental effects on the level of business activity.

One very crude way of estimating the relative
sizes of the two markets is to assume that the flow
of cash transactions occurs principally in the unorganized markets and that those transactions settled
by check take place in the organized markets. As a
strict proposition this assumption is certainly not
true. The two types of markets are both complemen-
tary and competitive. Moneylenders borrow from the
banks by writing checks on their demand deposits,
and many transactions taking place within the unorganized markets employ postdated checks or similar
devices as collateral. Nor is it true that indices
related principally to the commercial banking system
exhaust the contribution of the organized markets to
the total flow of finance. Still, in most of the
developing countries commercial banks are by far the
most important component of the organized financial
markets, and they also indirectly finance other institutions.

One index, suggested by U Tun Wai, seeks to measure the size of the organized markets (and thus, by
implication, that of the unorganized market) by calculating two ratios over time, the ratio of currency
held by the public to total money supply and the
ratio of commercial bank credit to domestic national
income (DNI). U Tun Wai uses the ratio of demand
deposits to money supply rather than that of currency.
This ratio considers matters from the liability side
of the bank's balance sheet, while the ratio of bank
credit to DNI (loans, overdrafts, discounts, and investments) relates to the asset side. Wai suggests
that the ratio of bank risk assets to national income
is a more reliable index of the two. However, given
the commercial banks' assets and liabilities, it is
quite simple to relate both indices. Thus, if M is

money supply, Y national income, D demand deposits, C risk assets, A and L total assets and liabilities, then:

$$D/M \quad [\; M/Y \quad (\underline{\underline{C}}/\underline{\underline{D}}) \;] = \underline{\underline{C}}$$
$$\qquad\qquad\qquad A \; / \; L \qquad\quad Y$$

In most developing countries the ratio of currency to money supply is about 50 per cent, compared with 20 or 30 per cent in the developed countries. The ratio of bank credit to national income hovers around a median of 28 per cent for all less developed countries. In 1963 this ratio was in the range of 40 to 45 per cent for such countries as Argentina, Brazil, Ceylon, Greece, the Philippines, Tunisia, and the UAR, but was less than 20 per cent for Ghana, Jamaica, Jordan, Korea, Malaysia, Mexico, Nicaragua, and Sudan. For the highly developed countries, the ratio ranged from 47 to 148 per cent.[27]

For Thailand, the ratio of currency to money supply appears to be within the range for countries in a similar stage of development; i.e., about 57 per cent. Somewhat more surprising is the rather low ratio of bank credit to national income. In 1963, this ratio was slightly higher than 16 per cent, which would put Thailand substantially below such countries as Ceylon, the UAR, and the Philippines. While this may be indicative, it has already been pointed out that the crude ratios are influenced by many considerations having little to do with either the stage of economic growth or the relative importance of unorganized markets.[28] For example, in some countries, such as Ceylon, Burma, or the UAR, a high ratio of bank credit to national income represents the large amounts of loans made by the banking system to the government whether under pressure of deficit financing or for other reasons.

However imperfect such crude indices may be when employed over a number of years, they do certify that an extension of the scope of the organized markets does, in fact, take place. This, however, is not sufficient in itself. Such an extension should not occur at the expense of eliminating or neglecting

functions hitherto performed in the unorganized markets. One indication whether such neglect or elimination has taken place comes from the structure and
pattern of interest rates, particularly in those markets which are known to be largely outside the organized ones. A sharp rise in the rate of interest on
agricultural loans, for example, even when accompanied by an increase in the ratio of bank credit to
national income, cannot be considered to be a movement in the desired direction. Only when over a
period of years there is a perceptible trend in the
ratio which suggests an increase in the scope of the
organized markets, accompanied by a shift to the
right of the schedule of lendable funds, can it be
asserted that there has been an improvement in the
efficiency of the financial markets.

The task of the development planner in the area
of financial markets is thus seen as one of devising
ways and means by which activities handled by the unorganized markets are gradually taken over by the
organized markets without impairing the level of economic activity and without causing social unrest.[29]
The extent to which the planner is successful can be
broadly gauged by indicators which, however crude, do
provide a reliable guide when observed over a period
of years.

FINANCIAL MARKETS AS A VEHICLE OF ECONOMIC GROWTH

In a country such as Thailand there are no ideological or cultural obstacles to reliance on financial markets as the primary vehicle to augment savings
and to channel them to more productive uses. Possible
alternatives, for example centralized direction and
coercion, are hardly indicated.[30] Not only has
Thailand been able to achieve an impressive record of
economic performance with little collectivist planning and little constraint on economic freedom; two
additional factors provide an added incentive to
avoid the alternative of centralized direction of the
saving-investment process. The first of these factors
is the considerable investment the country already
possesses in financial institutions and instruments of

all kinds. The other is the circumstance that foreign capital available to Thailand now and in the
foreseeable future can best be transmitted through
the financial institutions of the kind prevailing
within the country. It is possible that these same
factors would operate in other small, export-oriented
economies provided ideological considerations do not
override the importance of these economic advantages.

It would thus appear that in Thailand, at any
rate, financial markets can be structured so as to
speed up the rate of economic growth. The conceptual
framework already developed at some length suggests
the following broad strategic principles:

1. The efficiency of the existing institutions
and instruments of the financial markets will be improved to the extent that the cost of long-term capital is lowered and the spread between the reward to
the saver and the cost to the investor is narrowed.

2. The availability of capital to finance the
small and medium-size manufacturer should be increased, particularly when such a manufacturer is engaged in the production of commodities in which the
country has (or could acquire) a competitive cost
advantage in world markets. One way to increase the
availability of such capital would be to deflect the
financing flows from those channeled into trade, construction, and speculative activities.

3. Organized financial markets should be so modified and reformed as to be able to compete successfully with the unorganized ones. In particular, organized markets should try to enlarge significantly
the scope of their operations in financing productive
activities by developing imaginative institutions and
instruments able to attract lenders and entrepreneurs
hitherto confined to the unorganized markets.

These broad strategic guidelines may be deemed
too imprecise to provide a blueprint for a reform of
the Thai financial markets. But this need not necessarily be a drawback, from an operational standpoint,
for at least two reasons. In the first place, the

Thai economy has had an excellent record of growth,
particularly in the 1960's, and there is no proof
that the imperfections of its financial structure had
the effect of preventing this growth from reaching a
high rate. In fact, it could be argued that the
structure and the orientation of the Thai financial
markets have mirrored the efficient growth path of
the economy in the past, its institutions and instruments adapting themselves remarkably well to the financing of trade and related activities. In the
second place, although the time may have come when
Thailand needs to shift its developmental emphasis
to the establishment of a manufacturing base and to
expanding markets for its manufacturing output, no
rigorous case has been made for such a shift in developmental strategy.

It would, therefore, be inappropriate to adopt
(in Karl Popper's terms) a holistic philosophy and to
attempt a major revision of the Thai financial markets; instead, the approach should be that of piecemeal social engineering.[31] The main structure of the
financial markets in Thailand should be taken as a
datum, and such modifications and improvements as
seem to be called for should be cautious and moderate
rather than major and drastic. To this end, the three
broad principles enunciated above appear quite adequate.

In welfare economic terms, the proposition is
that the present situation is short of the optimal
point-set boundary. Given both uncertainty in the
dynamic sense and lack of firm knowledge about the
precise position of this boundary, a movement in the
northeast direction is best calculated to avoid gross
errors and eventually to reach the desired goal.

In short, the position taken here is that it is
both possible and desirable to modify the structure
of the Thai financial markets without perfect knowledge of the exact magnitudes prevailing either before
or after the change, provided the direction of the
change is known and provided that the change leads to
results implicit in the conceptual framework developed
in this chapter.

NOTES

1.   "A monetary system and especially its commercial banking component has commonly been the first
significant financial intermediary," J. G. Gurley and
E. S. Shaw, "Financial Aspects of Economic Development," American Economic Review (September, 1955),
p. 520.

2.   See Raymond W. Goldsmith, "The Determinants
of Financial Structure," Development Center Studies
No. 2 Revised (Paris: Organization for Economic
Cooperation and Development, July, 1965), p. 2.
(Mimeo.)

3.   Goldsmith's index measures the relation between the value of total financial assets and national wealth. This "financial interrelations ratio"
(FIR) is a composite of several determinants which
include GNP, a monetization ratio, a capital formation ratio, the ratio of new issues of nonfinancial
units to their capital formation, the ratio of new
issues of financial instruments by financial institutions to new issues by nonfinancial units, the ratio
of total issues of financial instruments to the issues
of nonfinancial units and others; ibid., pp. 6-7.

4.   In the United States, in 1962, 40 per cent
of family units earning less than $5,000 a year held
claims against life insurance and pension funds, compared with 85 per cent of families with annual income over $25,000 holding such claims. With respect
to stocks and other investment assets, 17 per cent
of those earning under $5,000 and 90 per cent of those
earning over $25,000 held them. For all families the
percentages holding claims against life insurance and
pension funds and stocks and other investment were
58 and 29 respectively. See Paul B. Trescott, Money,
Banking and Economic Welfare (New York: McGraw-Hill,
1965), p. 293.

5.   On the importance of "financial innovation"
in economic development, see Rando Cameron, et al.,
Banking in the Early Stages of Industrialization
(Oxford: Oxford University Press, 1967), pp. 1-9.

6. United Nations, <u>Economic Bulletin for Asia and the Far East</u>, XIII, 3 (December, 1962). Unfortunately Thailand was not one of the countries which had conducted savings surveys in response to the request by the Economic Commission for Asia and the Far East (ECAFE).

7. Irma Adelman and Cynthia Taft Morris, "Performance Criteria for Evaluating Economic Development Potential: An Operational Approach," <u>Quarterly Journal of Economics</u> (May, 1968).

8. The normalized version of the discriminant function (D_1) was equal to 127F plus 65K plus 108M plus 72L, where F is the degree of improvement in financial institutions, K is the degree of improvement in physical overhead capital, M the degree of modernization of outlook, and L the leadership commitment to development; <u>ibid</u>., p. 273.

9. Almost every book on economic development has a section dealing with the inadequacy of voluntary saving stemming from social and political, as well as economic, conditions prevailing in the less developed countries. Among the more assertive in stressing the effect of noneconomic factors on voluntary saving are Ragnar Nurske, <u>Problems of Capital Formation in Underdeveloped Countries</u> (Oxford: B. Blackwell, 1953), pp. 60ff; W. Arthur Lewis, <u>The Theory of Economic Growth</u> (London: Allen & Unwin, 1955); and Marion J. Levy, "Some Social Obstacles to Capital Formation in Underdeveloped Countries," in National Bureau of Economic Research, <u>Capital Formation and Economic Growth: A Conference of the Universities</u> (Princeton: Princeton University Press, 1955), pp. 441-520. A notable exception to the view that saving is the main limiting factor in capital formation and economic growth is propounded by Albert O. Hirchman, who holds that it is the "ability to invest" rather than to save which is holding back a more rapid rate of growth; see <u>The Strategy of Economic Development</u> (New Haven: Yale University Press, 1958), pp. 35ff.

10. For Taiwan, see The Central Bank of China, Taiwan Financial Statistics Monthly (June, 1965), p. 56; on Moslems, see R. Firth and B. S. Yamey, Capital Saving and Credit in Peasant Societies (London: Allen & Unwin, 1964).

11. "It is at least conceivable that under conditions of forced economic growth and industrialization, capital and hence capital formation may be viewed as limited to plant, equipment, and inventories that are directly serviceable as tools"; Simon Kuznets, "International Differences in Capital Formation and Financing," Capital Formation and Economic Growth: A Conference of the Universities (Princeton: Princeton University Press, 1955), p. 19.

12. See Gurley and Shaw, op. cit. In most ECAFE countries more than two-thirds of total saving comes from households, but the proportion of those savings held in financial claims is low and is positively correlated with both the level of per capita income and the ratio of household saving to disposable personal income; ECAFE Bulletin, pp. 8-10.

13. For the ECAFE countries surveyed the proportion of household saving directly transmitted to users in other sectors in 1959-1960 ranged from less than 4 per cent in Ceylon to 13 per cent for Korea; ECAFE Bulletin, p. 11. In 1946-1954, the corresponding proportion in the United States was 23 per cent, and this proportion actually declined sharply from the 1920's; R. W. Goldsmith, "The Formation of Saving in the U.S.," Proceedings of the Second International Savings and Investments Congress (Brussels: Secretariat of the Congress, 1959), p. 44. Financial markets in performing their transfer function also extend the availability of entrepreneurial talent by enabling people to obtain funds other than their own.

14. See, for example, Charles P. Kindleberger, Economic Development (New York: McGraw Hill, 1958); in this leading text on the subject, the author states: "One of the major tasks of the monetary

authorities in development is to support the gradual
expansion and proliferation of the machinery--commer-
cial banks, saving banks, investment banking, insurance companies, government bond market, private bond
and share markets, etc.--which link surplus and deficit spending units" (p. 191).

15.   Adelman and Morris, op. cit., p. 269.

16.   For an earlier attempt in this direction see
Alek A. Rozental, "Internal Financing of Economic
Development," American Journal of Economics and Soci-
ology (August, 1958); and "Mobilization of Domestic
Saving," in Proceedings of the Asian Section of the
International Chamber of Commerce (Karachi, 1960);
reprinted in Center for Development Planning, National Planning Association, Reprint Series #6 (Washington, D.C., 1967).

17.   See Tibor Scitovsky, Welfare and Competition:
The Economics of A Fully Employed Economy (Chicago:
Richard D. Irwin, 1951), pp. 223-225; and John A.
Buttrick and H. Williamson, Economic Development:
Principles and Patterns (New York: Prentice Hall,
1954), pp. 178-182.

18.   For a discussion of these nonpecuniary fac-
tors, see D. M. Wright, "Econometric Models in Rela-
tion to Social Setting," American Economic Review
(May, 1952); Henry G. Aubrey, Industrial Enterprise
in Underdeveloped Countries (New York: National
Bureau of Economic Research, November, 1953) (Mimeo.);
United Nations, Formulation and Economic Appraisal
of Development Projects (1951), pp. 90ff; R. I. Crane,
Aspects of Economic Development in South Asia (New
York: International Secretariat, Institute of Pacific
Relations, 1954), p. 47.

19.   In India, moneylenders exact interest rates
varying between 12 and 50 per cent; rates of loans
by the Pathans are reported to be as high as 300-400
per cent; see International Monetary Fund, "Financial
Institutions in India," Staff Papers (February, 1950),
pp. 39-45. In Cuba, rates on loans for processing
sugar range from 2.5 to 4 per cent, as compared with

mortgage loans of from 9 to 12 per cent. More significant is the fact that a small industrial producer
is unable to obtain bank accommodation at any price;
see IBRD, Report on Cuba (Baltimore: The Johns
Hopkins Press, 1953), p. 586. In Greece, interest
rates on industrial loans reach 30 per cent; see
Hollis B. Chenery, "Application of Investment Criteria," Quarterly Journal of Economics (February,
1953).

20. Thus, for example, Adelman and Morris, in
devising indicators of the performance of financial
institutions in the developmental context, attach
considerable importance to the way in which these institutions transfer long-term capital to agriculture
and manufacturing; see Society, Politics and Economic
Development (Baltimore: Johns Hopkins Press, 1967).

21. Speech delivered at the Seminar on Economic
Development and Investment Opportunities sponsored
by the Thailand Council of the Asia Society at the
Plaza Hotel, New York, October 5, 1966.

22. National Economic Development Board, The
Second National Economic and Social Development Plan
(Bangkok, 1967), p. 165.

23. For a first approximation to such a theory
see Alek A. Rozental, "Prolegomena to Growth Theory
of Dualistic Open Economics," Tunghai Economics, III
(1969). (Tunghai University, Taichung, Taiwan).

24. "All this is merely another way of stating
our argument that we need to have a more systematic
study of how the market forces actually work of fail
to work in the different types of underdeveloped
country. Applied to the majority of the underdeveloped countries at the earlier 'pre-take-off' stages
of economic development, this now assumes a special
significance. The degree of effective control that
the government of such a country can exercise over
the rest of the economy depends more clearly than
elsewhere on the growth of suitable monetary, fiscal,
and market institutions through which it can extend
its control"; Hla Myint, "Economic Theory and the

Underdeveloped Countries," Journal of Political Economy (October, 1965), p. 494.

25. This is not to suggest that institutions typically operating in the organized financial markets are invariably responsible and competent. In fact, it is quite possible that some direct financing takes place in the unorganized markets because an institution under public scrutiny has been discredited in the eyes of would-be borrowers. Inasmuch, however, as it is true that the bulk of unorganized financing is for the purpose of consumption and speculation, and to the extent that there is awareness that such financing deflects resources to less productive uses, there is little that responsible authorities can do about it as long as these transactions remain outside the orbit of public policy. To quote U Tun Wai, "In the unorganized money markets of the developing countries, most of the borrowings are for financing consumer expenditures. About 80 or 90 per cent of the supply of funds is from non-institutional sources such as professional money lenders, traders, shopkeepers, landlords, relatives, and friends who charge exorbitant rates of interest. Furthermore, the link between the unorganized and the organized money market is poor, and central banks are unable to influence the terms and conditions of loans in the former"; U Tun Wai, "Role of Money Market in Supplementing Monetary Policy," in David Krivine, ed., Fiscal and Monetary Problems in Developing States: Proceedings of the Third Rehovoth Conference (New York: F. A. Praeger, 1967), p. 161. See also Adelman and Morris, Society, Politics and Economic Development, op. cit., pp. 118-119.

26. ECAFE Bulletin, op. cit., p. 23.

27. U Tun Wai, op. cit., pp. 163ff.

28. Ibid.

29. "Unorganized finance that survives effective competition is worth preserving"; J. G. Gurley, H. T. Patrick, and E. S. Shaw, The Financial Structure of Korea (Seoul: United States Operation Mission/Korea, 1965), p. 85.

30. For an illuminating discussion of such alternatives and of the "dark side of finance," see
J. G. Gurley, "Financial Structure in Developing Economics," in <u>Fiscal and Monetary Problems in Developing</u>
<u>States</u>, <u>op. cit</u>.

31. See Karl Popper, "The Poverty of Historicism
III," <u>Economica</u>, XII, 6 (May, 1945), pp. 69-89.

CHAPTER **2** THE FINANCIAL NEXUS
AND THE THAI ECONOMY

Before examining in detail the structure and
functions of the financial markets in Thailand, it
is necessary to consider the background against which
the financial markets operate, the economy in general
and the financial nexus in particular.

This chapter will provide a brief account of the
Thai economic structure with emphasis on those aspects of the economy which are particularly relevant
to the generation of savings and the allocation of
investment.

THE THAI ECONOMY: RECORD OF RECENT YEARS

As Table 2.1 shows, Gross Domestic Product (GDP)
increased at an annual rate of 7.9 per cent in the
period 1962-1967, compared with the 4.7 per cent rate
in the preceding five years. In the more recent
period the higher rate of growth was due to rapid increases in value added of most sectors of the economy, with the notable exception of agriculture, services, ownership of dwellings, and administration
(including defense).

Agriculture, even though increasing far more
slowly than the other segments of the economy, still
accounts for almost a third of the national income,
trade is second in importance in proportion of total
value added. Exports account for nearly a sixth of
the GDP, with gross investment running, in recent
years, at some 20 per cent of total expenditures on
goods and services.

TABLE 2.1

Gross Domestic Product by Industrial Origin, 1962-1967
(billion baht; 1962 market prices)

Industrial Sector	1962	1963	1964	1965	1966	1967	Change 1962-1967 in % p.a.
Agriculture	22.7	25.0	26.4	27.1	27.4	29.6	4.6
Crops	15.8	17.6	18.5	18.7	18.7	20.7	4.7
Livestock	3.8	3.8	3.9	3.9	4.1	4.1	1.3
Fisheries	1.2	1.5	1.8	2.1	2.3	2.5	13.3
Forestry	1.9	2.1	2.2	2.4	2.3	2.3	3.4
Mining, quarrying	1.0	1.1	1.1	1.3	1.6	1.7	9.6
Manufacturing	7.1	8.5	9.6	11.3	12.3	13.8	11.8
Construction	2.7	3.4	3.7	4.3	5.5	6.3	15.6
Electricity, water supply	0.4	0.4	0.5	0.6	0.8	1.0	17.2
Transport, communication	4.4	4.5	5.2	5.8	6.3	7.0	8.1
Trade	11.4	12.7	14.8	15.9	16.8	20.4	10.4
Banking, insurance, real estate	1.9	2.1	2.3	2.7	3.2	3.7	11.9
Ownership of dwellings	2.9	2.9	3.1	3.2	3.4	3.5	3.2
Public administration, defense	3.0	3.3	3.5	3.7	3.9	4.4	6.6
Other services	5.7	6.1	6.4	7.1	7.7	8.2	6.3
Gross domestic product	63.2	70.0	76.6	83.0	88.9	99.6	7.9
Net factor income from abroad	-0.1	-	-0.1	-	-0.1	0.2	-
Gross national product	63.1	70.0	76.5	83.0	88.8	99.8	8.0

Source: Based on World Bank compilations derived from information provided by the National Economic Development Board.

The most remarkable fact about the recent performance of the Thai economy is that in spite of its high rate of growth it was able to generate an internal rate of saving which was more than adequate to finance private capital formation by voluntary savings and which contributed to the saving shortfall in the public sector. The excess of public investment over public saving was financed in the main by private and public capital inflow from abroad.

In the period 1963/64, the most recent for which comparative data are available, Thailand's ratios of saving to income were the highest among the developing nations of Asia and the Far East, while its compound growth rate for the period 1956/64 was exceeded only by that of Taiwan (see Table 2.2). Moreover, among the nine nations included in Table 2.2, Thailand is the only one that, throughout the entire period, maintained a stable level of prices and avoided any foreign exchange problems.

Thus, during the 1960's Thailand managed to sustain a high rate of growth, both aggregate and per capita (annual population increase was estimated to be in the neighborhood of 3 per cent per annum), while maintaining a very stable level of internal prices and while actually accumulating foreign exchange reserves.[1]

THE THAI ECONOMY: PROSPECTS

It was suggested in Chapter 1 that the impressive record of the Thai economy to date may not be maintained unless the economy develops a more viable manufacturing base with a substantial proportion of manufacturing output going to export markets. The past performance was the product of many circumstances, some of them fortuitous and some of them possibly non-recurrent.[2]

Less than 1.5 per cent of the value of total exports in recent years consisted of manufactured goods, and a closer scrutiny of these goods suggests that most of them were of the low capital intensity type.

TABLE 2.2

Ratio of Gross Domestic Saving to GNP, 1955/64,
Selected Asian Countries

Country	Annual Compound Rate of Growth of GNP at Constant Prices 1956/64	Ratio of Saving to GNP (two-year average)		
		1955+1956	1959+1960	1963+1964
Burma	4.7	18.2	17.7	20.7
Ceylon	3.8	16.7	12.2	11.2
China (Taiwan)	7.5	14.7	17.7	19.3
India	4.0	15.4	16.1	15.6
Korea, Republic of	5.5	9.5	10.0	13.5
Malaya, States of	5.6	17.8	20.8	16.8
Pakistan	4.3	5.7	9.8	14.9
Philippines	4.5	7.4	9.8	17.5
Thailand	6.7	14.9	15.5	21.1

Source: United Nations, Economic Survey of Asia and the Far East 1966, Bangkok, 1967.

While manufacturing increased faster than GNP in
the period 1962-1967 (Table 2.1), its higher rate of
growth seems to be the result of several rather special developments. Thus, the establishment of a major oil refinery in 1963 not only added some 7 per
cent to total value added in manufacturing but also
contributed substantially to the over-all growth rate
for the period 1961-1967.

Similar effects were due to establishment of a
tin smelter in 1965. Moreover, items such as "machinery and equipment" or "chemicals and chemical prod-
ucts" include a very high proportion of assembly
(automobiles) and packaging (pharmaceuticals) plants
(see Table 2.3).

The same pattern of reliance on activity which
is primarily for the purpose of satisfying the consumption demand of the urban middle class in the intermediate rather than the long run, and which does
relatively little to develop the native productive
base, emerges from a breakdown of capital formation
by type of capital goods. Construction accounts for
over 40 per cent of all capital formation in recent
years, and that proportion is understated in that
some of the imported "capital goods" are directly related to construction activity (e.g., cranes, drills,
and possibly elevators). Much of the "transport
equipment" is passenger vehicles or parts for them,
thus overstating even further the relative share of
"capital goods" in capital formation (Table 2.4).

In any case, and even if the view that Thailand
should shift its strategic emphasis from crop exports
to manufacturing based on local resources and oriented toward world markets is not accepted, there are
reasons to believe that continuing rapid growth of
the economy, on the lines followed in the past, cannot be taken for granted. As Forrest E. Cookson puts
it:

> For the past ten years the Thai economy
> has made remarkable progress; the society
> has achieved an internal economic equili-
> brium in which development could proceed

TABLE 2.3

Gross Domestic Product Originating from Manufacturing, 1961-1965
(million baht)

Product	1961	1962	1963	1964	1965	1966
Food	2,370.8	2,705.1	2,510.8	2,402.6	2,529.8	3,279.5
Beverages	689.3	794.9	880.8	927.3	995.5	1,190.7
Tobacco	865.9	996.8	1,008.5	1,031.3	1,235.4	1,348.3
Textiles	170.7	191.3	254.9	372.5	457.2	542.0
Footwear, other wearing apparel, and made-up textile goods	279.0	287.3	296.8	306.9	317.2	330.2
Wood and cork products, except furniture	293.8	348.4	472.0	558.9	620.4	609.1
Furniture and fixtures	86.4	100.1	100.5	104.9	108.1	116.7
Paper and paper products	21.5	18.8	24.4	44.9	48.8	55.8
Printing, publishing, and allied industries	148.3	148.7	176.4	213.7	227.2	262.1
Leather and leather products except footwear	120.6	120.5	124.7	131.4	135.2	140.5
Rubber products	239.2	210.5	219.9	216.2	223.5	228.2
Chemicals and chemical products	459.1	467.1	521.6	621.9	734.3	854.6
Petroleum refining	-	-	-	166.5	637.5	795.9
Nonmetallic mineral products except products of petroleum and coal	373.1	424.4	486.8	579.8	715.9	840.9
Basic metal industries	18.1	16.6	8.0	8.7	13.0	24.6
Electrical machinery, apparatus, appliances, and supplies	32.5	40.4	29.1	26.3	27.2	32.9
Machinery and equipment	253.3	245.9	442.7	630.0	668.0	736.8
All other	220.4	320.4	316.2	360.5	372.7	393.7
Total value added	6,642.0	7,437.2	7,874.3	8,704.2	10,066.9	11,782.4

Source: National Economic Development Board, National Income of Thailand, 1966 Edition (Bangkok, 1967).

TABLE 2.4

Gross Fixed Capital Formation by Type of Capital Goods, 1961–1966
(million baht; 1962 prices)

Type of Capital Goods	Gross Fixed Capital Formation					
	1961	1962	1963	1964	1965	1966
Imports of capital goods	2,633.4	3,041.5	4,013.1	4,525.2	4,899.6	5,465.4
Transport equipment	793.7	947.6	1,022.7	1,270.6	1,347.2	1,519.9
Machinery and other eqpt.	1,075.8	1,304.1	1,882.3	2,220.4	2,396.7	2,716.5
Industrial raw materials	763.9	789.8	1,108.1	1,034.2	1,155.7	1,229.0
Construction	5,031.0	5,982.0	7,783.2	8,475.3	9,292.7	9,893.6
Private construction activity	3,087.8	4,001.3	5,118.5	5,546.5	5,967.8	6,137.1
Construction in urban area	1,965.3	2,932.4	4,050.9	4,399.7	4,747.9	4,912.0
Construction in rural area	741.5	706.8	753.8	874.3	941.7	948.9
New lands	381.0	362.1	313.8	272.5	278.2	276.2
Public construction activity	1,943.2	1,980.7	2,664.7	2,928.8	3,324.9	3,756.5
Public construction	1,936.6	1,971.9	2,654.7	2,919.4	3,315.3	3,746.8
Cost of reafforestation	6.6	8.8	10.0	9.4	9.6	9.7
Other domestic capital formation	2,254.0	2,615.6	3,281.2	3,763.4	3,992.3	4,238.1
Agricultural tools of dom. origin	215.8	215.1	243.2	234.3	245.6	250.0
Value added of transport eqpt.	221.1	244.6	304.8	398.5	481.3	513.9
Trucks, buses, and cars	89.9	117.1	164.0	290.3	363.2	389.2
Domestic vessels	102.7	100.0	110.5	78.3	86.2	93.0
Rolling stock	28.5	27.5	30.3	29.9	31.9	31.7
Other tools & eqpt. dom. produced	42.0	39.4	61.4	60.6	68.5	71.9
Office eqpt. dom. produced in the public sector	145.6	173.3	115.9	155.2	152.7	169.3
Additional costs[a]	1,629.5	1,943.2	2,555.9	2,914.8	3,044.2	3,233.0
Gross fixed capital formation	9,918.4	11,639.1	15,077.5	16,763.9	18,184.6	19,597.1

[a]Import duties, insurance, transportation, markups, installation, sales and municipal taxes.

Source: National Economic Development Board, National Income of Thailand, 1966 Edition (Bangkok, 1967).

38

at a rapid pace. At present, however,
it appears that a variety of factors,
some inherent to the economy and some
external, are converging in such a way
that internal equilibrium could be
seriously upset and continued growth
threatened.[3]

MONETARY ACCOUNTS

Turning from the broad picture of the Thai economy to a somewhat more detailed account of its monetary aspects, it may be convenient to begin by pre-
senting a consolidated statement of the monetary
system (Table 2.5).

A consolidated monetary statement is useful on
at least two counts. It gives a summary of the assets and liabilities of the organized money market
and thus a glimpse into the nature of the financial
instruments and institutions of that market, and it
also provides some insight into the elements which
underlie changes in the money supply.

In preparing its consolidated statement Thailand
follows the International Monetary Fund (IMF) conven-
tions. Items which are assets of one monetary sector
and liabilities of another are excluded from both
sides of the account. Thus, for example, commercial
banks' holdings with the Bank of Thailand are exluded,
and so are their borrowings.

Table 2.5 gives assets and liabilities of the
monetary system for the period 1956-1967 arranged by
three sectors, foreign, government, and private. The
difference between the assets of the system and its
nonmonetary liabilities is the money supply, consisting of coins, paper currency, and demand deposits
held by the private sector. It is almost impossible,
in practice, to derive the consolidated statement
from the component series published independently in
Thai statistics. Much careful reconciliation is
necessary to come fairly close.[4]

TABLE 2.5

Consolidated Statement of the Monetary System, 1956-1967
(million baht)

Class of Assets or Liabilities	Amount on December 31											
	1956 (1)	1957 (2)	1958 (3)	1959 (4)	1960 (5)	1961 (6)	1962 (7)	1963 (8)	1964 (9)	1965 (10)	1966 (11)	1967 (12)
Foreign assets (net)	6,261.5	6,384.6	5,985.1	5,943.4	6,834.4	8,406.0	9,653.2	11,010.0	12,744.9	13,991.9	17,182.4	18,230.6
Net IMF position	62.5	62.5	62.5	225.0	225.0	225.0	225.0	234.0	234.0	395.2	494.0	494.0
Claims on government	5,093.9	5,552.0	5,974.4	6,520.0	4,545.6	4,379.2	5,184.4	5,026.0	5,580.3	6,587.4	9,325.4	10,394.3
Claims on private sector	3,219.3	3,712.5	4,353.6	4,912.7	5,761.7	6,586.6	7,791.6	8,908.1	10,553.7	12,611.6	14,701.1	17,043.4
Unclassified assets	428.7	519.0	695.5	695.0	1,031.8	1,166.5	1,135.4	1,277.2	1,465.7	1,580.5	1,508.1	2,122.5
Assets = liabilities	15,065.9	16,230.6	17,071.1	18,296.1	18,398.5	20,763.3	23,989.6	26,455.3	30,281.6	35,166.6	43,211.2	48,284.8

Money	7,728.4	8,196.6	8,451.9	9,076.1	10,088.4	11,075.4	11,093.3	11,881.0	12,919.0	14,332.1	16,657.8	17,874.1
Quasi-money	1,191.9	1,473.1	1,769.9	1,899.0	2,312.1	2,945.0	4,632.1	5,881.0	7,151.3	8,568.6	11,536.5	14,290.2
Govt. deposits (incl. official entities)	596.3	656.9	703.3	908.1	1,479.0	1,800.3	2,566.0	2,234.3	3,369.7	4,560.0	6,921.5	7,163.3
Bonds (savings, etc.)	71.3	86.8	105.4	133.7	168.4	213.7	301.6	430.7	590.6	712.5	846.0	978.2
Counterpart funds	351.8	452.7	375.5	451.1	464.1	544.0	566.6	483.9	382.8	164.2	53.2	55.8
Exchange difference	3,178.4	3,163.0	3,163.0	3,163.0	1,004.3	–	–	–	–	–	–	–
Capital accounts	1,583.0	1,868.1	2,152.5	2,268.9	2,505.7	3,728.0	4,064.1	4,606.2	4,791.9	5,317.8	5,951.6	6,604.4
Unclassified liabilities	364.8	333.4	349.6	396.2	384.8	456.9	765.9	938.2	1,076.3	1,513.2	1,244.6	1,318.8

Source: Bank of Thailand.

In the period 1956-1967 all items, with the exception of counterpart funds, increased substantially
in amount. The greatest increase took place in government bonds and in quasi-money. But bonds still
account for a minor proportion of total liabilities,
whereas quasi-money (time and saving deposits) rose
in relative importance from 8 per cent in 1956 to
over 29 per cent in 1967.

The nature and significance of the various assets and liabilities will be examined in detail in
later chapters. What will be briefly discussed here
are the changes in the money supply.

As mentioned before, in the period 1957-1967
Thailand's price level was so stable that, for all
practical purposes, it could be taken as given, thus
dispensing with the need, so urgent in analysis of
the financial structures of other countries, to distinguish between "real" and "nominal" financial flows
and stocks. The stability of the price level can be
traced directly to the management of the country's
money supply.

Money supply rose during the period under discussion by 86 per cent, but its share in total liabilities actually fell from 51 per cent in 1956 to
41 per cent at the end of 1965.

As a matter of fact, the increase in money supply
barely kept pace with the growth of the GNP. A simple linear regression of money supply on GNP shows
that a 10 per cent increase in GNP was associated
with an 8 per cent increase in money supply (and an
8 per cent increase in currency and a 15 per cent
increase in demand deposits).

Indeed, such increase in money supply as did take
place was due entirely to the increase in foreign
exchange assets. In both the public and the private
sectors, increases in some assets were more than offset by increases in liabilities, the net result being
that these two sectors actually contributed negatively
to the changes in money supply. In the public (government) sector an increase in government indebtedness

to the Bank of Thailand was more than offset by a
sharp increase in the public deposits at the banking
system. In the private sector, while loans and advances of the commercial banks increased substantially over the period under discussion, the sector's
time and savings deposits increased at nearly twice
the rate of loans and advances. The increase in
quasi-money, combined with what appears to have been
a deliberately deflationary policy of accumulating
large idle balances, kept the money supply to a level
which prevented prices from rising.

FINANCIAL INTERMEDIATION

The stability of the price system, together with
the rapid growth of the economy in a climate favorable to trade, played a part in generating a high
level of voluntary savings and a corresponding high
rate of private capital formation. Yet only a small
fraction of these savings and investment can be traced
through the financial intermediaries of the organized
financial markets.

As seen in Table 2.6, financial assets holdings
by the private sector were some 31 billion baht at
the end of 1966, an increase of 6 billion from the
preceding year. This represented only 25 per cent
of estimated private savings in that year.

Table 2.6 brings out the overriding importance
of the commercial banking system in organized financial intermediation. In 1966 demand and time deposits
of the commercial banks accounted for over half of all
the liabilities, currency accounting for an additional 30 per cent. Other liabilities were less than 20
per cent of the total outstanding. An increasing
proportion of private sector savings was channeled
through the commercial banks, and the proportion going
through other intermediaries declined throughout most
of the period 1957-1967.

Table 2.7 shows, however, that the commercial
banks, even though they are by far the most important
intermediary of the organized financial markets,

TABLE 2.6

Outstanding Amounts of Private Sector Savings as Represented
by Financial Asset Holdings, 1956-1967
(million baht)

| Year | Monetary System | | Govt. Savings Banks | Commercial Bank Time Deposits | Govt. Bonds & Bills | Life Insurance Fund | Total |
	Cash	Demand Deposits					
1956	5,420.7	2,275.1	730.0	349.4	189.3	225.5	9,190.0
1957	5,568.2	2,593.6	867.0	438.5	222.7	263.7	9,953.7
1958	5,543.2	2,917.5	949.0	621.7	261.0	290.7	10,583.1
1959	5,779.9	3,267.9	1,023.0	774.6	338.6	314.3	11,498.3
1960	6,043.9	4,022.7	1,248.0	1,025.7	480.5	328.1	13,148.9
1961	6,511.7	4,563.7	1,448.0	1,485.3	655.0	325.3	14,989.0
1962	6,573.4	4,519.9	1,698.0	3,140.0	770.9	333.5	17,034.8
1963	6,711.8	5,167.2	1,975.0	4,253.0	921.0	366.8	19,394.8
1964	7,202.9	5,535.8	2,311.8	5,614.3	1,227.2	386.9	22,278.9
1965	8,183.5	6,168.2	2,773.0	6,406.8	1,372.8	430.1	25,334.4
1966	9,438.4	7,219.4	3,443.5	8,814.8	1,583.3	485.9	30,985.5
1967	9,910.9	7,963.2	4,173.5	10,965.3	1,390.8		

Source: Compiled from data supplied by the Bank of Thailand.

TABLE 2.7

Selected Indicators of Investment Flows, 1957-1967
(amounts in billion baht)

Indicator	1957	1958	1959	1960	1961	1962	1963	1964	1965	1966	1967
Gross investment	7.1	6.6	7.8	9.3	9.7	12.2	15.2	16.9	17.7	23.8	30.4
Private	5.6	5.2	5.8	6.8	6.7	9.2	11.5	12.2	12.6	18.4	23.7
Public	1.5	1.4	2.0	2.5	3.0	3.0	3.7	4.7	5.1	5.4	6.7
GDP (Gross Domestic Product)	47.8	46.0	50.7	55.3	59.5	64.9	68.4	74.1	79.7	93.2	107.5
Index of GDP	100.0	96.2	106.1	115.7	124.4	135.8	143.1	155.0	166.7	195.0	224.9
Gross investment as % of GDP	14.9	14.3	15.4	16.8	16.3	18.8	22.2	22.8	22.2	25.5	28.3
Private gross investment as % of GDP	11.7	11.3	11.4	12.3	11.3	14.2	16.8	16.5	15.8	19.7	22.0
Index of gross investment	100.0	92.9	109.9	131.0	136.6	171.8	214.1	238.0	249.3	335.2	428.2
Index of private investment	100.0	92.8	103.6	121.4	119.6	164.3	205.4	217.9	225.0	328.6	423.2
Gross private sector borrowing from banks	0.49	0.64	0.56	0.85	0.83	1.20	1.12	1.64	2.10	2.09	2.34
Index of private sector borrowing from banks	100.0	130.6	114.3	173.4	169.4	244.9	228.6	334.7	428.6	426.5	477.6
Private sector borrowing as % of private investment	8.8	12.3	9.7	12.5	12.4	13.0	9.7	13.4	16.7	11.4	9.9

Source: Compiled by the World Bank from data provided by the National Economic Board.

45

accounted at the end of 1967 for less than 10 per cent of the volume of private investment.

In calculating the sources of private capital formation during the period of the second five-year plan (1967-1971), the planners allotted less than 10 per cent of total requirements to the organized financial institutions of the total estimated requirement of some 93 billion baht. Foreign sources were estimated to provide 10 billion, financial institutions 9 billion, the remainder to come from "self-finance."[5]

NOTES

1. International reserves increased continuously from 1961, reaching US$898 million at the end of 1968, equivalent to nine months of imports at the 1968 rate: Bank of Thailand, Annual Economic Report, 1968 (Bangkok, 1969), p. 22.

2. For a summary of these circumstances, of which the rapid growth in export markets appears to have been the most significant, see Forrest E. Cookson, "Prospectus--The Development of the Economy of Thailand, 1950-1965" (Washington: National Planning Association, Center for Development Planning, January, 1968). (Mimeo.)

3. Ibid., p. 15.

4. See Paul B. Trescott, "The Structure of Thai Monetary Accounts" (Mimeo; circa 1967).

5. National Economic Development Board, The Second National Economic and Social Development Plan 1967-1971 (Bangkok, 1967), p. 69.

CHAPTER **3** FINANCING OF RURAL
HOUSEHOLDS

Even though the share of agriculture in the Thai
economy shows a decline when measured as a proportion of GNP, agriculture continues to provide employment and income for at least three-fourths of the
labor force, and agricultural output provides much
of the wherewithal of the economy. The rhythm of the
monsoon still permeates the cycle of credit throughout the economy. In centers remote from primary agricultural production, credit continues to be tightest
in June and July, just before the planting season,
and eases considerably in the last quarter of the
calendar year when the rice harvest is being gathered.
The primary agricultural producer may borrow little
from the commercial banks directly, but those who
sell to him and who buy from him depend on bank credit
to varying extents.

In no other sector of the economy does the unorganized market play such an overriding role as in
agriculture. Most of the financial transactions between farmers and others, be they buyers or sellers,
are handled outside institutions subject to regulation, supervision, and control of the public. Most
of these transactions are in cash, and most of them
are done on the basis of private agreement, often implicit rather than explicit, and frequently sanctioned
by many years of usage and still adhered to, even
though the original rationale is but dimly perceived
or has disappeared altogether.

It is in agriculture that the pattern and the
structure of interest rates appear to be the most ir-
regular and discontinuous. Side by side with the substantial proportion of loans carrying a zero interest

charge there are others which, if computed in terms
of money and translated into annual rates, would show
fantastically high interest charges, upward of 600
or 800 per cent per annum. It is also in agriculture
that the many imperfections of the financial markets
in the less developed countries appear in their most
acute form and seem least capable of speedy improvement and least amenable to rational planning for economic development. Capital markets in the urban centers may be in an embryonic stage, but they are well-
nigh nonexistent in the countryside. In the cities
there is, prima facie, a substantial degree of competition among lenders, but such competition is much
weaker among those who supply credit to the farmer.

The role of debt in the financing of rural households is crucial. Much of the income-generating activity in the countryside would not be possible were
it not for inputs coming from other sectors and obtained through the use of the facilities of the financial nexus. Even when the borrowing is used for
purposes of consumption, it often indirectly finances
the productive process by providing the rural households with the wherewithal during the period of production of agricultural output. Thus, borrowing, by
affecting both the level of agricultural income and
the level of consumption, influences the level of
saving. Moreover, inasmuch as rural households do
have some choice in the form or in the timing of loans,
agricultural credit affects not only the level but
also the composition of rural saving. For these reasons, much of the discussion in this chapter revolves
around the magnitude, composition, and distribution of
agricultural credit and relies heavily on the findings
of the sample survey of agricultural credit conducted
in 1962-1963 and published under the title Agricultural Credit in Thailand, Theory, Data, Policy,
henceforth referred to as Agricultural Credit.[1]

THE MARKET FOR LENDABLE FUNDS IN AGRICULTURE

There is a dearth of reliable information regarding almost every significant magnitude of the market
for lendable funds in agriculture.

The chief reason for this statistical hiatus is
the fact that in agriculture, the bulk of borrowing
and lending is done outside institutions subject to
public scrutiny and control.* This situation is far
from being unique to Thailand.[2] Even in the United
States some 40 per cent of agricultural credit is
from noninstitutional sources.

U Tun Wai has devised a series of indicators relating the size of rural debt outstanding to a variety of economic variables. Table 3.1 applies these
indicators to Thailand and extends them to the years
1962-1963. The figures fail, however, to give a clear
idea of the size of the unorganized markets, as well
as of changes in size over time. For Thailand, at
any rate, no perceptible trend emerges from the table.

In the sample survey of agricultural credit in
Thailand for 1962-1963, the proportion of loans contracted by farmers from institutions of the organized
markets is estimated at 7.9 per cent of the number of
loans and 5.5 per cent of their value. Details are
given in Table 3.2.

Even though it is not possible to mark off clearly
the boundaries of the unorganized market in Thailand
agriculture, it is difficult to escape the impression
that it is the dominant force on both the supply and
the demand side in the market for lendable funds in
the countryside. Fortunately, the sample survey does
provide some valuable information about the characteristics and the operations of the unorganized markets and thus gives a factual background to a discussion of its nature and its role in the development
process.

---

*Among the unknown aspects of what one is tempt-
ed to call the "organization of unorganized markets"
are the interrelations of various lenders, their
sources of funds, the tie-in with commercial banks
and other institutions, and the degree of formal or
informal collusion.

TABLE 3.1

Farm Household Debt in Relation to
Economic Variables

Economic Variable	Debt (%)		
	1934-35	1952-54	1962-63
Commercial bank loans, overdrafts, and discounts	29	143	113
Currency in circulation in private hands	69	56	136
Income (output) originating in agriculture	23	14	34
Net national income at factor prices	12	8	15
Debt (million baht)	100	2,059	9,122

Sources: For earlier years, based on U Tun Wai,
          "Interest Rates Outside the Organized
          Money Markets of Underdeveloped Countries,"
          IMF Staff Papers (November, 1957), Table
          8. For 1962/63, computed by the writer.

UNORGANIZED MARKETS

Supply

As seen in Table 3.2, noninstitutional lenders
to farm households are about equally split between
commercial and noncommercial purveyors of resources
represented by neighbors and relatives. Relatives
are the single most important type of lender in every
region when the value of loans is taken into consideration. The percentage of loans extended by relatives ranges from a low of 22.5 per cent in the
Central Plain to a high of 58.5 per cent in the Northeast. It is assumed, although this is by no means

TABLE 3.2

Sources of Credit by Region
(percentage)

Type of Lender	Central Plain % of Loans	Central Plain % of Value	North % of Loans	North % of Value	Northeast % of Loans	Northeast % of Value	South % of Loans	South % of Value	Total % of Loans	Total % of Value[a]
Relative	17.8	22.5	44.8	47.0	50.0	58.5	40.2	43.0	39.9	32.5
Neighbor	14.0	16.7	24.1	19.9	12.1	4.3	15.1	12.9	15.7	15.5
Commercial lender	65.9	57.8	20.6	23.3	30.5	26.4	31.8	30.6	36.5	46.5
Local store	39.2	13.9	4.1	3.0	12.1	4.6	12.1	10.9	16.5	
Crop buyer	8.2	7.9	5.2	10.1	9.1	6.5	13.7	13.8	8.6	
Landlord	6.6	10.7	0.0	0.0	1.5	5.2	0.0	0.0	2.1	
Moneylender	8.0	14.3	7.8	8.9	3.3	7.5	3.0	1.5	5.4	
Other	3.9	11.0	3.5	1.3	4.5	2.6	3.0	4.4	3.9	
Institutional lender	2.3	3.0	10.3	9.8	7.6	10.8	12.9	13.7	7.9	5.5
Credit cooperative	1.4	2.0	10.3	9.8	7.6	10.8	12.1	12.9	7.5	
Other government agency	0.9	1.0	0.0	0.0	0.0	0.0	0.8	0.8	0.4	
Commercial bank	0.0	0.0	0.0	0.0	0.0	0.0	0.0	0.0	0.0	
Total	100.0	100.0	100.0	100.0	100.0	100.0	100.0	100.0	100.0	100.0

[a] In the published study the figures following the decimal point were missing, with the result that the addition of the component percentages yielded 98 per cent; hence the addition of 0.5 to each of the four components shown.

Source: Pantum Thisyamondol, Virach Arromdee, and Millard F. Long, Agricultural Credit in Thailand, Theory, Data, Policy (Bangkok: Kasetsart University, 1965), p. 37.

universally true, that loans extended by relatives
are made on terms and conditions vastly different
from those extended by other lenders. In particular,
it is alleged that these loans are often made without
security and without any interest cost to the borrower.

   Neighbors are often the more prosperous farmers
and not infrequently part-time landlords. In some
parts of the country, those with greater acreage will
let others work their land at certain times of the
year and will advance cash or supplies at other times.
The proportion of loans made by neighbors to the total value of loans is highest in the North (19.9 per
cent) and lowest in the Northeast (slightly over 4
per cent). The low figure for the Northeast is in
part explained by the high ratio of loans made by
relatives and partly by the presumed infrequency of
better-off farmers. It is in the North where the
practice referred to above is the most widespread
owing to the prevalence of multicropping in that area
and the correspondingly lesser emphasis on the production of annual staple crops. The point that neighbors
may double as part-time landlords in the North because
of the importance in the area of intermediate crops
such as garlic, fruit, and soybeans is made here to
account for the puzzling fact, shown in Table 3.2,
that no loans by landlords were found in the sample.

   The various categories of commercial lenders show
a more differentiated picture regionally. Commercial
lenders include shopkeepers, crop buyers, landlords,
moneylenders, and others. Commercial lenders are distinguished from relatives, neighbors, and institutional lenders. Local shopkeepers are the most numerous
commercial lenders in the country, as a whole, and in
two of the four regions. As a proportion of value of
loans, however, credit extended by shopkeepers diminishes in importance, suggesting that, while they make
numerous and frequent advances to the farmers, these
advances are generally for small sums or, what is actually the case in most instances, that the aggregate
value of the commodities which they sell for credit
is relatively small. This is seen in Table 3.3

TABLE 3.3

Sources of Credit by Type of Commercial Lender

Type of Lender	Number of Loans as % of Total Loans	Average Size of Loan (baht)
Shopkeeper	16.5	782
Crop buyer	8.6	1,921
Landlord	2.1	3,531
Moneylender	5.4	3,425
Other	3.9	1,328
All loans	36.5	1,727

Source: Derived from Agricultural Credit, pp. 37-38.

Somewhat surprising is the finding, shown in Table 3.3, of the relatively minor role played by crop buyers as suppliers of credit to farmers. Non-institutional suppliers of credit were often alleged to force the farmer into disadvantageous commercial relationships of various kinds.[3] Thus, for example, in Thailand, the practice of "rice baiting," whereby the farmer borrows against the security of his crop with the proviso that the crop, or a fraction of it, will be sold to the lender, was believed not only to be widespread but also to result in gross exploita-tion of the farmer. The practice of borrowing from crop buyers is most widespread in the Central region, which is both the most commercialized of all regions in Thailand and one where cultivation of annual crops, notably rice, predominates. Forty-five per cent of Central Plain farmers reported borrowing from this source. Of these, however, only 7 per cent were ob-ligated to sell the crop to the buyer.[4] Disregarding the determination of what constitutes "exploitation," Table 3.4 brings out clearly the fact that repayment of both principal and interest in kind is not an im-portant method of settling debts.

TABLE 3.4

Method of Repayment by Type of Lender
(percentage)

Type of Lender	Repayment of Principal			Repayment of Interest		
	Cash	Crop	Crop Sales	Cash	Crop	Crop Sales
Relative	95.4	1.6	3.0	83.2	12.6	4.2
Neighbor	92.1	4.0	3.9	77.3	17.9	4.8
Commercial lender	76.5	8.9	14.6	69.2	16.1	14.6
Local store	77.4	8.9	13.7	71.5	13.5	15.0
Crop buyer	67.4	5.1	27.5	64.1	12.8	23.1
Landlord	73.7	8.8	17.5	62.0	18.0	20.0
Moneylender	75.0	15.5	9.5	65.8	26.6	7.6
Other	93.0	4.7	2.3	79.5	17.9	2.6
Institutional lender	98.8	1.2	0.0	98.7	1.3	0.0
Credit cooperative	100.0	0.0	0.0	100.0	0.0	0.0
Other govt. agency	88.9	11.1	0.0	80.0	20.0	0.0
Commercial bank	-	-	-	-	-	-
All loans	84.8	6.3	8.9	75.4	15.0	9.6

Source: Agricultural Credit, p. 41.

Landlords play a minor role in the supply of credit to farmers except in the Central region, where 10.7 per cent of the value of all loans is provided by them (Table 3.2). In other regions tenancy is not widespread, and the landowners are often farmers themselves.

The catch-all category of "other" lenders includes itinerant traders and peddlers who, in certain areas, are important sources of credit to the farmers. They are the most important exception to the general situation that seems to be peculiar to Thailand: moneylenders not only reside in villages but are, for the most part, ethnically Thai.

Two-thirds of all loans extended to farmers were of less than one-year maturity.[5] Among noninstitutional lenders only relatives could be counted on to wait longer than one year for repayment, and in this case it is probable that the duration of the loan was determined less by the initial contract than by the willingness of the lender to wait.

The foregoing discussion of the structure of the supply side of the unorganized market for agricultural credit is believed to provide a fairly reliable picture of the situation in Thailand.

Although comparison with the surveys made in other countries is difficult, owing to differences in the definitions employed, and cannot be conclusive because of quite different conditions prevailing in such countries as India, Pakistan, Taiwan, and the Philippines, the findings for Thailand appear to be consistent with the findings elsewhere when modified by the specific conditions existing in Thailand. The emerging picture is that of a variety of lenders, and thus of some choice for the farmer, however limited in practice, landlords playing a much smaller role than in other countries and relatives a much greater role. Most important, crop buyers apparently exercise a lesser degree of monopsony power than is commonly believed. The relative importance of the various types of lenders seems to be geographically heterogeneous, commercial lenders predominating in areas of commercialized agriculture and of relatively high income per farm household (which is, in turn, correlated with area cultivated per farm) and relatives predominating in areas where over-all debt is low. Finally, the bulk of the supply of loans from commercial lenders is of relatively short duration; only 26.5 per cent of loans from this source are available for periods exceeding one year.

Demand

If commercial moneylenders predominate in the more prosperous regions rather than, as might have been expected, in the poor areas, it would seem that in the prosperous, commercialized areas the demand for credit is greater than the available supply from the preferred sources--institutions, relatives, friends, and neighbors. Conversely, in areas where total demand for credit is low, the preferred sources supply a larger proportion of the total. This suggests an important aspect of the demand for credit; namely, that it is strongly correlated with both income and area cultivated.

Table 3.5 deals with potential rather than effective demand for lendable funds. Farmers' responses indicate that the desire to borrow increases continuously and directly with respect to both area cultivated and net income. The proportion of farmers wishing to borrow (or saying so) would seem to be substantially greater than of those actually borrowing. After all, the willingness to borrow has to contend with the availability and the cost of funds and with other requirements of lenders which, on occasion, are beyond the capacity of the borrower to meet. Hence, an unexpected finding of the Thailand sample survey is that the proportion of all farmers desirous of borrowing is almost exactly the same as the proportion of farm households who actually borrow, 68.19 per cent versus 68.06 per cent. There is a strong presumption that "desire to borrow" was construed as tantamount to actively seeking a loan.

For those whose actually incur debts, the size of the debt increases with income as well as with

area cultivated per farm. It is worth noting that
the relationship between the size of debt and each
of the other two variables is not entirely symmetri-
cal. The modal loan size for the richest farmers is
in excess of 20,000 baht, and the corresponding figure for farmers with the largest farms is between
5,000 and 10,000 baht. It appears that the more prosperous the farmer, the more he is willing to borrow
and the greater the amount of debt he will contract.

TABLE 3.5

Agricultural Credit Sample Survey: Proportion
of Borrowers Desiring Loans by Income
and Area Cultivated

Proportion Desiring Loans			
By Net Income		By Area Cultivated Per Farm	
Income (baht)	Per Cent	Area (rai)	Per Cent
1-1,999	56.64	1-5	49.09
2,000- 4,999	61.33	5-10	54.00
5,000- 9,999	75.86	10-20	57.39
10,000-19,999	76.79	20-50	72.49
20,000 and over	87.50	50 and over	90.85
All incomes	68.19	All areas	68.19

Source: Derived from data contained in Agricultural
Credit.

While the sample survey did not explicitly relate the purpose to which the loan proceeds are devoted to indices of farmers' prosperity, there are
indications that here, too, the correlation is positive; i.e., the more prosperous the farmer, the
more productive the purpose for which he borrows.

Over two-thirds of loans contracted by Thai farmers are short-term in nature, of less than one year's duration. In fact, 76 per cent of all loans were for sums under 2,000 baht; and of those above 2,000 baht, only 13 per cent were for over one year or "indefinite."[6] Given the seasonal nature of needs for funds under annual crop cultivation, the type of cultivation still preponderant in the country, one would expect that the peak of demand for loans would take place during the planting season and the bottom reached during the harvest season. (Four seasons, each one of about three months duration, can be distinguished in the rice cycle of cultivation in Thailand. The harvest season extends roughly over the first three months of the calendar year, followed by the dry, the planting, and the growing seasons.) It is somewhat surprising to find that cash loans were fairly evenly spaced over time. As shown in Table 3.6, the proportion of loans contracted during the third quarter (the planting season), 26.5 per cent, was only slightly higher than the 22.2 per cent contracted during the first quarter (the harvest season). This suggests, among other things, both greater liquidity and lesser dependence on annual staples than is commonly supposed. For loans contracted in kind, however, the seasonal pattern is much more pronounced. During the peak demand season, 58.6 per cent of all loans are incurred, compared with only 6.8 per cent following the harvest.

TABLE 3.6

Date of Borrowing by Type of Loan
(percentage)

Loan Type	Quarter				Total
	1	2	3	4	
Cash	22.2	23.6	26.5	27.6	100
Kind	6.8	12.5	58.6	22.1	100
All loans	17.3	20.2	36.6	25.9	100

Source: Agricultural Credit, p. 27.

If the demand for cash loans in the country as
a whole does not diverge very much from a moving
average, the purpose for which the loans are made
tends to differ considerably both by region and by
time period. In general, in areas where the farmers
have to wait a full year for the bulk of their earnings to come in, loans for consumption purposes predominate. These are contracted during periods preceding the rice and corn harvests. In other areas,
where intermediate crops provide a considerable part
of farmers' income throughout the year, loans for
variable inputs play a more important role and are
contracted throughout the year.[7]

In the North, where intermediate crops are perhaps more important than rice, loans for living expenses constitute less than 10 per cent of the value
of short-term loans and less than 4 per cent of the
value of long-term loans. In the Central region,
on the other hand, where rice still dominates the
regional economy (and where little double cropping
is practiced), some 28 per cent of short-term borrowing was for consumption purposes and over 20 per cent
of long-term borrowing was used to pay for current
living expenses. Conversely, the North uses the
greatest proportion of its short-term loans for variable inputs even though, when long-term loans are
included, it is the Central region which forges
ahead.

Social expenditures account for only 4.17 per
cent of short-term and 3.45 per cent of long-term
borrowing. These are rather insignificant proportions for purposes which, allegedly, account for much
of farmer indebtedness in other countries.[8] This low
proportion does not mean that the Thai farmer does
not spend much on weddings, funerals, or bouns (local
temple festivals) but rather suggests that the Thai
rural society has developed means other than borrowing to cope with these expenditures; an earlier survey of rice farmers in the Central region established
that the proportion of ceremonial expenses to total
consumption expenditures was 13 per cent.[9] Thus, for
example, in the Northern provinces, in the event of
a death in the family, fellow villagers each

contribute 3 or 4 baht toward the funeral expenses
of the bereaved. Elsewhere, a communal fund is established, often made up of unsold paddy, out of
which certain emergency expenses of villagers are met.

From the sample survey, as well as from other
sources, the impression is gleaned that the demand
for loans increases as the farmer becomes more oriented toward commercial agriculture and as he learns
that an increased effort to enhance his productivity
will result in substantially higher cash income. The
extent to which this orientation will actually be
translated into effective demand depends on the supply of funds available to him and the terms at which
he can borrow.

Loan Terms: Collateral and Interest Rates

In this section two aspects of the terms of credit in the unorganized market will be discussed: the
pattern of interst rates and the security for a loan.
The method of repayment and the duration of loans
have been briefly discussed in other contexts.

While it is true that all aspects of rural credit are related and that the terms at which lendable
funds are transferred are both the product and the
influence behind the demand and supply schedules, the
connection between the collateral and the interest
rate is particularly intimate, even though the relationship is not necessarily a simple one.[10] For
example, while, in general, the better the quality
of the collateral the borrower can muster, the lower
the interest rate he has to pay, other things being
equal, it is not unusual to find that the most favorable terms are offered borrowers who proffer no collateral whatsoever. This is not surprising when it
is realized that the need to produce a security with
which to supplement a promise to repay is in itself
an admission that one's credit standing is not of the
highest order. It is, after all, only the Triple-A
American corporation which can sell unsecured debentures to the public. In the majority of cases, however, the credit rating of rural borrowers is such
that the quality and the kind of collateral he is
able to offer is an important determinant of the rate

of interest he will be asked to pay. It is difficult
to establish this proposition empirically, however,
because the data are not collected in a way which relates rigorously the quality of collateral to the interest rate under ceteris paribus conditions. Moreover, in practice, it is well-nigh impossible to
preserve these conditions when dealing with aggregates.
In the sample survey of Thai agricultural credit there
appears, however, some indirect confirmation, shown
in Tables 3.7 and 3.8, that the quality of the collateral influences the rate of interest. Table 3.7
shows that security of land, considered the best of
all securities, is given for most larger loans. As
Table 3.8 shows, it is the largest loans which carry
the lowest interest rate. Conversely, as seen in
these two tables, the greatest proportion of the
smallest loans (under 2,000 baht) involve no collateral whatsoever. Of these smallest loans, 54 per cent
are unsecured; of the largest loans (5,000 baht and
over), only 16 per cent are unsecured.

Table 3.7 shows that land as a security constituted only 17.3 per cent of all loans. Nearly half
of all loans granted were made with no security whatever. The picture is slightly clouded by the high
proportion of loans, particularly small loans, for
which no responses were given with respect to collateral, but it is likely that many loans in this category were made between parties related by kinship
and other ties. The high proportion of unsecured
loans is a circumstance found in a number of other
countries and reflects the poverty of the borrowers
and a shortage of marketable assets.[11] Of some interest is the very low proportion of loans secured
by jewelry in Thailand. In other countries, particularly India, gold and jewelry are much more important forms of security.[12] The small proportion of
crop collateral shown in Table 3.7 probably understates the real position. It is likely that many of
the smaller loans represented in the "no answer" column are, in fact, secured by crops in one way or another.

The high regard in which land mortgage is held by
the lenders is in itself a reflection of the scarcity
of transferable assets in the hands of the farmers.

TABLE 3.7

Security by Size of Loan
(percentage)

Size of Loan (baht)	Type of Security								
	Land	Crops	Farm Capital	Jewelry	Note	No Security	No Answer	Other	Total
1-1,999	8.1	1.2	1.1	1.4	1.6	53.7	32.0	0.9	100
2,000-4,999	37.2	1.0	1.0	0.3	3.4	40.5	15.6	1.0	100
5,000 and over	75.0	2.2	-	-	2.2	16.3	2.2	2.2	100
All loans	17.3	1.3	1.0	1.1	1.9	49.1	27.3	1.0	100

Source: Agricultural Credit, p. 28.

TABLE 3.8

Rate of Interest by Size of Loan
(percentage)

Size of Loan (baht)	Mean Interest Rate	Interest Rate (monthly)						
		0.0-0.9	1.0-1.9	2.0-2.9	3.0-4.9	5.0-9.9	10.0 and Over	Total
1-499	3.2	51.1	4.3	8.5	12.8	15.6	7.7	100
500-999	2.6	34.9	10.8	19.9	19.9	13.3	1.2	100
1,000-2,999	2.3	34.3	14.7	27.4	14.7	8.1	0.8	100
3,000 and over	1.9	26.3	26.8	30.8	11.1	4.0	1.0	100

Source: Agricultural Credit, p. 32.

In Thailand, however, land is considered the superior type of collateral for yet other reasons. It is preferred security by commercial banks and other institutions; it is required by the primary cooperative credit associations; and it is an asset whose value has been appreciating over time. This preference for land mortgage is a limiting factor in the development of rural credit both because of supply conditions and also because of the cumbersome procedures involved in the valuation and registration of real estate mortgages. On the other hand, rural lenders in unorganized markets are, in Thailand, rather reluctant to acquire land for themselves, to start eviction proceedings, and to bring about repossession. Their preference for land mortgage derives from their knowledge that a borrower who pledges an asset several times the value of the loan will do his utmost to repay it rather than risk proceedings against his land. In fact, moneylenders and others are much more flexible than institutions of the organized market in the way they deal with this collateral.

The inverse relation between the size of the loan and the interest rate is a well-known phenomenon of rural credit in the less developed countries. In part, as argued above, this relation is a function of the collateral available to small borrowers, but it also has much to do with the higher administrative cost of collection and with the nature of small loans, which imply a greater risk of delay or an inability to repay. The mean interest rate according to the size of the loan ranges, as shown in Table 3.8, from 3.2 per cent per month for loans under 500 baht to 1.9 per cent for those 3,000 baht and over. The extent of this range is almost certainly telescoped by the inclusion in the Thai sample of interest-free loans from relatives and others. It is this which accounts for the high proportion (51.1 per cent) of loans under 500 baht paying less than 1 per cent per month. In a 1955 study in the Philippines by Leopoldo P. De Guzman that involved a large sample of farm families and a total of 1,914 short-term loans, interest-free loans were excluded. The range of interest rates, all of which were inversely related to the size of the loan, extended from 55.4 per cent per annum for the smallest loans to 14.4 per cent for the largest.[13]

The inclusion in the Thai sample survey of agricultural credit of loans from relatives, landlords, and others which carry a zero interest rate is also responsible for the murky appearance of the relationship between the income of the borrower and the rate of interest. Contrary to what may have been expected, those with annual incomes of 20,000 baht and over, a high net income by Thai standards,* pay a mean monthly interest rate of 2.7 per cent, compared with the 2.3 per cent rate paid by those with net annual incomes ranging from 2,000 to 5,000 baht.[14] It is reasonable to assume, however, that a substantial number of the loans contracted by these lower-income borrowers and bearing a monthly interest charge under 1 per cent (57.6 per cent of all loans made to this income group) were, in fact, zero-interest loans.

The inverse relationship between the rate of interest and the size of the loan stems from the incidence of "sound" collateral, from the fact that administrative overhead is relatively invariant with respect to the size of the loan, and from the presumption that small loans are those demanded by the less provident farmers.

No such readily apparent connection exists for the relationship between the duration of the loan and the rate of interest. The rate of interest tends to be lower for loans made for periods in excess of one year than for short-term loans.[15] The De Guzman study brings out the relationship between the duration of loans and the interest rate in greater detail. In the nine categories into which De Guzman divides his sample (by average interest rate per annum and by average period of loans in months), the inverse relationship is, with only one exception, monotonic.

The reasons for the inverse relation between the duration of loans and the interest rate are somewhat conjectural. Shorter-term loans have been shown to be often made for less productive purposes than loans

---

*Per capita GNP in 1963 was estimated at slightly over 2,300 baht.

of longer duration. Shorter-term loans are associated with borrowers who are, on the whole, less provident, less prosperous, and, hence, less reliable
than borrowers for longer-term loans. It is the
longer-term loans that most often are associated with
collateral in the form of a land mortgage. Last but
not least, an interest charge, when computed on an
annual basis, makes little sense to an anxious borrower who needs the use of a loan for only two or
three months. The lender finds it easier to charge
a higher rate of interest when the absolute amount
added to the principal is still a small sum.

According to the sample survey of agricultural
credit in Thailand, the mean monthly rate of interest
on all loans and for all regions was 2.4 per cent in
1962/63. The breakdown by regions and by frequency
distribution is given in Table 3.9. Unlike certain
other data contained in the published results of the
sample survey, Table 3.9 weighs the number of loans
by their baht value. The data given in the table
appear to be consistent with findings in other countries; for example, U Tun Wai states that "weighted
average rates of interest . . . in rural areas in
underdeveloped countries . . . [are] usually between
24 and 36 per cent per annum."16

Even a brief scrutiny of Table 3.9 suggests that
there can be no simple explanation of the determinants of the interest rate. Thus, the Northeastern
region, considered to be the poorest and most de-
pressed area of Thailand, enjoys a lower mean rate
than the relatively prosperous North. The highly
commercialized and relatively well-to-do farmers in
the Central Plain pay more, on the average, than
farmers in the South. A very high proportion of
Southern borrowers pay less than 1 per cent a month,
suggesting a high incidence of interest-free borrowings from relatives and landlords (plantation owners). One possible reason for the low mean rate in
the South is the substantial proportion of Moslems
living in that region. The Northeast, which also enjoys a high proportion of interest-free loans, has
a substantial percentage of loans with very heavy
monthly interest costs.

TABLE 3.9

Rate of Interest by Region
(percentage)

Region	Mean Interest Rate	Rate per Month						Total
		0.0–0.9	1.0–1.9	2.0–2.9	3.0–3.9	4.0–4.9	5.0–9.9	10.0 and over	
Central Plain	2.2	30.1	15.6	28.1	8.3	6.5	9.4	2.2	100
North	3.3	39.7	9.5	4.3	15.5	13.8	13.8	3.4	100
Northeast	2.7	56.8	2.4	8.8	3.2	2.4	17.6	8.8	100
South	1.5	63.6	12.9	6.8	5.3	0.8	7.8	3.0	100
All loans	2.4	38.5	12.9	20.6	8.1	6.1	10.6	3.2	100

Details may not add up to totals because of rounding.

Source: Agricultural Credit, p. 30.

In the absence of data which would permit a more
rigirous statement regarding the determinants of interest rates, only observations of a general character can be made here.

In the first place, it is a truism that the rate
of interest is given by the intersection of the demand and supply functions. For any given supply of
lendable funds for a specific kind of loan, it will
be the quantity demanded of this type of loan which
will determine its price. The implication of this
is that in the South the mean cost of lendable funds
is lower than in the Central region because the demand for loans is much greater in the latter. Of
course, it is more than likely that the supply of
funds is also unequal, but presumably the relation
of demand to supply is determining. This tautology abstracts from differences in risk, which is in itself
a composite of many complex factors. It does, however, help to explain the high rate in the North.
By all standards, Northern borrowers seem to be the
most credit-worthy of all, yet they pay more for
loans than those in the Northeast. There must be
something in the nature of the demand for funds in
the North which exerts upward pressure on the level
of interest rates and which, to the extent that it
persists over time, is not fully alleviated by tem-
poral and spatial arbitrage on the supply side. In
fact, as suggested earlier, it would seem that the
nature of the cultivation in the Northern provinces,
with main reliance on the production of subsidiary
cash crops and the importance of long-maturing fruit
crops, puts a particularly heavy demand on the market
for lendable funds. For one reason or another, the
suppliers of funds have not yet adjusted to a situation where above-average profits could be made.

For Thailand as a whole the highest rates of interest are those charged by the local shopkeepers
and, somewhat surprisingly, by landlords. The lowest
rates are those obtained by relatives, although the
rate of 1.8 per cent per month given in Table 3.10 is
the weighted mean of all loans made by relatives, including the substantial, if unknown, proportion of
loans made without any interest charge. The pattern

of regional dispersion from the mean rates, according
to the source of loans, shows no particular surprises.
One would expect moneylenders to charge a much higher
rate of interest to farmers in the Northeast than to
those in the Central Plain. Both the risk and the
limitations on supply are greater in the former region.

TABLE 3.10

Monthly Interest Rates by Region
and Type of Lender
(percentage)

| Type of Lender | Monthly Interest Rate | | | | Mean Rate All Areas |
	Central Plain	North	North-east	South	
Relative	1.7	2.6	1.8	1.1	1.8
Neighbor	2.4	3.3	3.3	2.3	2.6
Commercial lender	2.3	4.8	4.3	2.0	2.9
Local store	2.7	5.4	6.2	2.7	3.5
Crop buyer	2.4	4.7	3.9	1.3	2.9
Landlord	3.8	–	1.8	–	3.5
Moneylender	2.1	5.0	7.3	3.6	3.3
Other	1.6	3.4	7.0	2.2	2.5

Source: Agricultural Credit, p. 40.

If one abstracts from the loans made among relatives, it would seem that the modal rate of interest
for loans in the Thai countryside is between 36 and
48 per cent per annum. This compares with the 24 to
30 per cent modal rate in the unorganized markets in
the urban areas. (See Chapter 7.) It is superfluous
to argue whether this differential is justified. The
very nature of the unorganized market is such that
elements of monopoly exist and some degree of exploitation does take place.[17] Perhaps the most significant finding of the sample survey is that the commonly employed forms of exploitation play but a minor
role in Thailand. Thus, in general, farmers have

access to more than one lender; "rice baiting" and
other types of borrowing and repayment in kind are
relatively unimportant; few farmers feel lenders take
undue advantage of them; and so on.[18]

Assuming a given level of effective demand for
loans, the interest rate will vary with the availability of funds in an area, with the cost of administration, and with the degree of risk. The fact that
rural rates are higher than those in the urban areas
must be primarily the function of higher relative
administrative costs and higher risks. It cannot be
due to lesser demand because this, if anything, would
militate against higher rates. It can be attributed
only partly to availability of funds because one
would expect funds to flow to the countryside, were
other factors comparable with those prevailing in
urban areas.

There can be little question that unit costs of
administration are greater in the case of agricultural credit than for comparable urban loans. Rural
loans are for smaller amounts and are made to a widely dispersed clientele which has little in the way
of easily assessable collateral and little sophistication in financial dealings. But, on the other hand,
rural lenders have developed a number of techniques
to reduce the unit costs of processing, of collection,
and of recovery. Most moneylenders are located in
the villages, right among their actual and potential
clients. They have developed simple and flexible
procedures and have adjusted in other ways to the peculiarities of their métier. Nevertheless, the administrative costs of rural loans probably remain
higher than those in urban centers, even though their
influence on the level of the rates of interest should
not be exaggerated.

Repayment Record

One indication of the creditworthiness of rural
borrowers and, hence, the degree of risk in agricultural credit may be obtained from the examination of
the repayment record of farmers. Unfortunately, data
on this point contained in the sample survey suffer

from a number of drawbacks. The published figures
do not specify whether "nonrepayment" means a delay
or a repudiation; if a delay, how long is it, and at
what point does it become a bad debt? The published
results also are not clear on whether the percentages
refer to the number of loans alone or whether these
are weighted by the amounts. Table 3.11 summarizes
such data as are available. It is seen that for the
country as a whole 18 per cent of farmers failed to
pay interest (on time?) but 43 per cent did not pay
back principal (on time?).

The higher proportion of those repaying interest
on time is not surprising. Even though in many cases
the terms of loans do not explicitly separate the interest from the principal, lenders make sure that any
partial repayment is first credited to interest, with
successive payments being applied to the capital value of the loan. What is surprising, however, is the
very high proportion of those who do not pay back
principal.

Were the figures in Table 3.11 to be taken as
pertaining to the actual loss experience of the lenders (rather than to a delay), then it would seem that
the rates of interest exacted in the Thai countryside
are far from being exorbitant. A loss ratio on both
interest and principal of the order of 20 per cent
effectively reduces the nominal interest rate (the
rate agreed on, either implicitly or explicitly, between the borrower and the lender) charged on a loan
by more than half. If R is the nominal rate, ϕ the
bad-debt ratio, and E the effective rate, then E =
$R - \phi - \phi R$. Thus, with a nominal rate of 50 per cent
per annum and with a bad-debt ratio of 20 per cent
(one in five borrowers fails to repay both interest
and principal), the effective return to the lender
is only 20 per cent per annum.

Table 3.12 shows the effective interest rates under various assumptions regarding the bad-debt ratio
and the nominal rate. In order for the lender to
realize an effective annual rate of 25 per cent annum, for example, he would have to charge the borrower
66.7 per cent if he believes that one out of four

farmers will fail to pay back the interest and the principal.

TABLE 3.11

Repayment Performance of Borrowers

Region	Percentage Repaying Principal	Percentage Repaying Interest
Central	49.6	77.6
North	77.8	95.8
Northeast	64.4	91.1
South	50.7	70.4
Total (465 borrowers)	57.0	81.9

Source: Derived from data in Agricultural Credit.

TABLE 3.12

Nominal and Effective Rates of Interest

Bad Debts as Per Cent of Loan Value	Nominal Rate of Interest			
	E^a 10	E^a 15	E^a 25	E^a 50
10	22.22	17.78	38.89	66.67
15	29.41	35.29	47.06	76.47
25	46.67	53.33	66.67	100.00
50	120.00	130.00	150.00	200.00

[a]Effective rate. $E = \dfrac{R + \phi}{1 - \phi}$. The formula does not consider compound interest, a minor consideration in the case of agricultural loans, which are typically of short duration.

In fact, however, the proportion of those who repudiate the debt is almost certainly lower than that shown in Table 3.11. Rural lenders do extend the maturity of the loan, particularly when nonrepayment is attributable to natural causes. All the same, uncertainty regarding these and other causes of nonrepayment do result, in the case of rural credit, in considerable disparity between nominal and effective rates of interest.

Other Aspects

The picture which emerges from the available empirical data suggests a large potential demand, on the one hand, and a limited supply of funds on the other. That a large need for funds exists is demonstrated both by the results of various surveys and by the published observations of keen students of agricultural credit, who point out low levels of income of farmers, little savings, uncertainties due to vagaries of weather and market, the seasonal nature of production--particularly of monsoon agriculture-- and the desire to maintain consumption at a scale dictated by custom and prestige.[19]

Because of the unavailability of collateral, limitations on the supply side, and other constraints, both institutional and cultural, effective demand is substantially below the potential need for funds. In particular, not enough credit is extended for purposes which will tend to enhance the productivity and the income of the farmer and particularly for purposes which would make the loan a self-liquidating one, in the sense of its proceeds adding to the value of output an amount in excess of the value of principal plus interest. To quote a passage from the Thai sample survey: "Actually, in an underdeveloped country, the agricultural credit problem is more likely to be too few debts than too many; the inability to obtain credit on terms they can afford may limit the farmers' possibilities of expanding output."[20]

The contention that the volume of credit demanded would have been greater had the terms been more favorable to the farmer suggests that the elasticity

of demand in terms of price (interest rate) is greater than unity. There is some evidence to suggest
that this indeed is the case. Thus, effective demand
for credit is greater in those areas where the rate
of interest is lower and where there is a greater degree of monetization of the economy.[21]

In any event, whatever the shape of the demand
function in the market for lendable funds in agriculture, a shift to the right of the supply function
would lower the cost of capital and increase the quantity of rural credit. As it is, it is contended that
the existing supply schedule has low elasticity. Those
who lend funds in the countryside are often persons
aware of alternative uses of capital which, given the
relative risks, they may find more attractive. The
institutional framework in which rural lenders operate
does not offer short-run possibilities of expanding
credit in a way possible in a fractional reserve
banking system. The links with the large, urban, organized market for funds are weak and uncertain.

An examination of the conditions under which lenders operate, however, lends little firm evidence to
support the contention that the prevailing terms of
credit are the results of some conspiracy rather than
the results of economic forces over which the lenders
themselves have but limited control. Even when lenders in the unorganized markets insist on land mortgage, they are often willing to accept the sort
of document which is not acceptable to the commercial
banks. In Thailand there exist three types of titles
to land. One is really a temporary squatter's permit,
unacceptable to all lenders; the second is a deed of
sale, which is not acceptable to organized-market
lenders but accepted by moneylenders; and the third
is a duly registered title, acceptable to all. The
moneylenders will not insist on registration, on appraisal, and on other formalities which farmers find
not only irksome and time-consuming but, equally important, sometimes impairing to their dignity and
standing in the community. One reason why relatively
good credit risks will borrow in the unorganized market rather than from banks or from an officially
sponsored institution is the more relaxed attitude

of the unorganized-market lenders toward this question of land collateral.

Frequently moneylenders will waive collateral but
will exact a higher rate of interest. Indeed, the
prevalence of some very high annual rates of interest
can, in the majority of cases, be traced to loans
made for small sums to farmers not noted for their
creditworthiness and devoid of any security. Such
loans are usually made for either emergency or current consumption, and there is little in the proposed
use of the loan which would diminish the risk to the
lender.

One subsidiary reason, not hitherto mentioned,
for the existence of high rates of interest is the
fact that many lenders in the unorganized markets
("moneylenders") lend out their funds for only a few
months in a year, there being no demand for credit
during the remainder of the year. Monthly interest
thus has to compensate for funds being idle during,
say, harvest months and yet provide an annual rate
of return which warrants the use of capital in agriculture.

The flexibility in the practices with respect to
collateral and the willingness to advance funds, at
a price, to less creditworthy farmers for consumption
purposes are among the two important reasons which
account for the fact that, in a country like Thailand,
perhaps 95 per cent of all loans are contracted outside the organized markets (see Table 3.2). Commercial bank loans to agriculture from January 1962 to
January 1964 rose by only 70 million baht;[22] not
many of these loans were made directly to farmers.

Other reasons for the prevalence of unorganized
markets in agricultural credit are found throughout
the vast literature dealing with rural conditions in
the less developed countries.[23] Moneylenders dispense
with many cumbersome procedures and with much paper-
work. They grant loans tailored to fit the borrower's
need of the moment. Most important of all, they can
disburse funds quickly and without recourse to an
authority other than their own. And they are amenable

to delays and postponements of repayment and will, on occasion, grant an additional loan to a debtor in temporary straits. Finally, moneylenders are ubiquitous, as contrasted with sporadic institutional lenders; they know their customers well and are well-known to them. Indeed, the relationship between the borrower and the lender outside the organized markets often involves a broader range of services, the lender performing valuable economic functions in the area of technical advice, storage, and marketing.

Be that as it may, elements of monopoly certainly exist, and many abuses do take place. Even in Thailand, where dispossession and loss of land through debt have been rare occurrences, in recent years at any rate, there are reasons to believe that farmers are not fully aware of the implicit cost of borrowing in such practices as sales of green paddy or repayment of loans in kind in farm produce. Moneylenders employ various techniques to hide the true cost of a loan from officialdom, such as lumping principal and interest in one promissory note with only one sum showing; deducting interest from the funds disbursed; postdating checks, which also lump interest and principal; issuing two promissory notes, one for interest, the other for principal, but both claiming to be for principal.[24] Some of these techniques rebound to the disadvantage of the less sophisticated and less alert borrowers.

Even though moneylenders frequently dispense with any security against the loan and will advance funds to improvident borrowers, they are not without recourse with respect to balky and recalcitrant debtors. In fact, while many of the methods employed to secure recovery shun courts and legal redress, they may appear to the farmer to be on occasion more ruthless than repossession proceedings, since they rely on social compulsion and exploit the farmer's concern about "face" and status in the village. Yet, by all accounts, defaults do take place, and they do so in a significant proportion of all loans granted.

But, if the often made assertion about the scourge of moneylenders and the plight of the farmer

who falls prey to them appears greatly exaggerated
(when it is not beside the point), it does not follow
that the status quo in agricultural credit is either
desirable or incapable of improvement. Much of the
desirable productive activity does not take place
because either the supply of finance is limited or
its terms are unacceptable. Yet much lending in the
countryside is for purposes which do little to improve
the lot of the farmer over time. The existing structure of credit tends to impede the flow of voluntary
savings on the part of the farmer in a variety of
ways. Farmers are compelled to borrow for a few
months every year merely to survive, and the necessity to do so inhibits the accumulation of cash savings, let alone entrusting them to a specialized
financial institution. The fact that most farmers
are perennially in debt robs them of an incentive to
save more, or indeed to work harder or more efficiently. There is little in the structure of unorganized
markets which would encourage longer-term productive
credit designed to increase the farmer's income and
thus his ability to save. Short-term consumption
loans are certainly more risky, but the risk is com-
pensated for by the high interest rate; and the lender who values liquidity prefers the existing pattern
of credit. To the extent that these lenders accumulate profits, they seldom use them for the development of productive enterprise but, rather, for ultimate enjoyment of consumption.

In short, the unorganized markets in agricultural
credit fulfill a static purpose.[25] They supply high-
cost, high-risk credit to many who otherwise would
not have been able to tide themselves over from one
year to the next. These markets are designed to maintain the existing asset structure with little growth
of either output or profits allowable over time.
Given the limited supply and a very large need for
funds for frequently nonproductive purposes, the unorganized markets do their job reasonably well, at
prices which appear consonant with conditions prevailing in them.

Given the nature of these unorganized markets,
it can hardly be expected that they will of and by

themselves gradually abandon their emphasis on consumption and short-term "asset maintenance" loans
and shift their emphasis into provisions of loans for
productive purposes. Yet, as argued previously, it
is the latter type of loan which is most likely to
increase the farmer's income over time and to generate voluntary saving capable of being channeled into
further productive uses. This being so, attention
should be devoted to devising ways and means of either
changing the character of these unorganized markets
or, alternatively, transferring some of their functions to markets which respond to developmental priorities. Some of these ways and means are suggested
in the concluding sections of this chapter. But, as
will be seen in the succeeding pages, the mere extension of the scope of the organized markets as they
perform at present is not likely to be very fruitful.
The organized markets require a considerable amount
of social engineering if they are to become more efficient and to increase their share in the market for
lendable funds in agriculture.

ORGANIZED MARKETS

Little is known about the inner structure of the
unorganized markets in agricultural credit, even
though this market provides the vast bulk of all the
funds to farmers. On the other hand, there is no
dearth of information about the structure of the institutions comprising the organized market, even
though only a fraction of total agricultural credit
flows through them. This situation is, of course,
implicit in the fact that the latter institutions,
being subject to public scrutiny, supervision, and
control, are surrounded by legislative enactments,
administrative statutes, and accounting requirements.
They have to publish financial statements at regular
intervals; they have to submit reports; and they are
frequently the subject of official discussions and
memoranda.

In no small measure these organizational constraints are responsible for the minor role which the
organized markets play in agricultural credit. The

constraints limit the area of operations, preclude
actions and policies which could extend the scope of
the institutions, and inhibit their flexibility and
freedom of movement. Yet the basic motivation of
these constraints, to direct the flow of funds in
agriculture to developmental ends consistent with the
national resources and objectives, is a sound one.
Hence, the study of the institutions in the organized
markets must bring out which of these constraints are
unavoidable and a necessary price to be paid for social control, and which are expendable or could be
reworked so as to provide maximum efficiency consistent with developmental aims.

The organized market for agricultural credit consists of three unequal parts. The bulk of credit
comes from the cooperative institutions. A small proportion is provided by various governmental departments and, in recent years, a small but growing amount
of lendable funds to the farmers have been made available by at least one commercial bank. In the aggregate the institutional loans to farm households have,
in recent years, reached about 500 million baht annually. It is doubtful whether this volume of lending represents any significant advance over the 5 or
6 per cent which was the proportion of borrowing from
institutional sources in 1962/63.

of the three components of the organized market,
the most highly structured is the cooperative institutional complex. At its base it consists of some 10,000
primary cooperative credit societies, of unlimited
liability type. At its apex it is represented by the
Bank of Agriculture and Agricultural Cooperatives.
The structure is, however, far from being a formal
pyramid. In fact, between the apex and the base there
are only two district agricultural banks or, rather,
federations of credit cooperatives, and some seven
production credit societies, a rather new and promising form of dispensing credit to the Thai farmer.

The supply of agricultural credit emanating from
governmental departments is uneven, intermittent, and
directed to achieving ad hoc goals. It is confined
to one or two ministries and is concentrated in the
Ministry of Agriculture.

So far, the commercial banks' direct loans to farmers have been limited to the activities of the Bangkok Bank Ltd., and to some special, regional activities on the part of some others. However, commercial banks do, of course, make loans classified as agricultural, which are usually confined to accommodation extended to processors, distributors, and exporters of agricultural crops.

The Cooperative Institutions

The introduction of cooperatives into Thai agriculture dates back to 1916. It was originally meant to be an experiment and was enacted through an amendment to the existing law on associations. By 1928, when the cooperative movement was already well on the way, a statute on cooperatives was promulgated. This statute, subject to minor amendments, is still in force.

In the history of the cooperative movement in Thailand there emerge three distinct stages. From inception to the revolution of 1932, the cooperative movement was an experimental, emergency device to protect the farmer from the imminence of dispossession and loss of land. Only after 1932 did the government undertake to promote actively the spread of cooperatives (including noncredit cooperatives), albeit still mainly on what may be termed welfare principles. In this, the second stage of the development of cooperatives, the formation of the Bank of Cooperatives in 1947 gave a fillip to the movement which lasted until about 1954 and produced a vigorous growth of credit societies. Since 1954, the beginning of the third stage, the cooperative movement has remained rather stagnant. The number of societies and the volume of loans outstanding has remained roughly constant. It is estimated that members of the credit cooperatives still amount to less than 10 per cent of rural households.[26]

Even though the village credit cooperatives accumulate a modest amount of deposits and reserves, the bulk of their funds for lending have come from other sources, first from the Bank for Cooperatives and then from its successor, the Bank for Agriculture and

Agricultural Cooperatives, which began operations in
1966. In the past the funds borrowed bore a 7 per
cent annual interest rate and were relent to members
at 10 per cent per annum, the differential covering
the costs of operation and accruing or contributing
to the cooperative reserve fund or else being used
for other functions the village cooperatives are supposed to perform, such as farm and cooperative education.

The Bank for Agriculture and Agricultural Cooperatives currently lends funds to cooperative societies at 9 per cent for relending to members at 12 per
cent, which is also the rate charged by the bank on
direct loans to farmers.

The interest rate charged by the village cooperatives to their members is a single rate regardless of
the duration of the loan or its purpose. In the past,
the bulk of the loans were for medium and long duration, up to ten years, and to a large extent for the
purpose of acquisition of land and debt consolidation.
In recent years, however, a greater emphasis has been
put on loans for the purchase of farm machinery and
land improvements and on short-term loans for general
farm operation.

The village societies are of the unlimited liability type. Even though each loan must be secured
by land mortgage, the borrower must attach two signatures of fellow villagers to his loan application.
In addition, the board of directors of the society,
usually of three or four members, must approve the
application, which is then submitted to the bank.
Bank officers, together with the officials of the
Ministry of Agriculture, approve and disburse the
loan. The village society membership is then supposed to see to it that the proceeds are spent according to the purpose set out in the application.

In spite of their relatively long history, the
village credit cooperatives remain of minor significance in the market for lendable funds in agriculture. They have done little to enhance the income
or the earning potential of their customers; their

influence on inculcating thrift habits and voluntary
saving has been negligible; and their impact on the
unorganized market has been barely perceptible.

A full discussion of the failure of the cooperative movement in Thailand to live up to its early
promise is beyond the scope of this study. But over-
shadowing all economic, political, or social factors
which account for the marginality of the cooperatives
in rural credit is the fact that they owe their formation and their continued existence to the initiative
of the government rather than to the expression of the
economic need of the Thai farmer. The concept of the
cooperative was borrowed from a different social and
economic setting and transplanted to a soil which
proved much less hospitable than that of Europe. Over
the years of its operations the cooperative credit
movement in Thailand has not developed much unofficial leadership, has not managed to tap private resources significantly, and, in fact, has hardly ever
ceased to be a governmental operation based on principles which have proved of little vitality in Asia.

It is largely because farmers consider cooperatives to be government-imposed institutions that they
often fail to repay loans, that they frequently misuse the proceeds of the loans, or that they simply
show a lack of interest either in joining a cooperative or approaching it for loans.

The governmental sponsorship and control over
credit cooperatives also accounts for the lack of
drive and vigor that sometimes characterizes those
entrusted with the task of fostering the cooperative
movement in the credit field. A district supervisor
has no special incentives to expand membership, to
increase the volume of business, or to experiment with
new ideas and practices. On the contrary, in many instances a man nearing retirement or anxious to maintain his civil service rating in the face of shifting
political winds will tend to minimize his risks and
his effort. There are, to be sure, many officials in
the cooperative movement who are well trained, well
motivated, and anxious to introduce long-delayed reforms. As will be seen below, their efforts have

borne fruit to some extent. But it remains true that
the nature of official control over the cooperative
movement militates against venturesomeness, provides
little incentive for expansionism and risk-taking,
and tends to perpetuate the status quo ante.

Attachment to the unlimited liability, Raiffesen
type of credit cooperative and to the ideology of the
cooperative movement rooted in the concept of welfare
rather than economic efficiency has further impeded
the growth of this type of credit. Most village cooperatives are too small and too understaffed to permit efficient management. Their amalgamation and
consolidation is, however, made difficult by the existing legal structure. The interest rate exacted
by village cooperatives bears no relation to market
conditions and, in fact, is one of the primary reasons
for the gradual drying up of funds. A farmer may prefer to pay a higher rate of interest provided he can
get the money, get it faster, and without many cumbersome procedures. In particular, the requirement
that each borrower must pledge his land severely restricts the scope of village credit societies, in
spite of certain relief given to cooperative mortga-
gors.

Other factors which help to explain the relative
stagnancy of cooperative credit in Thailand include
the farmers' lack of understanding of cooperative
principles and practices, lack of adequate cooperative education and training, insufficient attention
to integration of credit with marketing, and shortcomings in legal provisions.[27]

Nevertheless, the continuing efforts of the more
vigorous and better motivated leaders of the cooperative movement, still within the government, began to
bear some fruit in the 1960's. Beginning in 1961,
more effort was expended to direct cooperative credit
activities into accommodation for the purchase of
productive inputs, to simplify procedures, to insure
group supervision, and to orient the granting of the
loan toward its purpose rather than the credit status
of the borrower. In spite of legal difficulties, consolidation and amalgamation was pushed forward and
the formation of multipurpose societies encouraged.

Production Credit Cooperatives

Perhaps the most promising development in the
field of cooperative credit was the growth and apparent success of production credit cooperatives. They
were originally launched in 1959, and by the end of
1965 six were in operation and flourishing. In spite
of their modest scope to date, the production credit
societies merit a more extended discussion.

In the first place, this new type of credit institution has an operating area which covers an entire amphur (district). It is, therefore, large
enough to serve a larger membership, to employ paid
personnel, and to man its own office.

A production credit cooperative operates on three
fundamental principles: limited liability, supervised
credit, and integration of credit with provision of
inputs and the marketing of outputs. Not all of these
principles are, as yet, fully operative in Thailand,
but their gradual implementation seems to augur well
for the future of this type of credit.

The principle of limited liability allows the
formation of larger groups and restricts the responsibility of the members to the amount of the loans
they underwrite. Typically, up to 4,000 baht can be
borrowed by any member without any collateral other
than the signature of fellow members. The interest
rate is 12 per cent per annum.

The principle of supervised credit relates the
granting of the loan to the purpose for which the
money is borrowed rather than to the social status of
the borrower. Technical advice is extended regarding
the best utilization of the proceeds and the best
means of disposing of the crop. Throughout the entire process, from the time of application until the
sale of the crop, supervision is exercised both informally by members of a group within the society and
formally by the supervisor from the Department of
Credit and Marketing Cooperatives.

Integration with provision of inputs and with marketing of output is still in its infancy in Thailand,

but some of the societies do handle, on indent basis,
fertilizers, improved seeds, and other inputs. Other
societies market their members' produce on an agency
basis.

It appears that, in spite of the rather elaborate
application procedures and the institution of careful
check incident to supervision, production credit cooperatives manage to approve and disburse loans within fifteen days from the date of application. The
repayment record to date has been excellent.

So far, the financing of the production credit
cooperatives has been on a somewhat artificial basis,
funds being provided to it partly out of budgetary
allocations and partly out of counterpart funds.
These funds have been obtained at a subsidized interest rate so as to insure a spread to the production credit societies sufficient to cover the rather
high cost of operation of supervised credit. Yet
the production credit societies have shown a profit
which, beginning in 1961, has increased every year.

As shown by the experience of a number of countries which instituted supervised credit on principles analogous to those in Thailand, this type of
credit is best calculated to achieve the objectives
of increasing the productivity and income of the farmer and orienting him toward voluntary saving and
toward acquisition of productive assets.[28]

Bank for Agriculture and Agricultural Cooperatives

The principles behind the formation and operation
of the productive credit societies bode well for
their future. The intensified formation and promotion of this type of credit is one of the chief tasks
of the Bank for Agriculture and Agricultural Cooperatives, which came into operation in the second half
of 1966.

The bank is the apex of a unified system of agricultural credit; it absorbed the assets and the functions of the Bank for Cooperatives. The unified credit
system, however, does not exclude the participation of

private financial institutions in the field of rural
credit. In fact, the bank is to insure coordination
among the various government departments and the private institutions which are already in the business
of lending to farmers or can be induced to enter it
in the future.

The Bank for Agriculture has adopted the principles of supervised credit as its operational policy.
It extends credit to individual farmers directly but
on a limited scale. These loans are made through
branches of the bank; the number of branches rose from
7 in 1966 to 25 at the end of 1968. A substantial
proportion of funds, however, is being channeled via
the existing cooperatives and those which the bank
hopes to encourage to form on production society lines.

In the meantime, great emphasis is being put on
the training of personnel of the competence and integrity necessary to man a large-scale system of supervised credit.

Table 3.13 summarizes the activities of the Bank
for Agriculture and Agricultural Cooperatives for the
first two full years of its operations.

TABLE 3.13

Summary of Activities of the Bank for Agriculture
and Agricultural Cooperatives, 1967 and 1968

Activity	1967[a]	1968[a]
Capital fund (million baht)	304	448
Assets (million baht)	476	746
Provincial branches	15	25
Clients	45,278	121,749
Loans, indiv. farmers (million baht)	121	3,801
Loans, coop. soc. (million baht)	125	135
Headquarters staff	110	143
Field staff	216	665

[a]End of year.
  Source: Compiled from information obtained from the
           Bank for Agriculture and Agricultural Coop-
           eratives.

Of the loans made to individuals 60 per cent were of medium-term duration (up to three years). Short-term loans were made up to one year. The average loan size was 4,000 baht.

The objective of the founders of the Bank for Agriculture and Agricultural Cooperatives was to cover about 11 per cent of farm households. In spite of this relatively modest objective, the bank may find the goal difficult to reach.

The main problem is that of obtaining operating funds to finance expanding operations. Like its predecessor, the Bank for Cooperatives, the Bank for Agriculture and Agricultural Cooperatives finds it difficult to obtain additional funds outside government sources. It was initially planned to reach a loan fund of 900 million baht by the end of 1971; of this, 400 million was to come from sources other than budgetary appropriations. So far, however, practically the entire capital fund has been obtained from the Ministry of Finance. The problem is, as it was for many years, that the interest rate structure, as constituted at present, makes it well-nigh impossible to compete for funds in the open market. To lend at 12 per cent, the Bank for Agriculture and Agricultural Cooperatives can hardly pay more than 9 per cent for its own obligations. This, at current market rates, is hardly more attractive to the lenders than when the Bank for Cooperatives lent to its customers at 10 per cent and had to raise outside funds at 7 per cent, at a time when government bonds were yielding 8 per cent.

Furthermore, inasmuch as the bank will still appear to farmers as a government institution, it will encounter many of the same impediments and obstacles to growth which have plagued the existing institutions and which have been discussed above. In particular, the bank will find it hard to resist pressures for loans of longer duration but less productive purposes, not to mention other, less focused but no less dangerous, pressures.

All the same, the tidyness of the present system and the recognition of the need for supervised credit

to be administered by viable primary units disposing
of skilled personnel is a step in the direction of
greater efficiency and vitality of the organized segment of the market for rural credit.

Government Departments

It appears to be almost impossible to obtain a
clear picture of the role of government departments
in agricultural credit. Data relating to past operations are incomplete and inaccurate.[29] There is no
coherent system of accounts, no demarcation of responsibility, and only occasional traces of audit.
Inasmuch as the lending activities of the several
government departments have developed in response to
varied pressures and stimuli, no single authority
took it upon itself to trace these activities over
time or to evaluate their effects.

Some exceptions do exist, however; and from frag-
mentary evidence gathered elsewhere, as well as from
the few reliable sources in existence, it is possible
to piece together a somewhat uneven pattern of activities of government agencies in the rural credit
field.

In the Ministry of Agriculture various circulating funds were set up from time to time to make loans
either to encourage a certain type of cultivation, to
introduce a new crop, or to make possible the purchase
of a specific kind of output. Thus about 16 million
baht was advanced to farmers between 1952 and 1954 to
propagate new varieties of rice. About 4 million
baht was advanced in the same period for the purchase
of fertilizer and about 7 million baht to buy farm
equipment. Somewhat earlier, a fund of about 15.4
million was lent for various inputs under a project
which shows about a 60 per cent ratio of bad debts.
Other circulating funds included slightly over 3 million baht lent to rubber cultivators and about 2 million baht lent to cotton growers. About 10 million
was lent to fishermen and another 20 million to livestock breeders in the late 1950's and early 1960's.
Again, the repayment record was not good, and the
entire financial record remains somewhat murky.

In the Ministry of the Interior, loans falling
roughly under the heading of agricultural credit were
made by the departments of Administration, Social
Welfare, and Community Development. No details are
available on the operations of the Department of Administration except for the prevailing impression
that a good deal of money was lost on various schemes
to promote hog raising and livestock marketing. The
Social Welfare Department disbursed about 16 million
baht in loan funds to 40,000 families in the ten-year
period ending in 1963. Less than 4 million baht has
been repaid to date. A similar welfare disbursement
of 4 million baht was made by the Community Development Revolving Fund.

Unlike the operations of the Agriculture and Interior ministries, the loan operations of the Ministry of National Development were made primarily to
the cooperative institutions. In addition to this
interest in cooperative credit, the ministry has also made loans to paddy marketing cooperatives out of
a revolving fund of about 38 million baht. The 110
paddy marketing societies incurred a loss of more
than 8 million baht by the close of 1963. Other
types of cooperatives borrowed about 36 million baht.
A certain proportion of these loans was counted as a
loss, as a number of cooperatives, unable to repay,
were liquidated.

Commercial Banks

Under the auspices of the government's Accelerated Rural Development Program a group of commercial banks in fourteen districts of the Northeast
agreed to make loans to farmers under a government
guarantee against losses. In 1968 about 8 million
baht of loans were disbursed under this program, compared with 5 million in 1967. Except for this program, the only commercial bank in Thailand actively
engaged in independent lending to farmers is the
Bangkok Bank, Ltd., the largest deposit bank in the
Kingdom.

Bangkok Bank, Ltd., entered the field of agricultural credit in January 1963, in part to establish

its influence more firmly in the countryside, which
it had somewhat neglected in its concentration on
branches in the urban centers and abroad.

It extends two kinds of credit. One, individual
loans to the more established and prosperous farmers,
is of the standard type. The prospective borrower
makes an application and offers collateral, usually
in the form of a registered land mortgage. The application is reviewed by the branch manager, but the
final approval must come from the head office. The
rate of interest ranges from 12 per cent, for production loans, to 15 per cent, for longer-term loans
for the purpose of settling debts. Intermediate
rates are charged for loans ranging from one to five
years for such purposes as purchase of heavy machinery and construction of warehouses. There is no set
limit on the amount of the loan.

The other kind of loan is of special interest
because it combines some of the most promising features of agricultural credit under the aegis of a
profit-making organization. This is the group loan
scheme of supervised credit for production purposes.
The program of the Bangkok Bank, Ltd., group loans
derives from the experience of the Farm Credit Administration in the United States, from the successful
experiments with supervised credit in a number of
Latin American countries, and from the pioneering
efforts of the production credit societies in Thailand itself.[30]

Under the scheme, loans are made both for short
terms and long terms to groups of farmers, of no less
than 5 and no more than 20 members, residing in the
same village or hamlet. Up to 3,000 baht can be borrowed by each of the group's members without collateral other than the security of the crop to be produced and the joint liability of the entire group,
limited to the amount of the debt outstanding. The
rates of interest are similar to those under the individual loan scheme. In addition to the interest
payable to the bank, the group members undertake to
pay an additional 1 per cent per annum to cover the
administrative costs of the group, mainly the costs

of travel of the group's selected representatives to
the branck office of the bank for meetings, confer-
ences, and so on.

The authority to grant the amounts requested by
the borrowers is vested not in the head office, as
for individual loans, but in the manager, assisted by
the agricultural credit officer of the branch. The
latter plays a key role in the implementation of the
entire program. It is he who will make the preliminary survey, who will advise the group on the best
means of using the loan proceeds, and who will offer
technical assistance throughout the life of the loan,
which is paid out in installments. These agricultural credit officers are graduates of the Kasetsart
University (Agricultural University) and are special-
ly trained to carry out supervisory functions.

An interesting feature of the group loan program
is its integration, whenever possible, with both marketing and the provision of inputs. Thus, in the
areas where the crop pattern allows it, the bank will
arrange for millers and processors to buy the crop
from its borrowers at a price guaranteed not to be
below the market. The loan account is then automatically credited with the amount of the sale. With
respect to inputs, the bank will provide them directly whenever the purpose of the loan calls for such
inputs as are handled by distributors who are also
clients of the bank.

The bank claims that this arrangement enables the
group to enjoy extra benefits in that a part of the
dealer's commission is passed on to the farmer. For
example, the usual dealer commission on a Fordson
tractor is 7.5 per cent. Under an arrangement with
the group wishing to borrow for a tractor, the dealer will get only 2.5 per cent commission but will
still service the tractor. The group will benefit
to the extent of getting a tractor, including servic-
ing, for 5 per cent less than the retail price. Still,
the borrower's choice of inputs is somewhat limited
as a result of such an arrangement. It is interesting that some 73 per cent of all group loans have
been allegedly used to secure labor inputs. This is

a very high proportion, indeed, and a suspicious mind
would seek some connection between this high percentage and the fact that labor inputs are not yet provided by the Bangkok Bank, Ltd.

Even though the program is still in its early
stages, it bears the mark of success. Strangely
enough, it is the group program which has proved the
more rewarding to the Bangkok Bank, and there is a
possibility that the program of individual loans will
be discontinued.

Table 3.14 summarizes the operations of the group
loan program. Even though the scope of the program
is confined to areas where there are branches of the
Bangkok Bank, the annual value of loans increased
nearly fortyfold in the space of only five years.
Even so, the limiting factors have proved to be the
shortage of qualified field personnel and the sheer
inability of the overworked credit officers to visit
those villages where there appears to be some interest in forming a loan group. As a matter of fact,
the bank appears to do very little proselytizing, yet
word of mouth spreads so effectively that in Chiengmai
province alone, perhaps 100 tentative loan groups
have formed but the branch officers have not even had
the time to conduct initial interviews with them.

Equally encouraging is the excellent record of
repayments shown by the groups. Some 96 per cent of
all loans are paid on or near maturity and, so far,
no group loan has remained unpaid for longer than four
months. This testifies to the importance of proper
technical advice combined with continuous supervision,
but also to the heavy drain on administrative and
technical personnel required under a successful supervised group program.

The officers of the Bangkok Bank, Ltd., estimate
that the costs of running the group loan program
amount to 4 or 5 per cent of the value of loans. This
seems to be a very high percentage, but it would seem
that a substantial proportion of these expenses may
be invariant with respect to volume of loans. Be that
as it may, the bank admits to making a modest profit
on the operation.

TABLE 3.14

Bangkok Bank: Summary of Operations of Group Loans, 1963-1968

Operations	1963	1964	1965	1967	1968
Number of groups	57	224	776	n.a.	n.a.
Number of members	851	3,091	8,122	21,332	31,861
Value of loans[a]	2,338,482	4,746,096	15,554,300	55,218,000	85,951,000

n.a. = not available.

[a]Amounts outstanding at end of year; in baht.

Source: Bangkok Bank Ltd. (Courtesy of Chusak Himathongkom, Chief, Agricultural Credit Division).

The success of the Bangkok Bank, Ltd., in the
field of supervised group credit should be viewed in
the proper perspective. Having the field to itself,
and disposing of great resources, the Bangkok Bank,
Ltd., could, as it were, skim off the cream of the
business. On the one hand, it could select its borrowers from those areas which present the best prospects and, on the other hand, it has had first pick
at the requisite personnel. Were the program to be
expanded substantially, with the participation of
other commercial banks, with nationwide coverage,
and with a vastly increased volume of loans, serious
problems would arise both with respect to risks and
with respect to the availability of personnel. All
the same, the experience of the Bangkok Bank, Ltd.,
has demonstrated that it is possible for a commercial bank to operate successfully in the field of
agricultural credit. This has, of course, been demonstrated in other countries. While the experience
of Australia and New Zealand may be of little relevance for Thailand, that of the Philippines should
be instructive.[31]

Implications for Developmental Planning

This survey of the organized market for agricultural credit shows that this market is dominated by
cooperative institutions which only recently and haltingly have begun to develop techniques and methods
which may reduce, sometime in the future, farmers'
dependence on the facilities available in the unorganized market. Even with the promise implicit in
the formation of the Bank for Agriculture and Agricultural Cooperatives, with its emphasis on supervised
credit and administrative efficiency, much of a dent
is not likely to be made in the unorganized market.
Yet that market cannot be relied on to nurture a dynamic kind of credit designed to lift the farmer's
income to a higher level, to provide him with incentives toward greater effort and productivity, and to
show him the connection between forbearance for the
present and a higher standard of living in the future.

It would seem that for the institutions under public control and scrutiny to encroach significantly on

the unorganized markets' domination of rural credit,
recourse must be had to financial entities not yet,
to any significant degree, involved in that market.
In Thailand it is the commercial banks which could
provide the type of finance the moneylender is either
unwilling or incapable of providing.

The Bangkok Bank, Ltd., which has successfully
promoted the kind of supervised group credit consonant with developmental objectives, is anxious to expand its operations to other provinces where, as yet,
it has not established its branches. The effort to
supplement the activities of the cooperatives cannot
and should not be confined to one commercial bank,
however aggressive and progressive that bank may be.
On the other hand, other commercial banks show little
desire to enter the field of rural credit. However,
the newly formed Krung Tai Bank is committed to entering the field. This bank was formed from a merger of
two government-sponsored banks, and its management
and control remain in official hands. The new bank
has a large number of branches in the provinces (see
Chapter 5). With the exception of the ARD program,
the commercial banks incorporated in Thailand (and
foreign chartered banks are probably not likely to
enter rural credit anyway) prefer to steer clear of
direct lending to farmers, citing lack of branches,
lack of trained personnel, or lack of capital as
their reason. Underlying all these reasons there is,
of course, the fact that banking is generally profitable in Thailand and that there are many attractive
opportunities outside rural credit, opportunities with
which the commercial bankers are much more familiar
by training and experience.

The obstacles to the entry of commercial banks
into the field of rural credit must be overcome, but
they are not likely to be overcome by a process of
suasion alone. To insure the active participation of
commercial banks the development planner could consider a system of rewards and incentives more or less
along the following lines:

The Bank of Thailand, one of the few central banking institutions in the developing countries not

already actively engaged in agricultural credit,
would announce a policy of support of commercial
banking operations in rural areas. First, however,
the Bank of Thailand might find it necessary to nudge
the banks in that direction by increasing the required reserves against deposits from the level of
6 per cent (raised to 7 per cent in May 1969) to,
say, 10 per cent but allowing the extra 4 per cent
to be kept in the form of agricultural paper. The
Bank of Thailand would proclaim its readiness to discount such paper at 5 per cent, provided the commercial bank rate did not exceed 15 per cent. Given
the generous spread which the Bank of Thailand would
allow in its rediscounting of agricultural paper,
the commercial banks should not suffer undue hard-
ships and might even find the business of rural lending a profitable line of endeavor.*

A 10 per cent spread between the commercial bank
rate and the Bank of Thailand rate should provide a
sufficient margin for risk, for heavy initial administrative expenses, and for lack of experience.
Equally important would be the Bank of Thailand's
determination that its new line of rediscounting not
be bogged down in red tape, administrative delays,
and the sort of requirements which, while in principle sound, in practice have the effect of grinding
the entire scheme to a halt. Subject to general rules
of eligibility, which should be few in number and
clear in intent, the Bank of Thailand should rediscount paper presented to it without any further credit
investigation but subject to post-audit and severe
penalties for willful misrepresentation.

----

*Tentative steps in the direction indicated were
taken by the Bank of Thailand beginning late in 1968.
The facilities offered are, so far, limited to the
Bank for Agriculture and Agricultural Cooperatives
and confined to financing of the production of rice
and maize. The Bank of Thailand stands ready to rediscount up to 80 million worth of promissory notes
at 7 per cent provided that the Bank for Agriculture
and Agricultural Cooperatives does not charge more
than 12 per cent for its discount facility.

It is possible that even with the crisp carrot
dangling from the stick, the commercial banks would
find it difficult to recruit and train technically
qualified and properly motivated personnel. The
problem is indeed a major one. In order to supervise
and administer loans of, say, a billion baht per annum, perhaps 2,000 men would have to be found. Of
course, not all of them would have to be available
at once. It would be unrealistic to expect the volume of agricultural loans handled by commercial banks
to reach the goal of one billion baht in a year or
two. This would take several years. Assuming that
one trained supervisor can handle fifteen or twenty
groups of rural borrowers per year, the task of providing supervisors should not be an impossible one.
Even so, the initial cost of recruitment and training
might prove prohibitive to some of the smaller banks,
and there might be real difficulty in locating suitable candidates. At the same time, there would be
great merit in conducting the training on fairly
standard lines, if only to facilitate the task of
passing on agricultural paper's eligibility. It
would seem that the primary responsibility for such
training should be assumed by the Bank for Agriculture and Agricultural Cooperatives. This institution
has the status and the resources to coordinate a vast
training program with the universities and might well
find that the outlay on the training program yields
greater returns than its direct lending activities.
The entry of the commercial banks, and of their more
than 500 branches, into rural credit should substantially change the existing structure of the market
for lendable funds in agriculture and should shift
the respective shares of the market in favor of the
organized lenders.

The proposal outlined above is designed to increase directly the share of organized markets in
financing rural households. But, as the discussion
of the unorganized markets has suggested, there appears to be scope for increasing the proportion of
loans made by organized markets indirectly by absorb-
ing certain of the activities of the unorganized markets in agriculture. One line of approach would be to
draw certain moneylenders into the institutionalized

orbit. One reason for the high rates of interest
charged by moneylenders is their inability to replenish their working capital at certain times of the
year plus the fact that their limited funds are employed only for a portion of the year. It might be
worthwhile to develop some mechanism whereby moneylenders could discount with commercial banks or public institutions certain kinds of paper. Such an arrangement could be a prelude to gradual integration of
at least a segment of the moneylending profession into
the organized network. To some extent, such integration has been taking place in most of the developing
countries; an interesting proposal on these lines
was made in connection with the Muda Project in Malaysia in 1967. Under the proposed "agricultural
bills scheme," farmers' IOU's would be endorsed by
the lenders, discounted by commercial banks, and rediscounted by the Central Bank. Certainly integration has been initiated in Thailand. But the entry
of the commercial banks into the field of agricultural credit on a large scale should provide many opportunities to speed up this process. The Thai commercial banking system, with its complex of branches,
agencies, and correspondents, appears singularly well
adapted to this task.

The measures so far discussed aim at channeling
a greater proportion, as well as a greater absolute
amount, of agricultural loans into productive uses.
But it must be recognized that there will continue
to exist a demand for loans for consumption purposes
which cannot be dealt with along sound banking principles. No doubt, a certain proportion of such loans
may be considered undesirable on social grounds, and
some sort of campaign to eliminate the demand for
them might well be instituted. But it would be naive
to suppose that such a campaign would be entirely successful. The fact is that, while it is important to
separate the demand for production loans from the demand for consumption loans, some device must be found
to meet the latter demand if an even greater burden
is not to be borne by those least able to bear it.
Again, while no detailed proposals will be made here,
there appear to be two promising avenues of approach
to the problem. One of them would actually attempt

to draw the poor, improvident farmer into the vortex
of productive activity, in the belief that once ex-
posed and immersed in such activity he will actually
have less need, as well as less desire, to borrow
for nonproductive purposes. One possibility would
be to set up a pilot system of communal credit run
on the lines of a corporate undertaking for a specific project. Say a storage silo is considered to be
a worthwhile project. A group of villagers might in-
corporate for the specific purpose of constructing,
managing, and maintaining the silo and exploiting it
for commercial uses. The group acquires an equity
in the undertaking in proportion to the resources it
contributes, with the important proviso, however,
that the poorer farmers can contribute labor, if nothing else. The value of such labor would be expressed
as an equity in the undertaking. The group obtains
a loan from an institution in the organized market,
covered by a joint guarantee of the group.

The other avenue of approach would be to set up
institutions dealing explicitly and exclusively with
consumption loans, loans for emergencies, and similar
demands. It would seem that rural pawnshops could
serve in this capacity, and such pawnshops could be
run either by the cooperatives or by licensed pawn-
brokers.[32]

It is not pretended here that these suggestions
would be easy to put into operation. No panaceas and
no easy and painless solutions exist to the manifold
problems of rural finance.

Above all, it cannot be overemphasized that credit
cannot operate in a vacuum. The best-thought-out and
the most soundly implemented credit system will do
little for economic development if the farmer is left
to the vagaries of the weather and of the market. He
cannot be left to fend for himself if one of the other
fails him in spite of his best efforts, for in that
case he will cease to care or to respond to stimuli
and incentives. It is incumbent on the development
planner to insure, as much as possible, that this does
not happen.

NOTES

1. Pantum Thisyamondol, Virach Arromdee, and Millard F. Long, Agricultural Credit in Thailand, Theory, Data, Policy (Bangkok: Kasetsart University, 1965). Hereafter referred to as Agricultural Credit.

2. See the relevant data for India, Pakistan, the Philippines, and other countries in Udhis Narkswasdi, Agricultural Credit Systems in Certain Countries (Bangkok: Kasetsart University, 1963), pp. 48-53.

3. See, for example, Frank J. Moore, "Money-lenders and Cooperators in India," Economic Development and Cultural Change (June, 1953), pp. 140-143.

4. See Agricultural Credit, p. 42.

5. Ibid., p. 39.

6. Ibid., p. 29.

7. Ibid., p. 23.

8. See Udhis Narkswasdi, op. cit., p. 23; and Frank J. Moore, "A Note on Rural Debt and Control of Ceremonial Expenditures in India," Economic Development and Cultural Change (June, 1954), pp. 408ff.

9. Ministry of Agriculture, Report on Economic Survey of Rice Farmers in Nakorn Pathom Province, 1955-56 (Bangkok: Agricultural Research and Farm Survey Station, 1959).

10. See Anthony Bottomley, "Premium for Risk as a Determinant of Interest Rates in Underdeveloped Rural Areas," Quarterly Journal of Economics (November, 1963), pp. 637-647.

11. See Udhis Narkswasdi, op. cit., pp. 41-43.

12. Ibid., p. 42.

13. See Leopoldo P. De Guzman, "An Economic
Analysis of the Methods of Farm Financing Used on
5,144 Farms: 1955," The Philippine Agriculturist,
XL (1958).

14. Agricultural Credit, p. 33.

15. Cf. Agricultural Credit, p. 32.

16. U Tun Wai, "Interest Rates Outside the Organized Money Markets of Underdeveloped Countries,"
in Staff Papers (International Monetary Fund, November,
1957), p. 102; see also Reserve Bank of India, Report
on Rural Credit Follow Up Survey, 1956-57 (Bombay:
Reserve Bank of India, 1960); N. B. Tablante, "Implications of Credit Institutes and Policy for Savings
and Capital Accumulation in Philippine Agriculture,"
Philippine Economic Journal, III (Second Semester,
1964), pp. 208-225; and F. H. King, "Agricultural
Finance and Credit in Taiwan" (n.d.) (Mimeo.)

17. See R. C. Blitz and M. F. Long, "The Economics of Usury Regulations," Journal of Political
Economy (December, 1965).

18. See Agricultural Credit, pp. 42-43.

19. See, for example, U Tun Wai, op. cit., p. 81.

20. Agricultural Credit, p. 19.

21. See Agricultural Credit, pp. 37ff.

22. Bank of Thailand, Annual Economic Report,
1964.

23. In addition to the sources already cited,
the most comprehensive and in many ways indispensable
reference is the Reserve Bank of India, All India
Rural Credit Survey, Vols. I and II (Bombay: Reserve
Bank of India Publications, 1954, 1956, and 1957).

24. See U Tun Wai, op. cit., p. 98.

25. See Horace Belshaw, Le Crédit Agricole Dans Les Pays Économiquement Sous-Développés (Rome: Food and Agriculture Organization, 1959), pp. 59ff.

26. For statistical data, source material, and additional detail pertaining to the discussion of cooperatives, see Alek A. Rozental, "Draft of Final Report on Finance and Development in Thailand" (Washington, D.C.: Center for Development Planning, National Planning Association, 1968). (Mimeo.)

27. Many of the shortcomings mentioned in the text are prevalent throughout Asia and are frequently more acute elsewhere. "Cooperation has failed, but Cooperation must succeed": Government of India, Summary Report on All-India Rural Credit Survey (New Delhi, 1960), p. 8.

28. See Horace Belshaw, op. cit., pp. 243ff; the previously cited sources from the Philippines and Taiwan also stress the apparent success of supervised credit.

29. This discussion of government departments relies heavily on National Economic Development Board, "Policy and Principles of National Agricultural Credit and Draft Act of the Bank of Agriculture and Cooperatives" (Bangkok, 1965). (Informal translation, mimeo. in Thai.)

30. Information about the operation of the Bangkok Bank, Ltd. credit program in agriculture was obtained through direct contact with the bank's officers and from field trips to the area of its most extensive operations; see also Bangkok Bank, Ltd., Agricultural Credit (November, 1964). The U.S. Operation Mission to Thailand has long attempted to orient the granting of credit to farmers along the lines of supervised credit. See John L. Wann, John W. Sims, and Fulton Want, eds., A Report on Agricultural Credit: Cooperative Organization, Management and Administrative and Agricultural Marketing (Bangkok: Thai-American Audiovisual Service, November, 1959); and W. J. Maddock,

"Agricultural Credit Thailand 1964" (August, 1964).
(Mimeo.)

31. See Jose E. Desiderio, "Rural Banking in the
Philippines," The Philippine Economic Bulletin
(November-December, 1963).

32. For some evidence that rural pawnships can,
in fact, operate successfully, see United Nations,
State Pawnshops in Indonesia (E/CN. 11/I&T/WP. 1/13);
and United Nations, Pawnshops in the Associated States
of Indochina (E/CN. 11/I&T/WP. 1/20).

CHAPTER **4** COMMERCIAL BANKING

Commercial banks have a threefold function to perform in the intermediation process. First of all, they borrow surpluses of the household units in exchange for the indirect securities they issue, i.e., demand and time deposits. Second, they transmit the funds so borrowed to deficit spending units in exchange for direct securities of these units. Finally, commercial banks facilitate the adjustment of portfolios of spending units by enabling them to hold the desired proportion of direct and indirect securities.*

In Thailand, it would appear that the relative importance of commercial banking in the organized financial market structure is greater than in most countries at a similar stage of development. There are two reasons for this. First, Thai banks have experienced a remarkable record of growth, particularly in the last ten years or so. Second, and perhaps more important, Thailand is singularly devoid of the many semi-official financial intermediaries which abound in several other countries. Thai authorities, perhaps wisely, have refrained from setting up and sponsoring a plethora of institutions whose contribution to economic growth is problematical, whose bewildering variety of instruments often confuses both savers and investors, and whose staffs constitute a

---

*Direct securities are those issued by spending units themselves, such as bonds, accounts payable, and bills. Indirect securities are those which represent claims against financial intermediaries, such as time and demand deposits, insurance claims, and unit trust certificates.[1]

real drain on the meager administrative and managerial resources of the developing countries. Moreover,
for historical and ideological reasons, Thailand has
been able to withstand the pressure for such measures
as compulsory insurance and industrial pension funds,
which elsewhere constitute a substantial proportion
of total financial securities circulating within the
economy.

The predominance of commercial banking in the
financial structure of Thailand is not likely to diminish in the near future. In preparing financial
estimates for the second five-year plan, the National
Economic Development Board assumed a total supply of
investible funds from the private sector of nearly 70
billion baht over the period 1966-1971. Of this total, the financial institutions as a whole are expected to supply 9.1 billion, the share of the commercial banks being 7.1 billion, or nearly two-thirds.
Even this probably underestimates the relative importance of commercial banking, inasmuch as the estimates
for investible funds to be provided by such institutions as the Industrial Finance Corporation of Thailand (IFCT) and the newly formed Bank for Agriculture
and Agricultural Cooperatives appear to be overly
generous.[2]

THE GROWTH OF COMMERCIAL BANKING

It is possible to distinguish three significant
phases in the history of commercial banking in Thailand. The initial phase, from the establishment of
the first bank in 1888 (a branch of the Hongkong and
Shanghai Banking Corporation) up to World War II, was
dominated by branches of large foreign banks engaged
mainly in financing export and import bills in the
European trade, which itself was largely controlled
by British, Danish, French, and German firms operating out of Bangkok. During this phase most local
banks were Chinese and their primary business was to
transmit remittances to the mainland. In the second
phase, these Chinese remittance banks were joined by
banks established by native entrepreneurs, very frequently merchants, traders, and exporters who were

enticed into the banking business by the large profits to be made in financing the booming postwar export trade. The entry of native entrepreneurs into
commercial banking was facilitated by three developments: (1) the changing pattern of foreign trade,
with its focus shifting away from Europe toward neigh-
boring countries and Japan; (2) the shutdown during
World War II of the Thai branches of the large European banks; and (3) the requirement that export proceeds be sold to the Bank of Thailand. It was this
last requirement which has enabled the small and in-
experienced bankers to grow and expand, inasmuch as
they, by guaranteeing their customers conformance
with the law, have been able to charge a handsome
commission on the export proceeds.

The last phase in the development of Thai commercial banking, and the one that will receive most attention in this chapter, may be termed the "modern"
phase. During this phase, commercial banks incorporated in Thailand forged far ahead of the branches of
foreign banks in volume of deposits, capital, and
accommodation to business. They began to establish
numerous branches in the country and to expand their
activities beyond making remittances and financing
foreign trade. Most important, they started to be
integrated into the monetary system of the country,
principally through a series of regulatory measures
which culminated in the Commercial Banking Act of
1962. While it is difficult to date precisely the
onset of the modern phase, it may be convenient to
regard the year 1955 as a demarcation point, inasmuch
as the period of multiple exchange rates ended that
year. It was, however, 1962 which really marked the
beginning of commercial banking in Thailand along
lines comparable with modern banks elsewhere.[3]

Of the 29 commercial banks currently (late 1960's)
doing business in Thailand, 13 are incorporated
abroad, 16 in Thailand. Two of those incorporated in
Thailand, the Agricultural Bank and the Provincial
Bank, merged under the name Krung Thai Bank, which
opened for business in March 1966. Only 4 of the 16
banks incorporated in Thailand received their charters
prior to World War II. Of these 4, one, the Wang Lee

Chan Bank, is not a commercial bank in the full sense
of the term but essentially a family concern not generally dealing with the public.[4]

The historical background of Thai commercial
banking has left three residual strains which are of
interest in the analysis of the current scene. The
first of these is that the great prestige and former
power of British banks remains as an influence on the
attitudes and practices of Thai bankers, particularly
those in positions of official authority. Not only
was the Hongkong & Shanghai the first bank chartered
in the country, but it and the Chartered Bank were
two of the three banks which up to 1903 could issue
notes. The Chartered Bank was the one in which, for
a time, both the royal family and the royal treasury
had open accounts. Up to at least 1941, all the principal financial advisers to the Kingdom were British.
Until very recently, the leading officials in the
field of finance and banking tended to be trained in
England. The second residual strain, perhaps related
to the first, is the compradore system; though now
somewhat on the decline, it still persists and seems
to have taken on forms which are at variance with its
original rationale (see Chapter 5 for a discussion of
the role of the compradore in Thai banking).

The third residual strain, also stemming from the
way in which commercial banking has developed in Thailand over the years, is the predominance of foreign
trade financing. To an extent perhaps greater than a
scrutiny of official data would indicate, Thai banks
are, with few exceptions, mainly interested in accom-
modating exporters and importers and those closely
connected with them. In the past, of course, this
was the commercial bank's raison d'être. It is much
less so at present, but habits and attitudes persist,
and skills and experience nurtured in a particular
tradition need time and careful tending before they
can be fruitfully transferred elsewhere.

ASSETS AND LIABILITIES OF COMMERCIAL BANKS

Table 4.1 presents a summary account of the principal balance sheet items of all the commercial banks

TABLE 4.1

Main Assets and Liabilities of Commercial Banks[a], 1955-1967
(million baht)

Year End	Deposits[b]				Cash on Hand and Balance with Bank of Thailand		Liquid Assets[d]		Loans and Discounts		Risk Assets[e]	Capital Account[f]	
	Demand	Time	Other[c]	Total	Amount	As % of D & T Deposits	Amount	As % of Total Deposits	Amount	As % of Total Deposits		Amount	As % of Risk Assets
1955	1,967.3	243.6	-	2,210.9	443.6	20.06	756.1	34.20	2,391.4	108.16	3,034.0	455.0	15.00
1956	2,180.7	371.0	315.3	2,867.0	502.0	19.67	883.0	30.80	2,839.3	99.03	3,210.1	458.7	14.29
1957	2,491.9	452.2	431.4	3,375.5	564.5	19.17	1,024.9	30.36	3,339.0	98.92	3,749.2	502.9	13.41
1958	2,886.7	649.1	423.8	3,959.6	538.7	15.24	947.8	23.94	3,977.7	100.46	4,631.2	518.3	11.19
1959	3,153.7	980.4	332.0	4,466.1	676.4	16.36	1,073.6	24.04	4,488.4	100.50	5,077.4	514.8	10.14
1960	3,840.5	1,223.6	385.4	5,449.5	743.5	14.68	1,333.9	24.48	5,397.3	99.04	6,374.8	561.0	8.80
1961	4,313.4	1,690.6	504.6	6,508.6	876.3	14.60	1,607.8	24.70	6,333.3	97.31	7,527.7	614.9	8.17
1962	4,233.8	3,347.0	226.3	7,807.1	1,004.4	13.25	2,174.6	27.85	7,459.3	95.55	8,681.6	813.3	9.37
1963	5,025.4	4,514.3	243.2	9,782.9	1,284.1	13.46	3,018.5	30.85	8,712.6	89.06	9,532.4	804.6	8.44
1964	5,615.5	5,614.3	232.3	11,462.1	1,295.6	11.54	3,187.6	27.81	10,546.3	92.01	11,274.3	1,085.8	9.63
1965	6,420.8	6,856.2	285.2	13,562.2	1,293.0	9.74	3,388.2	24.98	12,762.0	95.11	13,382.3	1,382.5	10.00
1966	7,513.5	9,364.3	315.8	17,193.6	1,457.1	8.63	5,120.6	29.78	15,036.4	87.45	15,567.4	1,612.4	10.36
1967	8,163.0	11,779.1	351.6	20,293.7	1,692.4	8.49	5,968.0	29.41	17,262.1	85.06	18,261.7	1,913.2	10.48

[a] Excluding those of Thai bank branches abroad; but data on risk assets and capital account as from May 1962 included.

[b] Excluding foreign currency deposits and inter-bank deposits.

[c] Comprising certified checks, cashiers' checks, marginal deposits, etc.

[d] Comprising cash on hand, balances at the Bank of Thailand, balances at banks abroad, gold and government securities other than those pledged or deposited as guarantee with the Bank of Thailand.

[e] From May 1962, as defined in the Commercial Banking Act, B.E. 2505.

[f] From May 1962, comprising paid-up capital, statutory reserves, other reserves, net profit after distribution, and capital funds of foreign branches.

Source: Bank of Thailand.

in Thailand for 13 calendar years, beginning with
1955 and ending with 1967. It should be borne in
mind that the composition of the banks has changed
slightly during the years, new banks being chartered
and old banks merging or changing their names. More
significant is the fact that the accounting procedures and practices have been changed, mainly as a
result of the passage of the Commercial Banking Act
of 1962. In particular, the data on demand and time
deposits prior to May 1962 are not strictly comparable with those following that date. The great increase shown in time deposits after 1962 must be
attributed, in part, to the reclassification of accounts which has taken place in connection with the
implementation of the Commercial Banking Act as well
as to other causes (this matter receives attention
below). After 1965, time deposits actually exceed
the demand deposits of commercial banks, a rather
unusual situation when compared with the distribution
of banking assets elsewhere.

It is interesting to note that at the end of 1967,
the ratio of cash on hand and balances with the Bank
of Thailand to total deposits was only about 40 per
cent of the 1955 ratio. The ratio of liquid assets
(which comprise, in addition, balances at foreign
banks, and gold and government securities other than
those pledged with the central bank) to deposits,
however, had declined only slightly, and was actually
higher at the end of 1967 than at the end of 1958,
unlike the former ratio, which showed a continuous
decline during the period. It should be noted that
the ratio of cash and balances to deposits at the
central bank is not the legal reserve ratio familiar
to students of the fractional reserve systems. In
Thailand, the commercial banks can keep a part of
their legal reserves in the form of government securities (fuller discussion of the commercial banks'
reserve position is found below).

While a fuller analysis of the behavior and significance of various balance sheet items of Thai commercial banks is made in subsequent sections of this
chapter, Table 4.1 reveals data on two other ratios
which merit immediate comment. The first of these is

the ratio of loans, overdrafts, and discounts to total deposits. The other is the ratio of capital account to "risk assets."

At the end of 1967, the ratio of loans, overdrafts, and discounts to total deposits stood at 85
per cent, and for most of the period surveyed oscil-
lated close to 100 per cent, exceeding it in three
out of the thirteen years. Prima facie, this ratio
appears abnormally high when compared to that of
American banks, for example, which hold a ratio of
loans, overdrafts, and discounts to deposits of some
70 per cent as a prudent maximum. But such a direct
comparison may be misleading. In the first place,
Thai banks, unlike American banks, lend a good proportion of their total accommodations in the form of
overdrafts. A customer will obtain a line of credit
against which he will overdraft. The difference between the line of credit and the actual overdraft
will not be shown as a deposit, as is the practice in
the United States, where "every loan creates a deposit."* This tends to understate the denominator
of the ratio.

In the second place, Thai banks can apparently
maintain what to an American banker would be a dan-
gerously illiquid situation because they can easily
obtain funds from foreign banks and the Bank of
Thailand.[5] Finally, to the extent that a greater
proportion of assets of Thai banks are in the form
of self-liquidating paper to finance exports and imports, they can, at least in principle, afford a higher ratio of earnings assets to deposits. This certainly applies to banks operating in Thailand which

----

*An interesting provision in the Commercial Bank-
ing Act of 1962 (Section 11) empowers the Bank of
Thailand to instruct the commercial banks to add the
unused balances of overdrafts to their deposits for
the purpose of determining the required cash reserve.
This power has never been invoked and, in fact, commercial banks do not report the amounts of unused
overdraft balances.

are incorporated abroad and to those locally chartered and soundly managed banks whose main business
is the financing of foreign trade.

The other ratio in the table which merits comment
at this juncture is the one shown in the last column.
Both the numerator and the denominator of the ratio
require explanation. The Commercial Banking Act
passed in 1962 was a generally successful attempt to
bring the practices of Thai banks into line with
those of other modern banking systems. It provided
that two separate "reserves" be maintained, both in
the interest of sound banking practice and so as to
furnish the central bank with means of control over
banking operations. The first of these reserve requirements obligated the banks to maintain a proportion of their deposits (both demand and time) in the
form of legal reserves, comprising cash and prescribed
government securities, within the range of from 5 to
50 per cent, the exact percentage to be determined
by the Bank of Thailand subject to approval by the
Minister of Finance. It was raised from 6 to 7 per
cent in May 1969, with government securities not to
exceed 50 per cent of the required reserves. The
second requirement specified that a commercial bank
maintain capital funds (the sum of paid-up capital,
reserves, including other reserves appropriated from
net profit, and undivided profit) as follows:

>   (1) total assets at a ratio not less
> than that prescribed by the Bank of Thai-
> land and approved by the Minister; such
> ratio shall be not less than five per-
> centum and not more than fifteen percen-
> tum; (2) each category of assets at a
> ratio not less than that prescribed by
> the Bank of Thailand and approved by the
> Minister (of Finance). Assets under
> paragraph (1) and (2) shall not include
> cash, deposits with the Bank of Thailand,
> Thai government securities and any other
> assets as the Minister may prescribe.[6]

The prescribed ratio of capital funds to these
"risk assets" is currently 6 per cent but the concept

of "risk assets" (or total assets less excluded
items) is now difficult to define with precision. In
general, they exclude preferred securities such as
those of the Treasury, the Industrial Finance Corporation of Thailand, Buffer Stock Certificates (issued
in connection with tin ore control), bank premises
and equipment, and, more importantly, a large proportion of the paper used in the financing of export
trade. There are now at least nine major regulations
in force which amend, amplify, and clarify the provisions of the act. On May 1, 1962, shortly after the
passage of the act, one such regulation provided for
several exemptions from total assets under Section
10.[7] (See Chapter 6 for a discussion of reservation
requirements.)

As seen in Table 4.1, the ratio of capital account
to risk assets stood at slightly over 10 per cent at
the end of 1967, compared with 15 per cent at the end
1955. However, since the passage of the Commercial
Banking Act of 1962, the ratio has remained fairly
steady, suggesting that the commercial banks, given
a steady increase in their risk assets, have had to
increase their capital resources rather substantially.

At the time the act of 1962 was being implemented,
the provision pertaining to the ratio of capital to
assets was the one that provided the most heated debates and caused the greatest consternation among
bankers. In particular, several bankers were faced
with the prospect of reducing their earning assets
within one year unless they could raise additional
capital.[8] As it turned out, there was little trouble
raising additional capital, especially insofar as the
monetary authorities were determined to restrict the
entry of new banks. It appears that due to a resolu-
tion passed by the Council of Ministers and advice
tendered by the financial advisers in the 1950's, no
more than one branch of a foreign bank per country
diplomatically represented in Thailand will be authorized in the future. Exceptions have been made, as in
the case of the Bank of Tokyo (with the Mitsui Bank
established in Thailand since 1952) and Chase Manhat-
tan (which, however, took over the charter acquired
by the Nationale Handelsbank). Since 1957, the only

really new local bank that has been established is
the Asia Trust Bank, established in 1966.

Detailed data on commercial bank assets and liabilities are presented according to sources and uses
of funds in Tables 4.2 and 4.3 Before considering
the data in these two tables, it may be useful to reconcile the definitions of Thai terms for certain
items which may be at variance with the usage familiar
to students of Western banking.

First of all, the summary balance sheet for all
the commercial banks in Thailand is not a truly consolidated account because it includes interbank balances. For a variety of technical reasons these are
not eliminated but are carried on both the sources
and the uses sides. "Cash on hand" (which is not
counted as part of the legal reserve against deposits)
includes foreign currency purchased by commercial
banks in their course of business. "Other" securities (securities other than Treasury bonds and bills,
carried at book value) includes debentures and equity
securities of private and state corporations, some of
which, such as those of the Industrial Finance Cooperation of Thailand, the commercial banks were encouraged to acquire. "Trust receipts" represents
mainly import bills which have fallen due but whose
maturity has been extended by the importer who issues
a trust receipt to the commercial bank to secure the
extension.

On the sources of funds side, "capital account"
is tantamount to the "capital fund," i.e., net worth.
With respect.to demand deposits, those classified as
"banks" include domestic as well as foreign banks'
deposits. Those classified as "government" are exclusively those of government departments. Deposits
of municipalities and state enterprises are lumped
together with those of business and individuals under
the "private residents" label. Demand deposits classed
as "nonresidents" include those of foreign embassies
and foreign government officials. The same classification applies to time deposits. "Other" deposit liabilities include cashier's and certified checks issued
by the banks and not yet collected, as well as marginal

TABLE 4.2

Commercial Banks: Uses of Funds, 1955-1967
(million baht)

Use[a]	1955	1956	1957	1958	1959	1960	1961	1962	1963	1964	1965	1966	1967
Cash on hand	135.6	174.9	205.4	211.8	234.8	262.9	287.1	309.1	369.8	369.2	360.4	403.4	467.5
Balance with banks:													
Bank of Thailand	309.6	328.0	359.4	328.5	446.7	480.6	593.9	701.7	919.7	940.0	942.2	1,071.2	1,247.2
Bank in Thailand	54.3	153.5	215.5	178.2	213.9	227.0	247.4	284.0	463.0	648.9	769.9	887.5	1,078.8
Banks abroad	170.9	264.2	265.0	253.2	248.7	283.8	283.0	372.7	508.8	540.6	679.0	799.8	777.3
Investment													
Treasury bills	53.5	94.1	79.8	43.7	16.1	23.5	80.0	195.1	304.3	267.7	197.0	390.9	514.7
Bonds	188.1	142.8	155.9	204.2	294.6	394.8	518.0	946.0	1,380.6	1,903.8	2,342.7	3,728.1	4,343.5
Others	22.7	23.2	21.8	29.9	27.9	40.8	–	56.2	128.8	156.2	201.1	223.5	255.3
Loans and overdrafts													
Bills	1,620.4	2,049.9	2,426.7	2,894.4	3,268.4	3,809.3	4,361.5	5,392.8	6,188.2	7,401.8	8,930.7	10,577.3	12,590.7
Domestic	250.1	284.5	289.9	360.8	317.9	497.5	681.0	6,605.0	751.0	905.2	995.7	1,352.0	1,631.0
Import	271.0	350.2	420.0	473.0	620.4	735.6	847.0	488.7	628.0	805.8	971.0	1,051.8	1,083.8
Export	249.9	163.7	202.4	249.5	281.7	354.9	443.4	446.7	572.7	719.9	929.5	851.9	704.4
Trust receipts	–	–	–	–	–	–	–	603.0	667.6	763.2	968.6	1,241.2	1,252.2
Fixed assets	161.9	170.3	213.1	256.4	322.2	458.1	514.4	626.5	779.9	880.7	897.7	1,058.1	1,197.8
Other assets	458.2	221.7	258.3	437.9	278.5	478.6	641.4	373.1	404.0	406.5	542.6	645.1	894.7
Total	3,946.2	4,412.0	5,113.2	5,921.5	6,571.8	8,047.4	9,498.1	11,400.6	14,066.4	16,709.5	19,728.1	24,281.8	28,038.9

[a]See text for definition of categories.

Source: Bank of Thailand.

TABLE 4.3

Commercial Banks: Sources of Funds, 1955-1967

(million baht)

Source[a]	1955	1956	1957	1958	1959	1960	1961	1962	1963	1964	1965	1966	1967
Deposits													
Demand													
Banks	42.3	141.2	191.6	164.0	114.9	170.1	149.4	206.6	243.6	358.1	617.4	891.0	964.7
Govt.	79.9	117.9	220.5	172.6	207.3	223.8	350.0	273.6	355.6	437.5	656.6	649.5	722.3
Private residents	1,885.7	2,042.6	2,343.9	2,753.2	2,939.9	3,619.1	3,963.5	3,980.0	4,627.0	5,127.6	5,709.1	6,774.1	7,371.8
Non-residents	21.4	56.4	3.7	11.8	35.0	20.2	26.8	43.9	68.7	74.3	75.6	153.7	118.7
Time													
Banks	–	55.3	32.2	66.3	82.5	141.9	111.8	112.3	136.0	176.7	194.7	137.1	123.0
Govt.	71.9	11.7	8.7	17.6	185.5	197.3	205.3	158.6	223.2	226.7	442.4	535.7	794.8
Private residents	168.0	349.4	438.5	621.7	766.7	1,025.7	1,485.3	3,148.6	4,255.0	5,368.3	6,406.8	8,825.5	10,979.4
Non-residents	3.7	9.9	5.0	9.8	28.2	0.6	11.7	52.6	42.8	29.2	39.1	33.0	51.4
Other	–	131.6	180.7	121.1	88.3	160.7	279.9	157.6	167.3	159.6	188.4	216.3	256.5
Borrowings													
Bank of Thailand	3.0	–	–	8.7	41.9	98.5	106.3	103.6	98.0	164.7	244.3	336.9	298.5
Banks in Thailand	56.0	99.1	95.1	101.4	252.8	202.2	243.4	293.1	370.2	326.4	241.4	198.5	154.4
Banks abroad	338.2	438.6	543.8	559.9	738.4	804.9	1,065.5	1,506.7	1,896.2	2,318.1	2,760.5	2,927.1	2,901.4
Other liabilities	821.1	499.6	546.6	795.1	575.6	821.4	884.3	589.2	759.2	969.6	893.2	1,123.2	1,529.3
Capital accounts	455.0	458.7	502.9	518.3	514.8	561.0	614.9	774.2	823.6	972.7	1,258.7	1,480.2	1,772.7
Total	3,946.2	4,412.0	5,113.2	5,921.5	6,571.8	8,047.4	9,498.1	11,400.6	14,066.4	16,709.5	19,728.1	24,281.8	28,038.9

[a]See text for definition of categories.

Source: Bank of Thailand

114

deposits of customers prior to opening of letters of
credit. "Borrowings from other banks" include loans
from the Government Savings Bank. "Other liabilities" consist of provident funds, suspense accounts,
and time bills under trust receipts. These are import bills that have been discounted by foreign banks
and remitted to Thailand for collection after the
importer has extended their maturity under the trust
receipt procedure.

Turning to the data on sources of funds: Table
4.3 shows that the greatest percentage increase occurred with respect to borrowings from the Bank of
Thailand. This has risen a hundredfold over the period. But the significance of this must tempered by
the realization that even in 1967, borrowings from
the Bank of Thailand still accounted for only 1 per
cent of all the sources of funds. Moreover, most of
the increase occurred before 1962. Even though the
Bank of Thailand has since then established several
new lines of credit to the commercial banks, their
rate of utilization has been somewhat disappointing.
Indeed, as mentioned earlier, foreign banks have been
a much more important source of funds. The proportion of borrowing from them rose from under 9 per
cent in 1955 to over 10 per cent in 1967. At the
end of 1967, commercial banks had borrowed only 299
million from the Bank of Thailand, while loans from
head offices and correspondent banks neared 3 million
baht.

Of prime importance as a source of funds to the
commercial banks of Thailand was the sharp increase
in time deposits of private residents. In fact, by
the end of 1967, these time deposits had become the
most important single source of funds when measured
as a percentage of total liabilities, accounting for
over one-fourth of the 28 billion total. With time
deposits now exceeding demand deposits, a variety of
explanations has been adduced to explain this rather
striking phenomenon. No doubt, the monetary and political stability, the growth of personal income and
confidence, and the sound stewardship of commercial
banks which the public came to expect from the Bank
of Thailand after 1959 have all played a part.[9] To

some extent, legislative enactments have also been
instrumental. The reclassification of accounts has
already been mentioned. Other observers attach considerable importance to the increase in the rate of
return which allegedly occurred during the period,
though the influence of higher interest rates payable
on time deposits is by no means a simple one.[10] While
it is true that the rates of interest payable on
three-month and six-month deposits increased from 3
to 5 per cent per annum after 1959, it should also
be noted that the return on the longest-term time
deposits (twelve months) was actually lowered in 1962
from 8 to 7 per cent. Probably at least as important
as the changes in interest rates was the legislation
passed in 1962 exempting interest on deposits from
income taxation.[11]

While the spectacular growth of time deposits
cannot be gainsaid, there are those who remain somewhat skeptical about the extent to which these deposits fully measure the growth of voluntary savings.
They view the rapid increase in time deposits largely
as a shift from demand deposits which has resulted
not merely because of the reclassification but also
because of the ease with which time deposits can, allegedly, be treated as checking accounts.[12]

Turning to the data on uses of funds: the most
striking development was the growth of investments in
government bonds. Their twenty-three-fold increase
over time is also reflected in the percentage distribution. From less than 5 per cent of assets in 1955,
government bonds rose to some 15 per cent in 1967.

Loans and overdrafts represent the most significant use of funds from the standpoint of financial
intermediation. Unlike commercial bills, loans and
overdrafts presumably indicate the supply of funds
used for purposes more related to development planning than is the financing of exports and imports.
In fact, these loans rose faster than did foreign
trade bills. They also moved upward at a faster rate
than did demand deposits, giving some credence to the
proposition alluded to earlier, namely, that an account in a time deposit does not necessarily forgo
all the advantages of a demand deposit.

Balances with other banks are an item that looms
large on both sides of the commercial bank balance
sheet, even though, as suggested earlier, it represents largely a "wash" transaction. It does, however,
indicate the importance of interbank transactions and
reflects some banks' need for funds, both to meet
demands for accommodation at short notice and for win-
dow dressing.

TIME SERIES ANALYSIS: COMPOSITION
OF BALANCE SHEETS

A scrutiny of the commercial bank's sources and
uses of funds, while instructive, fails to relate the
structure of the banking system to the trend of the
economy as a whole. The two economic variables which
best put the changing composition of the commercial
bank's balance sheets into perspective are the GNP
and the money supply. Accordingly, simple regressions of selected balance sheet items on these two
variables will be presented and briefly discussed in
this section. The analysis does not extend beyond
1965, the last year for which data were available at
the time the computer program was set up. A subsequent manual check of variables selected at random
did not warrant any substantive modifications in the
results of the regressions.

Table 4.4 presents some of the results of time
series analysis. The first conclusion which appears
to emerge from the table is that, for analytical purposes, it seems largely superfluous to use two independent variables, inasmuch as GNP and money supply
yield almost identical results, suggesting that these
two variables are highly correlated with each other
(correlating MS with GNP yields a coefficient of 0.98).
This conclusion may be a little too hasty. The slopes
of regression on the two variables do differ from each
other and thereby justify the inclusion of both in
the analysis.*

_____

*In fact, the slopes of the regressions may be
of greater significance throughout this analysis of
time series where all relevant magnitudes show an

TABLE 4.4

Commercial Banks: 1955-1965 Time Series Analysis

Dependent Variable (y) (Simple Correlation Coefficients)	Independent Variable (x)	
	GNP	Money Supply
Private demand deposits as % of total liabilities	-8.9489	-9.2177
Loans, overdrafts & discounts as % of total assets	-4.3369	-4.8057
Total deposits as % of total liabilities	9.1952	9.3270
Loans, overdrafts, discounts & investments as % of total assets	7.0260	6.8507
Time deposits as % of total liabilities	9.6589	9.5005
Private deposits as % of total liabilities	-8.9489	-9.2177
Private time deposits as % of total liabilities	9.6589	9.5005
Demand deposits as % of total liabilities	-8.8804	-8.9457
Investments as % of total assets	7.7593	8.2443
(Slope of Regression)[a]		
Private demand deposits as % of total liabilities	-6.1018	-7.8336
Loans, overdrafts & discounts as % of total assets	-2.00784	-17.8503
Total deposits as % of total liabilities	2.6034	3.2914
Loans, overdrafts, discounts & investment as % of total assets	72.0616	56.3739
Time deposits as % of total liabilities	23.4514	28.7502
Private deposits as % of total liabilities	-6.1018	-7.8336
Private time deposits as % of total liabilities	23.4514	28.7502
Demand deposits as % of total liabilities	-5.2580	-6.6017
Investments as % of total assets	5.0254	4.2840

[a]Defined as per cent change in y associated with 10 per cent increase in x; minus sign indicates an inverse correlation.

Source: Based on data provided by the Bank of Thailand.

   With few exceptions, the selected balance sheet
ratios in Table 4.4 show very high correlations both
with GNP and the money supply, even though in four
instances the correlation is an inverse one. Thus,
the ratio of loans, overdrafts, and discounts to total assets and the ratio of demand deposits, both
private and total, to all liabilities are inversely
correlated, indicating a steady decline in their relative importance over time. This is not surprising.
On the liabilities side, time deposits have increased
relative to the total much faster than demand deposits, and on the assets side, the share of loans, overdrafts, and discounts to the total diminished steadily
over time relative to that of investments. The lower
value of correlation coefficients for the ratio of
earning assets to total assets (negative for earning
assets, less investments) suggests a more erratic
behavior over time, the numerator or the denominator
changing direction, and, hence, the sign of the ratio
in some years.

   Slopes of regression, as defined here, are perhaps of greater interest for analytical purposes than
simple correlation coefficients, which merely indicate
the conformance of observations to a straight trend
line. While the relationship mentioned above, of
course, holds here as well, it is perhaps useful to
note that as money supply and/or GNP increases, the
relative share of time deposits among total banking
assets increases at over twice their rate and that of
investments at five times the rate of increase of the
independent variables.

   Thus, Table 4.4 emphasizes and underlines the
points made in the preceding section. Thai commercial

----

upward trend throughout the period. An attempt to
introduce an explicit time variable into the regression analysis did not yield meaningful results. The
use of ratios (of a given balance sheet item to total
assets and total liabilities) was resorted to in order
to reduce somewhat the influence of time over the
values of the regression coefficients.

banks have grown with the national income and the
money supply. But the composition of their portfolios and debts has changed significantly. Time deposits and borrowings have become the most important
sources of funds, and investment in government securities has been the most important use to which these
funds were put. "Important" in this context means
relative to other assets and liabilities. From the
standpoint of development finance, one could question
the importance of purchases of government securities
over loans to business, agriculture, and industry.
While these, too, have grown over time, as have indeed all items on the balance sheet, they have not
grown as fast as investments relative to national income or the money supply.

TIME SERIES ANALYSIS: EXPANSION OF CREDIT

The changing structure of sources and uses of
commercial bank funds was related in the preceding
section to the trend of national income and the money
supply. Now an analysis of some of the factors which
appear to have been significant in the expansion of
credit by the banking system as a whole will be attempted. A fractional reserve banking system expands
the means of payment in the hands of the public by
creating debts against itself, primarily through the
crediting of demand deposits. The usual difficulties
of time series analysis are further compounded in this
instance by the fact that expansion of bank credit
affects the level and rate of growth of national income and, even more directly, of money supply. In
the case of Thai banks, moreover, there are two additional considerations which cast further doubts on
the validity of any findings derived from this method
of analysis. In the first place, the distinction between time and demand deposits remains somewhat vague,
at least in some years; secondly, the nonreporting of
unused overdraft balances obscures somewhat the concept of demand deposits in the hands of the public.
Accordingly, the observations made in this section
must be regarded as very tentative.

The economic significance of the ability of the
commercial banks to create credit lies, from the

standpoint of the saving-investment process, in the
fact that it enables them to issue their liabilities
to deficit spending units in exchange for portfolio
assets, and to do so in excess of initial cash resources. This is the one reason why bank loans, overdrafts, and discounts can increase faster than income
and money supply. In the period from 1955 to 1965,
a 10 per cent increase in GNP was associated with a
26.2 per cent increase in loans, overdrafts, and discounts, and this rate was even greater when related
to a 10 per cent increase in money supply--to be exact, 37 per cent. It follows from the fact that
money supply increased at a slower rate than income
in the period under consideration.

As seen in Table 4.5, expansion of earning assets of commercial banks is very highly correlated
with both cash and deposits. Here again, it is the
slopes rather than the coefficients which appear to
be of greater analytical interest. While an increase
in cash at banks and in the hands of the public are
both associated with a relatively greater increase
in earning assets, it is the latter which is accompanied by the more significant increase of earning
assets. This is somewhat surprising because the traditional banking theory would lead one to expect that
it is the bank's cash resources which are more directly associated with its ability to expand earning assets. The finding provides a somewhat flimsy basis
for the speculation that the Thai banks' ability to
expand credit is not necessarily highly correlated
with their willingness to do so. This point will be
discussed more fully later.

A 10 per cent increase in time deposits is associated with a 20 per cent increase in all earning
assets, while the same increase in demand deposits
is linked to an increase in earning assets of only
7 per cent. This is to be expected because even if
many loans were given in the form of overdrafts, other
loans would take the form of demand deposits. One
possible implication here is that (to the extent that
a regression equation may be said to have any predic-
tive value) a continuing growth of time deposits
ahead of demand deposits may be expected to result in

TABLE 4.5

Commercial Banks: 1955-1965 Time Series Analysis

	Time Deposits	Demand Deposits	Currency at Banks	Currency Held by Public
Simple Correlation Coefficients				
Loans, overdrafts, discounts & investments	9.9251	9.9062	9.7597	9.7597
Loans, overdrafts, & discounts	9.9366	9.9303	9.7257	9.7257
Slope of Regression[a]				
Loans, overdrafts, discounts, & investments	20.0754	6.5319	24.167	24.167
Loans, overdrafts, & discounts	20.8293	6.7858	24.959	24.959

[a]Defined as the percentage change in y associated with a 10 per cent increase in x.

Source: Based on data provided by the Bank of Thailand.

a rate of growth of earning assets which will be
slower than that experienced in the past.

Inasmuch as cash and deposits are those elements
which presumably underlie the ability of the banks to
expand credit to the private sector, Table 4.6, which
relates the banks' cash resources to their deposits,
is of interest here. The table shows that the correlation coefficients are uniformly high, as could have
been expected. The values of the slopes indicates a
greater elasticity of time deposits than of demand deposits. A 10 per cent increase in bank cash resources
corresponds to a less than 10 per cent increase in demand deposits, but represents a 28 per cent increase
in time deposits.* This suggests that the expansion
of time deposits adds more to cash resources than the
expansion of demand deposits, hardly an unexpected
finding inasmuch as the latter constitute a liability
more directly convertible into cash in the hands of
the public than the former.

TABLE 4.6

Commercial Banks: 1955-1965 Time Series Analysis

Dependent Variable y	Cash on Hand, Foreign Currency & Balances with Bank of Thailand (x)	
	Simple Correlation Coefficient	Slope[a]
Demand deposits	.96928	9.4354
Time deposits	.98786	27.9778

[a]Defined as the percentage change in y associated
with a 10 per cent increase in x.

Source: Based on information provided by the Bank
of Thailand.

---

*The slopes as expressed here do, of course,
give elasticities when the decimal point are adjusted. Thus, a slope of regression of all deposit on
cash and deposits at the Bank of Thailand of 15.2
indicates an elasticity of 1.52. (All correlations
were calculated in log-log space.)

In Thailand, cash held by banks does not count
as part of the legally required reserve against deposits. Deposits held at the Bank of Thailand form
a part of the reserve, together with the commercial
banks' holdings of government securities. Since mid-
1966, the required reserves have been allowed to consist of deposits of cash at the central bank and of
government securities in the commercial banks' portfolios, in equal parts. As mentioned earlier, Thai
commercial banks do have total legal reserves that
are no less related to earning assets and deposits
over time than are the cash resources themselves. In
fact, as shown in Table 4.7, the association is striking. The rate of increase of total deposits is three
times that of excess reserves. While it is true that
reserves, hence excess reserves, contain government
securities, so do earning assets. Table 4.7 hints
that excess reserves have been used to expand holdings of government securities rather than that of
loans, overdrafts, and discounts.

TABLE 4.7

Commercial Banks: 1955-1965 Time Series Analysis

Dependent Variable y	Excess Reserves (Independent Variable, x)	
	Simple Correlation Coefficient	Slope[a]
Loans, overdrafts, discounts, & investment	.85472	24.5660
Government securities	.91262	39.2350
Deposits (demand and time)	.9326	30.1234

[a]Defined as percentage change in y associated with
a 10 per cent increase in x.

Source: Based on information provided by the Bank
         of Thailand.

This proposition is worth exploring. Unfortunately, detailed information about the composition of the commercial banks' required and excess reserves has been available only since 1962; this information is presented in Table 4.8. What this table, in effect, strongly suggests is that excess reserves were invested in government securities rather than used to expand other earning assets. This point will be elaborated further below.

What, then, are the findings of this section? Subject to the qualification made above, it can be conjectured that during the "modern" phase, the expansion of credit by commercial banks was made possible by the rapid expansion of time deposits of private residents. However, this expansion of credit did not realize its full potential, as evidenced by the maintenance of substantial excess reserves which were used primarily to purchase government securities far beyond the quantities required against total deposits.

An attempt was made to arrive at a more rigorous expression of the relationship between excess reserves and various balance sheet items by multiple regression analysis. Unfortunately for this sort of analysis, however, all the pertinent variables are dominated by a strong upward trend. The resulting multi-collinearity makes it statistically difficult to distinguish the influence of one variable from another. A number of multiple regressions were run, but only the following one may be said to be statistically meaningful and even in this one the size of standard errors does not inspire great confidence:

If E = excess reserves

X_1 = commercial banks cash assets

X_2 = loans and discounts

and X_3 = government securities

$$E = 195.10 + .1575X_1 - .0195X_2 + .0889X_3$$
$$\quad\quad\quad\quad (.205) \quad\quad (.0188) \quad (.0541)$$

TABLE 4.8

Commercial Banks: Legal, Required, and Excess Reserves, 1962–1967
(million baht)

Year and Quarter		Reserves		Reserve Requirement (3)	Excess Reserves (4)
		Thai Govt. Securities (1)	Cash Deposits at BOT (2)		
1962	December	117.9	681.8	484.5	315.2
1963	March	114.4	598.3	496.5	216.2
	June	126.8	676.6	527.9	275.5
	September	125.1	675.7	550.1	250.7
	December	139.5	805.8	595.8	349.5
1964	March	137.3	721.3	618.7	239.9
	June	147.0	754.3	646.1	255.2
	September	164.5	731.1	676.2	219.4
	December	174.5	957.0	708.8	422.7
1965	March	168.4	736.7	723.2	181.9
	June	334.6	708.9	746.9	296.6
	September	370.3	736.8	797.2	309.9
	December	403.5	864.8	847.4	420.9
1966	March	425.9	879.3	894.5	410.7
	June	454.7	1,159.3	947.9	661.1
	September	486.1	910.4	1,026.2	370.3
	December	511.0	943.3	1,088.7	365.6
1967	March	512.2	951.5	1,110.6	353.1
	June	542.2	1,028.8	1,161.3	409.7
	September	581.1	1,005.7	1,204.2	382.5
	December	613.7	1,263.8	1,269.9	607.6

Source: Bank of Thailand.

126

CROSS-SECTION ANALYSIS: JULY 1962 AND 1966,
BANKS OPERATING IN THAILAND

Given the severe limitations of time series analysis, it may be useful to supplement that analysis
with an examination of the balance sheets of the commercial banks at points of time. July 1962 has been
chosen because it was the earliest month for which
reasonably consistent and comparable data were available, even though only in raw form. For purposes of
comparison, a similar set of data was prepared for
July 1966, the last month for which raw data were
available at the time the analysis was undertaken.
The data are presented separately for banks incorporated in Thailand and for those with head offices
abroad.

The data are not exactly comparable to those
presented earlier for all banks, mainly because, for
purposes of cross-section analysis, it was possible
to net out private deposits and, in the case of banks
locally chartered, to adjust for operations of foreign branches of banks with headquarters in Thailand.
The difference between the totals given in this section and those given in the Bank of Thailand Monthly
Bulletin (on which Table 4.2 is based) is of the
order of 5 per cent.

Table 4.9 gives the principal items of the balance sheets of the sixteen incorporated banks operating in Thailand as of July 1962. The degree of disparity with respect to size is considerable. Capital
funds range from 3 to over 110 million, deposits from
6 million to substantially more than 1 billion baht,
and loans and overdrafts from less than 100 million
to over 1 billion. As mentioned previously, Wang Lee
Chan Bank, whose capital, deposits, and loans are by
far the smallest, is more properly regarded as a family bank than as a commercial bank.

Table 4.10 provides similar data for those banks
which have head offices abroad but maintain branches
in Thailand (these "foreign" banks operate in Thailand out of branches located in Bangkok, with the
single exception of the Chartered Bank, which operates

TABLE 4.9

Comparative Statement of Condition,
Banks Incorporated in Thailand, July 1962
(million baht)

Bank	Capital and Liabilities				Assets							Total Capital & Liabilities or Assets
	Capital Fund	Deposits	Borrowing	Other Liabil.	Cash	Govt. Sec.	Other Sec. Invest.	Loans & Advances	Bills Receivable	Bank Prem. & Eqpt.	Other	
	1	2	3	4	5	6	7	8	9	10	11	12
Siam Com. B.	113.9	477.8	-	13.4	177.7	17.0	13.1	286.5	58.4	32.3	20.2	605.1
Wang Lee Chan B.	3.0	6.4	-	0.3	2.3	0.3	0.1	6.6	-	0.1	0.3	9.5
Bank of Asia	48.3	268.5	1.1	9.2	48.8	35.6	3.2	139.6	19.2	46.1	34.6	327.1
Siam City B.	19.7	347.3	4.0	25.2	89.9	40.0	0.5	151.2	84.4	14.6	16.2	396.8
Provincial B.	41.8	759.9	90.6	47.1	76.7	13.6	1.7	671.7	98.1	65.6	12.2	939.5
Bangkok B.	106.0	1,363.3	722.9	182.2	208.5	181.6	19.0	1,005.7	826.0	90.0	42.9	2,373.7
Bangkok B. of Com.	27.1	445.3	-	52.5	118.8	52.8	0.7	235.3	58.4	28.2	30.3	524.6
B. of Ayudhya	27.0	415.9	81.1	43.2	43.7	16.0	8.2	325.7	105.8	30.8	37.1	567.3
Thai Farmers B.	35.1	384.2	17.3	36.0	80.1	57.1	1.0	145.9	141.9	36.3	10.0	472.5
Laem Thong B.	33.5	159.5	39.5	11.5	21.5	13.6	1.9	166.0	32.1	8.6	0.4	244.3
Union B. of Bangkok	17.1	217.2	34.5	44.5	42.3	33.0	1.1	104.0	97.0	17.4	18.4	313.2
Thai Danu B.	25.7	134.4	-	21.6	20.1	24.3	0.6	91.3	25.3	7.5	12.8	181.7
Agricultural B. Bangkok	21.1	929.4	107.8	49.7	127.2	180.1	2.1	562.0	62.3	150.7	23.7	1,108.1
Metropolitan B.	35.2	226.2	198.6	86.0	62.6	31.0	6.3	157.6	272.2	4.5	9.9	544.1
Thai Military B.	20.2	230.5	7.9	29.2	65.5	52.9	0.3	101.6	58.2	2.8	6.3	287.5
Thai Developmt B.	11.5	224.1	13.6	40.3	31.7	10.0	0.5	157.4	54.2	14.8	21.3	289.5
Total	586.2	6,589.9	1,317.1	691.9	1,217.4	758.9	60.3	4,308.1	1,993.5	550.3	296.6	9,184.5

Source: Compiled from data provided by the Bank of Thailand.

TABLE 4.10

Comparative Statement of Condition,
Banks Incorporated Abroad, July 1962
(million baht)

Bank	Capital and Liabilities				Assets							Total Capital & Liabilities or Assets
	Capital Fund	Deposits	Borrowing	Other Liabil.	Cash	Govt. Sec.	Other Sec. Invest.	Loans & Advances	Bills Receivable	Bank Prem. & Eqpt.	Other	
	1	2	3	4	5	6	7	8	9	10	11	12
The Hongkong and Shanghai B.	24.0	200.8	24.7	44.7	17.1	4.8	0.2	149.4	103.4	19.6	0.2	294.7
The Chartered B.	17.7	223.6	57.0	136.2	18.9	13.0	0.2	254.8	138.1	2.5	6.8	434.4
Banque de L' Indochine	0.9	67.8	43.4	18.6	26.5	5.2	0.4	72.0	23.1	0.3	3.1	130.6
Sze Hai Tong B.	16.9	17.0	29.8	3.8	16.9	7.5	0.2	15.2	27.3	0.1	0.4	67.5
The B. of Canton	1.0	32.7	23.0	3.2	12.9	5.0	–	22.0	19.8	0.2	0.1	60.0
Mercantile B.	–	66.3	61.5	10.7	7.7	7.2	0.2	90.5	26.7	6.2	0.1	138.5
The B. of China	3.8	38.3	89.9	10.7	32.3	14.5	–	45.0	45.5	2.4	2.9	142.6
The Indian Overseas B.	–	41.1	29.9	1.8	8.9	5.6	0.2	27.8	29.3	0.6	0.3	72.7
The Chase Manhattan B.	5.6	136.9	28.9	7.9	12.5	7.5	–	113.2	39.3	–	6.7	179.2
The B. of America	–	270.5	35.0	19.2	54.4	69.5	–	169.5	26.9	2.5	1.8	324.7
The Mitsui B.	–	58.2	111.0	42.5	11.8	14.0	0.2	176.8	6.9	1.3	0.8	211.7
The B. of Tokyo	–	6.4	30.4	0.6	1.1	21.9	–	10.6	0.4	2.1	1.2	37.4
The United Malayan B.	–	–	–	–	–	–	–	–	–	–	–	–
Total	69.9	1,159.6	564.5	299.9	221.0	175.7	1.6	1,146.8	486.7	37.8	24.4	2,094.0

Source: Compiled from data provided by the Bank of Thailand.

a branch in Phuket). For these banks, the differences with respect to size are no less pronounced.
Data for capital fund could not be obtained on a consistent basis for 1962. The act of 1962 changed
rather drastically the provisions with respect to
capital assets to be maintained in Thailand by foreign banks as well as the method of accounting for
them.

In Tables 4.11 and 4.12 comparable data are
provided for July 1966. Again, the differences in
relative size of the banks are very pronounced. A
question of interest is whether the growth of individual banks, in terms of total assets, earning assets,
or deposits, is in any way related to the bank size,
its capital resources, or its cash position.

Insofar as available data permit a firm conclusion, the answer appears to be that there is no perceptible connection between, say, cash and deposits,
or capital and loans, as explanatory variables of
growth of individual banks. In other words, the bank
whose cash resources increased most from 1962 to 1966
is not necessarily the one whose deposits or loans
have grown most. In Tables 4.13 and 4.14 are given
the Kendall rank correlation coefficients which have
been computed for the relevant variables. The choice
of Kendall rather than Spearman rank correlation was
dictated by the number of observations.

Even though the results of rank correlation
analysis yield such meager numerical values, they are
not without relevance to an inquiry into the role of
Thai commercial banking in the financial intermediation process. The results are consistent with the
proposition already hinted at in the course of time
series analysis, namely, that as an industry, banking
in Thailand operates below capacity. That is, it is
suggested that the ability of an individual bank to
expand loans has not been hampered by its inability
to obtain additional cash or capital and, conversely,
that an individual bank's superior performance in expanding its assets has not been dependent on its performing equally well with respect to raising additional capital or retaining sufficient cash resources.

TABLE 4.11

Comparative Statement of Condition, Banks Incorporated in Thailand, July 1966
(million baht)

Bank	Capital and Liabilities				Assets							Total Capital & Liabilities or Assets
	Capital Fund	Deposits	Borrowing	Other Liabil.	Cash	Govt. Sec.	Other Sec. Invest.	Loans & Advances	Bills Receivable	Bank Prem. & Eqpt.	Other	
	1	2	3	4	5	6	7	8	9	10	11	12
Siam Com. B.	142.2	1,283.4	—	26.7	243.3	562.3	50.5	505.5	22.3	47.1	21.3	1,452.3
Wang Lee Chan B.	3.5	5.9	—	0.6	1.5	0.9	0.1	6.4	—	0.1	1.0	10.0
Bank of Asia	90.1	307.9	1.1	45.2	51.8	20.2	3.8	237.6	89.8	38.1	3.0	444.3
Siam City B.	53.9	826.2	19.6	61.3	160.4	101.9	2.3	416.4	172.5	38.2	69.3	961.0
Krung Thai B.	146.7	3,258.3	162.8	63.5	339.9	1,198.6	24.4	1,641.4	193.8	308.5	24.7	3,731.3
Bangkok B.	291.9	3,570.9	1,004.5	392.1	639.4	448.6	100.0	1,970.5	1,803.3	214.5	82.7	5,259.4
Bangkok B. of Com.	63.0	1,035.6	1.8	86.4	197.7	175.3	8.7	548.8	135.2	63.6	57.5	1,186.8
B. of Ayudhya	145.1	1,066.7	375.3	55.8	193.4	250.0	16.6	703.2	318.4	84.5	76.8	1,642.9
Thai Farmers B.	78.0	888.0	4.3	382.1	104.2	210.0	20.1	391.9	542.2	17.3	16.7	1,352.4
Laem Thong B.	41.5	239.6	17.1	26.0	28.5	29.4	6.8	226.0	10.8	19.8	2.8	324.2
Union B. of Bangkok	48.2	386.3	34.2	20.2	79.6	90.0	4.4	168.8	98.7	20.9	26.5	488.9
Thai Danu B.	57.8	340.0	3.7	46.6	44.8	115.3	7.3	206.9	32.9	7.1	33.8	448.1
Bangkok Metropolitan B.	60.6	647.7	382.4	30.1	124.9	160.5	10.2	405.7	385.8	19.1	14.6	1,120.8
Thai Military B.	79.5	489.5	37.6	87.2	153.1	122.0	7.2	314.7	85.2	3.9	7.7	693.8
Thai Development B.	39.5	630.5	13.2	32.4	76.3	33.0	4.1	458.1	78.7	44.0	21.4	715.6
Asia Trust B.	44.4	126.9	183.3	4.5	58.3	15.6	2.0	62.5	202.4	15.6	2.7	359.1
Total	1,385.9	15,103.4	2,240.9	1,460.7	2,497.1	3,533.6	268.9	8,264.4	4,172.0	942.3	462.5	20,190.9

Source: Compiled from data provided by the Bank of Thailand.

TABLE 4.12

Comparative Statement of Condition,
Banks Incorporated Abroad, July 1966
(million baht)

Bank	Capital and Liabilities				Assets							Total Capital & Liabilities or Assets
	Capital Fund	Deposits	Borrowing	Other Liabil.	Cash	Govt. Sec.	Other Sec. Invest.	Loans & Advances	Bills Receivable	Bank Prem. & Eqpt.	Other	
	1	2	3	4	5	6	7	8	9	10	11	12
The Hongkong & Shanghai B.	46.5	220.4	-	12.7	28.7	33.0	1.1	131.8	52.1	32.4	0.5	279.6
The Chartered B.	49.5	300.8	0.7	49.6	35.6	43.5	1.1	226.7	86.4	5.2	2.1	400.6
Banque de L' Indochine	33.0	77.8	27.1	10.4	7.4	15.2	1.0	80.4	34.3	6.9	3.1	148.3
Sze Hai Tong B.	26.6	30.0	22.8	6.7	21.4	11.5	0.6	15.0	36.9	0.1	0.6	86.1
The B. of Canton	9.1	70.0	7.7	2.6	39.2	5.0	-	18.1	26.3	0.1	0.7	89.4
Mercantile B.	26.2	69.9	5.8	11.5	21.1	10.0	0.2	48.9	26.9	6.1	0.2	113.4
The B. of China	46.4	66.9	82.4	22.5	72.3	14.0	-	66.3	60.8	1.9	2.9	218.2
The Indian Overseas B.	11.6	43.7	5.4	4.3	20.0	8.3	0.3	14.0	21.5	0.5	0.4	65.0
The Chase Manhattan B.	99.4	173.7	4.7	14.2	31.7	43.0	7.0	133.7	67.8	1.6	7.4	292.0
The B. of America	104.1	399.6	-	18.9	118.1	66.5	-	195.1	95.5	2.8	44.6	522.6
The Mitsui B.	90.2	241.0	70.7	26.5	34.8	65.0	1.1	317.3	6.8	2.0	1.4	428.4
The B. of Tokyo	60.3	283.2	56.2	18.3	17.4	56.9	1.1	301.5	37.6	1.5	2.0	418.0
The United Malayan B.	54.0	230.4	100.6	25.4	27.8	28.0	0.4	236.6	110.5	4.3	2.8	410.4
Total	656.9	2,207.4	384.1	223.6	475.5	399.9	13.9	1,785.4	663.4	65.4	68.7	3,472.0

Source: Compiled from data provided by the Bank of Thailand.

TABLE 4.13

Rank Order of Index of Assets and Liabilities,
Banks Incorporated in Thailand, July 1966,
Matrix of Kendall Coefficients
(1962 = 100)

	Deposits	Cash	Capital Fund	Government Securities	Loans & Advances	Bills Receivable	Other Secur. & Investments
Deposits	1.0	0.4857	0.2190	0.3905	0.3143	0.0440	
Cash		1.0		0.1048		0.0989	0.2000
Capital fund			1.0	-0.0476	0.3619	0.1868	
Government securities				1.0			
Loans & advances					1.0		
Bills receivable						1.0	
Other securities & investments							1.0

Source: Computed from data underlying Tables 4.10 and 4.11.

133

TABLE 4.14

Rank Order of Index of Assets and Liabilities,
Banks Incorporated Abroad, July 1966,
Matrix of Kendall Coefficients
(1962 = 100)

	Capital Fund	Deposits	Cash	Government Securities	Loans & Advances	Bills Receivable
Capital fund	1.0	-0.2857		-0.1515	0.2424	0.3030
Deposits		1.0	0.2727	-0.0303	0.5455	0.2424
Cash			1.0	-0.0909	0.1818	0.1212
Government securities				1.0		
Loans & advances					1.0	
Bills receivable						1.0

Source: Computed from data underlying Tables 4.10 and 4.11.

Admittedly, the empirical evidence is too thin to
sustain fully such a far-flung proposition, but such
evidence as that provided in Tables 4.13 and 4.14 is
at least compatible with it.

For the purposes of present discussion, the capacity of the Thai banking industry may be taken to
mean its ability to attract additional deposits, on
the one hand, and its ability to expand earning assets, on the other. To the extent that attracting
deposits is only in part amenable to the decision-
making of the individual commercial banks and insofar
as, in Thailand, the economically significant earning
assets would exclude the purchases of government securities, the index of capacity would be the ratio of
loans, overdrafts, and discounts actually made to
that amount which could potentially be made.

This clearly overstates the case. Banks do have
some ability to attract deposits through variations
in the rates of interest they pay, the quantity and
quality of service they provide, and so on. Conversely, the ability to expand loans is limited by the
willingness of the public to borrow. As will be
argued later, however, the Thai banks do seem to compete for deposits, but their competition for loans
and so forth seems to be rather more subdued in the
face of what is alleged to have been sustained and
continuing high demand for accommodation on the part
of the public.

Thai banks are restricted in their ability to
make loans by both legal and economic constraints.
Among the economic constraints are the willingness
of their customers to borrow, the quality and quan-
tiey of would-be borrowers, and the need to maintain
liquidity and a balanced portfolio. The legal constraints are much easier to quantify. These are the
ratio of cash and government securities to total deposits and the ratio of capital funds to risk assets.
(See above. Other constraints are available in the
act of 1962 but have not yet been invoked. A fuller
discussion of these constraints is given in Chapter
6.) It may be worthwhile to consider some of these
relevant ratios, both for domestic and foreign banks,

as they are presented for 1962 and 1966 in Tables
4.15 and 4.16.

Taking domestic banks first, it is interesting
to note that, at least in the case of the bigger
banks, the ratio of loans, overdrafts, and discounts,
to deposits actually declined from 1962 to 1966, even
though the ratio of cash to deposits declined but
slightly and that of capital to earning assets actually increased. The slight drain on total cash resources is explained both by the high purchases of
government securities and the fact that these securities could be used as part of legal reserves in increasing quantities.

Foreign banks, even more than the domestic ones,
appear to have steered shy of their full potential.
Despite the increase in both cash resources and capital fund relative to deposits and risk assets, respectively, their ratio of loans, overdrafts, and
discounts to deposits decreased rather significantly
over the period 1962-1966. This is the more striking
because the foreign banks showed a rate of growth of
deposits much below that of the domestic banks. (See
Figure 4.1). This lag continues up to the present
and applies particularly to time deposits.

In addition to cash on hand and deposits with
the Bank of Thailand, cash resources of commercial
banks also include balances with banks abroad and
gold. Thus, the concept of "liquid assets" as defined in Table 4.1 cannot be applied to them because
Thai government securities are excluded. Between
1962 and 1966, most domestic banks showed a decline
in relation to deposits; however, three, including
the largest domestic bank, actually managed to increase the ratio of cash to deposits (see Table 4.15).
Almost all foreign banks, on the other hand, did increase their ratio of cash to deposits, and one of
those that did not actually showed cash resources in
excess of its total deposits (see Table 4.16).

As mentioned before, since mid-1966, cash deposited with the Bank of Thailand has not needed to
exceed 3 per cent of total deposits. It is clear that

TABLE 4.15

Commercial Banks Incorporated in Thailand,
Key Balance Sheet Ratios, 1962 and 1966

Bank	A		B		C		D		E	
	1962	1966	1962	1966	1962	1966	1962	1966	1962	1966
Siam Commercial Bank	0.72	0.41	0.78	0.89	0.37	0.19	0.33	0.27	0.30	0.12
Wang Lee Chan Bank	1.03	1.08	1.09	1.25	0.36	0.25	0.45	0.55	0.43	0.47
Bank of Asia	0.59	1.06	0.74	1.14	0.18	0.17	0.30	0.28	0.24	0.26
Siam City Bank	0.68	0.71	0.79	0.84	0.26	0.19	0.08	0.09	0.07	0.08
Krung Thai Bank	0.83	0.56	0.94	0.94	0.12	0.10	0.05	0.08	0.04	0.05
Bangkok Bank	1.34	1.05	1.49	1.21	0.15	0.18	0.06	0.08	0.05	0.07
Bangkok Bank of Com.	0.66	0.66	0.78	0.84	0.27	0.19	0.09	0.09	0.08	0.07
Bank of Ayudhya	1.04	0.96	1.09	1.21	0.11	0.18	0.06	0.14	0.06	0.11
Thai Farmers Bank	0.75	1.05	0.90	1.31	0.21	0.12	0.12	0.08	0.10	0.07
Laem Thong Bank	1.24	0.99	1.34	1.14	0.13	0.12	0.17	0.18	0.16	0.15
Union Bank of Bangkok	0.93	0.69	1.08	0.94	0.19	0.21	0.09	0.18	0.07	0.13
Thai Danu Bank	0.87	0.71	1.05	1.07	0.15	0.13	0.22	0.24	0.18	0.16
Bangkok Metropolitan Bank	1.90	1.22	2.06	1.49	0.28	0.19	0.08	0.08	0.08	0.06
Thai Military Bank	0.69	0.82	0.92	1.08	0.28	0.31	0.13	0.20	0.09	0.15
Thai Development Bank	0.94	0.85	0.99	0.91	0.14	0.12	0.05	0.07	0.05	0.07
Asia Trust Bank	-	2.09	-	2.23	-	0.46	-	0.17	-	0.16
Total	0.96	0.82	1.08	1.08	0.18	0.17	0.09	0.11	0.08	0.09

A – Ratio of loans, overdrafts, and discounts to deposits.

B – Ratio of loans, overdrafts, discounts, and investments to deposits.

C – Ratio of cash to deposits.

D – Ratio of capital fund to loans, overdrafts, and discounts.

E – Ratio of capital fund to loans, overdrafts, discounts, and investments.

Source: Computed from data in Tables 4.9 and 4.11.

TABLE 4.16

Commercial Banks Incorporated Abroad,
Key Balance Sheet Ratios, 1962 and 1966

Bank	A 1962	A 1966	B 1962	B 1966	C 1962	C 1966	D 1962	D 1966	E 1962	E 1966
The Hongkong and Shanghai Bank	1.26	0.83	1.28	0.99	0.09	0.13	0.09	0.25	0.09	0.21
The Chartered Bank	1.76	1.04	1.35	1.19	0.08	0.12	0.05	0.16	0.04	0.14
Banque de L'Indochine	1.40	1.47	1.49	1.68	0.39	0.10	0.01	0.29	0.01	0.25
Sze Hai Tong Bank	2.50	1.73	2.95	2.13	0.99	0.71	0.40	0.52	0.34	0.42
The Bank of Canton	1.28	0.63	1.43	0.71	0.39	0.56	0.02	0.20	0.02	0.18
Mercantile Bank	1.77	1.08	1.88	1.23	0.12	0.30	–	0.35	–	0.30
The Bank of China	2.36	1.90	2.74	2.11	0.84	1.08	0.04	0.37	0.04	0.33
The Indian Overseas Bank	1.39	0.81	1.53	1.01	0.22	0.46	–	0.33	–	0.26
The Chase Manhattan Bank	1.11	1.16	1.17	1.45	0.09	0.18	0.04	0.49	0.04	0.40
The Bank of America	0.73	0.73	0.98	0.89	0.20	0.30	–	0.36	–	0.29
The Mitsui Bank	3.16	1.34	3.40	1.62	0.20	0.14	–	0.28	–	0.23
The Bank of Tokyo	1.72	1.20	5.14	1.40	0.17	0.06	–	0.18	–	0.15
The United Malayan Banking Company	–	1.51	–	1.63	–	0.12	–	0.16	–	0.14
Total, foreign banks	1.41	1.11	1.56	1.30	0.19	0.22	0.04	0.27	0.04	0.23
Total, domestic banks	0.96	0.82	1.08	1.08	0.18	0.17	0.09	0.11	0.08	0.09
Total	0.60	0.86	0.68	1.10	0.11	0.17	0.08	0.14	0.07	0.11

A – Ratio of loans, overdrafts, and discounts to deposits.

B – Ratio of loans, overdrafts, discounts, and investments to deposits.

C – Ratio of cash to deposits.

D – Ratio of capital fund to loans, overdrafts, and discounts.

E – Ratio of capital fund to loans, overdrafts, discounts, and investments.

Source: Computed from data in Tables 4.10 and 4.12.

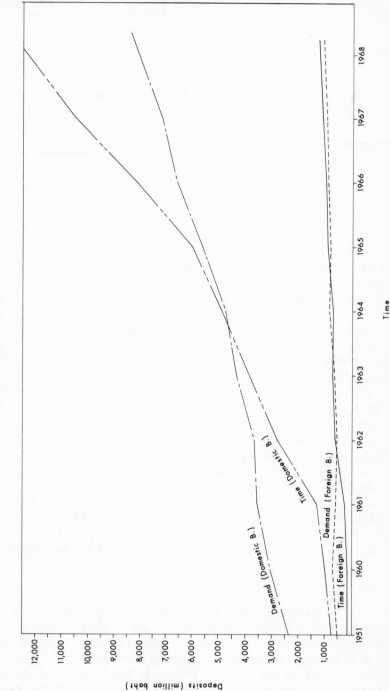

FIGURE 4.1

Time and Demand Deposits of Foreign and Domestic Banks
Operating in Thailand, 1951-1968

Source: Based on information provided by the Bank of Thailand.

139

every one of the Thai commercial banks could multi-
ply its total deposits without running up against
any cash constraints. This point is worth making
because, even though the domestic banks as a whole
may have had the capacity to expand credit, the ability of individual banks to expand their liabilities
through expansion of credit could have varied significantly.

COMMERCIAL BANKS AND UNUSED CAPACITY

In order to quantify the concept of unused capacity, Tables 4.17 and 4.18 give the results of an instructive, if admittedly not very rigorous, exercise.
"Unused capacity" may be defined as the difference
between the level of deposits maintained in fact and
the level which could, in theory, be maintained,
given the banks' reserves and the continuation of the
present reserve requirements. In Tables 4.17 and
4.18, potential expansion of credit is calculated
first on the basis of banks' liquid assets and then
on the basis of capital fund. Both calculations are
approximate. Not all liquid funds could possibly be
converted into legal reserves against deposits, and,
further, the legal definition of risk assets (or capital funds, for that matter) does not coincide with
that employed in the tables.* More important, the
calculations given in the tables do not pretend to
provide a normative guide to Thai commercial banks.
Clearly, no one would seriously suggest that an expansion of credit on the scale indicated either could
have or should have been provided (if only from the
standpoint of monetary stability). The tables are
merely intended to dramatize the proposition that
commercial banks could have substantially increased

---

*Excess of liquid funds over reserve require-
ments is, of course, much greater than "excess reserves" as defined, say, in Table 4.8. There, only
amounts actually deposited at the Bank of Thailand
count as reserves. As seen in Table 4.1, liquid assets are nearly three times the size of the legal
reserves.

TABLE 4.17

Potential Expansion of Credit,
Banks Incorporated in Thailand, July 1966
(million baht)

Bank	Excess Reserves (Liquidity)	Potential Expansion	Excess Reserves (Capital Fund)	Potential Expansion (Capital Fund)
Siam Commercial Bank	728.60	12,143.33	36.73	612.17
Wang Lee Chan Bank	2.04	34.00	0.72	12.00
Bank of Asia	53.52	892.00	21.46	357.67
Siam City Bank	212.72	3,545.34	72.17	1,202.83
Krung Thai Bank	1,343.00	22,383.33	223.09	3,718.17
Bangkok Bank	873.74	14,562.34	70.77	1,179.50
Bangkok Bank of Com.	310.86	5,181.00	80.06	1,334.33
Bank of Ayudhya	379.40	6,323.33	100.00	1,666.67
Thai Farmers Bank	260.92	4,348.67	22.05	367.50
Laem Thong Bank	43.52	725.34	8.39	139.83
Union Bank of Bangkok	146.41	2,440.33	31.35	522.50
Thai Danu Bank	139.70	2,328.34	26.51	441.83
Bangkok Metropolitan Bank	246.54	4,109.00	13.79	229.83
Thai Military Bank	245.72	4,095.33	12.39	206.50
Thai Development Bank	71.46	1,191.00	33.19	553.17
Asia Trust Bank	66.28	1,104.67	2.41	40.17
Total	5,124.43	85,407.35	755.08	12,584.67

Source: Based on data in Table 4.11.

TABLE 4.18

Potential Expansion of Credit,
Banks Incorporated Abroad, July 1966
(million baht)

Bank	Excess Reserves (Liquidity)	Potential Expansion	Excess Reserves (Capital Fund)	Potential Expansion (Capital Fund)
The Hongkong and Shanghai Bank	48.48	808.00	21.07	351.17
The Chartered Bank	61.04	1,017.33	11.49	191.50
Banque de L'Indochine	15.20	253.33	3.12	52.00
Sze Hai Tong Bank	31.10	518.34	2.41	40.17
The Bank of Canton	40.00	666.66	1.86	31.00
Mercantile Bank	26.90	448.34	1.75	29.17
The Bank of China	82.28	1,371.33	2.83	47.17
The Indian Overseas Bank	25.68	428.00	1.23	20.50
The Chase Manhattan Bank	64.28	1,071.33	3.09	51.50
The Bank of America	160.62	2,677.00	29.96	499.33
The Mitsui Bank	85.34	1,422.33	16.05	267.50
The Bank of Tokyo	57.30	955.00	16.85	280.83
The United Malayan Bank	41.98	699.67	13.73	228.83
Total	740.20	12,336.66	125.44	2,090.67

Source: Based on data in Table 4.12.

the size of their lending operations had they so
wished.

Why should the commercial banks not desire, if
indeed they do not, to expand their lending operations? Certainly, very few bankers would be willing
to acknowledge that they are less than anxious to expand their earning assets. It is equally certain
that most of them would, when queried as to why their
earning assets are below full potential, reply that
it is due to the lack of creditworthy borrowers, or
adequate collateral, or applicants, or any of a dozen
other plausible factors which might prevent them from
making additional loans. Nevertheless, after all
these explanations are accounted for and given due
weight, there still exists a prima facie case for the
contention that Thai bankers, whether deliberately
or subconsciously, are less interested in expanding
earning assets than objective circumstances would
seem to warrant.

For example, the existence of unused capacity
does not appear to arise from an inadequate demand
for the product. Judging from the high level of interest rates and, even more, their persistence over
time, the demand continues strong relative to supply
(see Table 4.19). It is also doubtful that the excess capacity results from the existence of too many
banks. Even in the mid-1950's the Thai government
imposed strong restrictions on the new entry, and it
seems unlikely that the number of banks operating at
present in the country is too great in relation to
the needs of the economy, although it is possible
that the facilities for financing foreign trade could
be provided with fewer banks. One bit of evidence
which indicates that there is little fear of over-
capacity, at least from the viewpoint of outsiders to
the industry, is the long waiting line of applicants
for banking charters. It is said, for instance, that
the (hypothetical) value of a new charter was in excess of 20 million baht in 1967. Add to that the sum
of at least 30 million required as capital, and it is
seen that the entry into banking is highly prized,
indeed.

TABLE 4.19

COMMERCIAL BANKS: RATES CHARGED ON ACCOMMODATION
(% per annum)

Type of Accommodation	Rate Charged on Accommodation					
	1962	1963	1964	1965	1966	1967
Call money	6-12	6-12	6-12	6-12	6-12	7-10
Commercial bills	15	15	15	15	14	14
Import bills	10-15	6-10	6-10	6-10	6-10	10
Export bills	8-12	8-10	8-10	8-10	8-9	9
Rice warrants	7	7	7	7	7	7
Bills on industrial raw materials	-	7	7	7	7	7
Bills or industrial credit bills	-	7	7	7	7	7
Loans & overdrafts	9-15	9-15	10-15	10-15	9-14	12-14

Source: Bank of Thailand.

Moreover, the industry is a highly profitable one, even on the basis of official and declared income data. As shown in Table 4.20, the average return on net worth (i.e., capital fund) for the 1956-1965 decade was over 10 per cent. (The rate seems to have declined rather sharply in 1965, but the figures for that year are preliminary.) It is somewhat surprising that the rate of return of foreign banks is much higher than that of domestic banks, even though the former are relatively more prominent in the financing of foreign trade, which is less risky and accordingly commands lower average accommodation rates. Foreign trade banking may actually be more profitable in the aggregate. In addition to the admittedly lower rates of interest, bankers charge fees for opening of letters of credit, exchange transactions fees, and so on, which make the total return on this type of business compare favorably with that obtained on more risky loans. The very high rates of return on capital shown by foreign banks may be accounted for, in part, by the vagueness of the capital concept regarding banks with headquarters abroad and, in part, by greater tradition of compliance in reporting corporate income that, perhaps, can be expected from foreign banks.

If, then, the usual economic explanations for excess capacity--too many producers, inadequate demand for the product, lack of alternative opportunities, and so on--do not seem to apply to Thai banking, the reasons for the Thai bankers' alleged lack of enthusiasm to expand their earning assets further must be sought elsewhere.

At this point, one is tempted to develop a hypothesis which, albeit difficult to prove, does fit with some of the observations so far brought to light. The hypothesis runs as follows:

Thai bankers do not maximize the long-run profits of the banks they control because, consciously or not, they do not fully identify their personal interests with those of the banks. Most of them are traders and manufacturers as well as bankers, and their economic position, social status, personal

TABLE 4.20

COMMERCIAL BANKS: PROFIT RATES, 1956–1965

(thousand baht)

Year	Net Profit (1) Banks Incorporated in Thailand	Abroad	Total	Net Worth (2) Banks Incorporated in Thailand	Abroad	Total	(1) as Percentage of (2) Banks Incorporated in Thailand	Abroad	Total
1956	33,841	26,380	60,221	409,200	49,500	458,700	8.27	53.29	13.13
1957	30,974	35,663	66,637	450,400	52,500	502,900	6.87	67.92	13.25
1958	31,592	32,324	63,916	462,600	55,700	518,300	6.82	58.03	12.33
1959	34,063	23,091	57,154	474,000	40,800	514,800	7.18	56.59	11.10
1960	43,755	19,890	63,645	508,000	53,000	561,000	8.61	37.52	11.34
1961	51,148	31,470	82,618	554,800	60,100	614,900	9.22	52.36	13.44
1962	61,730	37,755	99,485	695,500	78,700	774,200	8.87	47.97	12.85
1963	70,182	34,718	104,900	742,900	80,700	823,600	9.45	43.02	12.74
1964	101,683	56,098	157,781	887,900	84,800	972,700	11.45	66.15	16.22
1965	62,198	29,264	91,462	1,152,100	106,600	1,258,700	5.39	27.45	7.26

Source: Based on information provided by the Bank of Thailand.

146

prestige, and the like may not always weigh most
heavily on the banking side of their activities (see
Table 4.21). A banker who is at the same time the
manufacturer of one product and the importer of yet
another could, for instance, feel that a vigorous
expansion of his earning assets, while possibly indicated from a banking standpoint, would run counter
to his manufacturing or trading interests. Even if
a loan or an advance were not made to a direct com-
petitor, it might be made to one who would eventually
compete with some of the nonbanking activities of the
lender or, in any case, add to the existing competitive pressures surrounding such resources as office
space or skilled help. Moreover, the Thai banker
may have an erroneous conception of the demand elasticity for bank credit. He may prefer to make fewer
loans at high average rates than try to compete for
a larger volume of loans at lower rates of interest.
(It is doubtful whether many bankers will long maintain this conception, provided they take their business of banking seriously. There are very few industries with a greater range of increasing returns to
scale.) The Thai banker's rational evaluation of demand elasticities may, further, be influenced considerably by less tangible, yet potent, considerations
which stem from a situation where money is scarce and
costly, where the loan-granting ability confers subtle
advantages, and where, finally, it is possible to reap
individually a pecuniary harvest that need not necessarily be shared with the bank.

    The Thai bankers have been able to maintain this
dichotomy of interests and behavior for a number of
reasons. In .the first place, banking is profitable
and, for persons making money elsewhere, there is
little pressure to maximize profits in banking per
se. Secondly, banking assets and liabilities have
shown a consistent upward trend, though, as argued
earlier, the main expansion took place with respect
to assets which have been used little to finance the
needs of the small manufacturer, farmer, or mining
operator. This apparent growth in banking accommodation has tended to obscure the degree of underutilization of capacity. Thirdly, a number of factors
have served to provide bankers with a convenient

TABLE 4.21

Outside Interests of Major Shareholders
of Banks, September 1967

Bank Post of Major Shareholder	Outside Interest	Outside Position
Vice Chairman	1. Trading	Director
	2. Hotel	Managing Director
	3. Trading	Director
	4. Finance	Director
	5. Weaving	Chairman
Managing Director	1. Distillery	Managing Director
	2. Chemical	Director
	3. Distillery	Director
	4. Trading	Chairman
	5. Distillery	Managing Director
	6. Export-Import	Managing Director
	7. Trading	Chairman
	8. Warehouse	Director
Managing Director	1. Trading	Director
	2. Building Contractor	Director
	3. Trading	Director
Asst. Managing Director	1. Chemical	Director
	2. Insurance	Director
Managing Director	1. Investment	Director
	2. Weaving	Chairman
	3. Sugar Industry	Managing Director
	4. Match Mfg.	Managing Director
Asst. Managing Director	1. Rubber	Manager
	2. Restaurant	Chairman
Managing Director	1. Insurance	Manager
	2. Rice Mill	Director
Managing Director	1. Rubber Mfg.	Director
	2. Paper Mill	Director

Bank Post of Major Shareholder	Outside Interest	Outside Position
Managing Director	1. Warehouse	Chairman
	2. Rubber	Managing Director
	3. Trading	Director
Vice Chairman	1. Import	Chairman
	2. Warehouse	Director
	3. Cinema	Director
	4. Trading	Chairman
Managing Director	1. Building Contractor	Director
	2. Sawmill	Director
	3. Liquor Agency	Director
	4. Provision, Food	Director
	5. Forestry	Managing Director
	6. Sawmill	Director
	7. Trading	Chairman
	8. Transport	Director
	9. Insurance	Director
	10. Motor Spare Parts	Director
	11. Building Contractor	Director
	12. Sugar Refinery	Director
	13. Warehouse	Director
	14. Mining	Director
Chairman	1. Liquor Agency	Director
	2. Trading	Director
	3. Agricultural Trading	Chairman
	4. Insurance	Director
Managing Director	1. Trading	Director
	2. Finance	Managing Director
	3. Finance	Managing Director
	4. Shipping	Director
	5. Motor Trade	Chairman
	6. Motor Trade	Chairman
	7. Warehouse	Director

Source: The Bank of Thailand and other sources.

rationalization for their alleged lackadaisical attitude toward the expansion of loans and advances.
Thus, existing traditions, practices, and standards
of Thai banks have enabled bankers to maintain that
the limitations of demand are responsible for restrict-
ing the expansion of loans. This, if true (and there
is no hard information on the number of applicants
turned down), operates on both sides of the schedule
for lendable funds. Prospective borrowers do not go
to a bank if, say, they lack the proper collateral,
and the bank, consequently, does not see them.

It has been suggested that an additional reason
for potential borrowers avoiding commercial banks is
the "halo effect." Many smaller manufacturers and
traders simply know too little about the resources and
practices of commercial banks and therefore do not believe that they qualify as borrowers even though their
business status and asset position may be quite sound.

To the extent that bankers consider banking operations tantamount to financing foreign trade, neither their skills nor their attitudes prepare them to
consider extending their operations beyond accommodations to exporters, importers, and wholesale traders.

Finally, underutilization of capacity has been
possible because the existing banking structure, together with policies of monetary management, has not
provided strong incentives for expanding loans and
advances to sectors other than foreign trade. For a
variety of reasons, the central bank has had to rely
mainly on moral suasion when dealing with commercial
banks. Its well-intended measures to develop a money
market have run counter to its avowed desire to reduce the cost of bank credit. Likewise, its commitment to monetary stability has militated against an
unduly large expansion of bank credit. (For a fuller
discussion of the relationship of Thai commercial
banks with the central bank see Chapter 6.)

OPERATIONAL POLICIES

As has been suggested, the hypothesis of deliberate maintenance of excess capacity is a tempting one,

but whether its validity can be established with a
high degree of confidence is doubtful. Yet the hypothesis does at least provide a convenient focus for
viewing the operations of commercial banks without
being bogged down in a maze of detail or concerned
unduly with developments of secondary importance to
economic analysis. In this section, some of the
points touched on in the closing paragraphs of the
preceding one will be discussed more or less in the
order in which they were made.

First, there is the matter of the profitability
of commercial banks. A relatively high rate of return on invested capital in commercial banking may
be simply a function of its efficiency and may not
be out of line with the rate of return in other sectors of a prosperous and buoyant economy. There are
no firm data regarding rate of return on invested
capital in Thailand. However, the profitability of
Thai banks appears to stem principally from the
spread between the average rate of interest paid on
deposits and the average rate charged for accommodations. While precise information is not available,
qualified observers think that the spread is of the
order of 5 to 8 per cent (of earning assets). Through
the courtesy of a leading commercial bank, it was
possible to obtain, but not publish, the results of
the bank's calculations of average costs and payments
of interest for 1962, 1963, and 1964. Taking the
average for the three years, total interest income
was 8 per cent of loans and advances; interest payments averaged slightly over 3 per cent of deposits.

Table 4.22 gives the rates of interest payable
by Thai banks on deposits.

Now a spread of five or six basic points is not
usually associated with very efficient banking operations. In the United States, commercial banks show
a rate of return on capital of about 9 per cent out
of a spread which is less than half that of Thai
banks. For example, in the period 1951-1960, the
average difference between the rate of return on
earning assets of member banks (members of the Federal Reserve System) and the effective rate paid on
time deposits (no interest is payable on demand

TABLE 4.22

Commercial Banks: Rates of Interest Payable on Deposits, 1962-1967
(% per annum)

Type of Deposit	Rate of Interest					
	1962	1963	1964	1965	1966	1967
Demand deposits	0.5	0.5	0.5	0.5	0-0.01	0.01
Limited demand deposits[a]	4-5	4-5	3	3	Cancelled	–
Savings deposits	4-5	4-5	4-5	4-5	3-5	3.5
Time deposits under under 3 months	5	0.5	0.5	0.5	0.01	0.01
3-6 months	6	5	5	5	5	5
6-12 months	8	6	6	6	6	6
over 12 months	8	7	7	7	7	7

[a]Subject to maximum drawing of four checks per month.

Source: Bank of Thailand.

deposits) was two percentage points. In 1951, for
instance, the rate of return on earning assets was
2.71 per cent and that paid on time deposits was 1.0.
In 1959, the former rate stood at 4.33 per cent and
the latter at 2.36 per cent.[13]

It could be contended that, even when not a reward for superior efficiency, a high rate of return
is necessary to compensate for risks. While risks
are, of course, taken daily, the record of Thai banks
does not seem to indicate that the business has been
subject to unduly large losses in the past. As seen
in Table 4.23, bad debts as a proportion of loans
averaged less than .5 per cent in the years 1956-1967.

It appears some caution is necessary in interpreting Table 4.23. The table may understate the
proportion of bad debts to the extent that some banks
will carry loans made for other than economic reasons
for years without writing them off, even though the
chances of repayment are very poor indeed. Still,
the proportion of bad debts is not likely to exceed
1 per cent. The risk on investments, which are primarily in the form of government securities, is, of
course, even less.

The fact that a considerable spread exists between interest paid by banks and interest payable to
them by borrowers may indicate that so long as the
relatively high level of the latter can be maintained,
there is little stimulus for the banks to improve operational efficiency. It also suggests that to the
extent that excess capacity in the industry is consistent with other motivations of the bankers, there
will be little competitive pressure to reduce the rate
of interest payable by borrowers. The official statistics which provide a breakdown of commercial bank
loans by purpose indicate that there has been some improvement in the relative share of loans going to manufacturing, at the expense of the shares going to
agriculture and mining. At the end of 1967 loans to
manufacturing were 16.5 per cent of all loans, compared with 14.9 per cent at the end of 1962. Agriculture and mining accounted for 5 per cent of the total
at the end of 1967 compared with 6.4 per cent in 1962.[14]

TABLE 4.23

Commercial Banks: Bad Debts as Proportion of Loans, 1956-1967

Year	Bad Debts (1)			Loans, Overdrafts, & Discounts (2)			(1) as Percentage of (2)		
	Banks Incorporated in Thailand	Abroad	Total	Banks Incorporated in Thailand	Abroad	Total	Banks Incorporated in Thailand	Abroad	Total
1956	10,808	2,889	13,697	2,015,200	824,100	2,839,300	.54	.35	.48
1957	10,901	3,337	14,238	2,351,500	987,500	3,339,000	.46	.34	.43
1958	10,964	3,793	14,757	2,899,600	1,078,100	3,977,700	.30	.35	.37
1959	18,368	8,908	27,276	3,344,300	1,144,100	4,488,400	.55	.78	.61
1960	28,313	6,957	35,270	4,067,600	1,329,700	5,397,300	.70	.53	.65
1961	34,503	5,075	39,578	4,769,100	1,564,200	6,333,300	.72	.33	.62
1962	30,292	4,563	34,855	5,883,800	1,652,500	7,536,300	.51	.28	.46
1963	31,689	6,436	38,125	6,941,400	1,866,100	8,807,500	.46	.34	.43
1964	32,552	539	33,091	8,443,100	2,152,900	10,596,000	.39	.03	.31
1965	53,841	1,841	55,682	10,143,500	2,788,500	12,932,000	.53	.07	.43
1966	78,376	10,072	88,448	12,265,200	2,808,900	15,074,100	.64	.36	.59
1967	120,791	10,871	131,662	14,184,200	3,077,500	17,261,700	.85	.35	.76

Source: Bank of Thailand.

154

But there is a strong feeling among students of Thai banking practice that such breakdowns are not very meaningful, inasmuch as the bankers themselves are often ignorant of the real purpose to which their funds are directed though fully cognizant of the Bank of Thailand's desire to increase the proportion of loans going into manufacturing. (The efforts of the Bank of Thailand in this direction are discussed in Chapter 6.)

One reason why commercial bankers may not always know the real purpose of the loan is that many have been nurtured in a tradition which attaches much more importance to the person of the borrower than the reason for his application. No doubt, the two aspects of the transaction are not unrelated. But very few, if any, banks will spend much time analyzing the project, its future flow of cash, or other conditions which might indicate the project's chances for success. Instead, they will concern themselves primarily with the asset position of the borrower, his past credit rating, and, above all, the type of collateral he can offer.

For really top-notch names among the business community, no collateral other than a signature or two may be required. But in most cases, certainly in over half of the loans by value, a tangible security is required by the banks, more often than not in the form of a land mortgage. This is shown in Table 4.24. The preponderance of land as a source of lendable funds has several consequences. As mentioned before, it tends to orient the bankers toward the nature of the collateral rather than the purpose of the loan. It makes obtaining funds more difficult for those who, for one reason or another, cannot own land. It makes investment contingent on the availability of unencumbered real estate and thereby directs the attention of a would-be investor to land and real estate development and away from more productive investment. Banks usually lend only about 30 per cent of the value of the collateral. In a period of rising land values, commercial banks do not mind repossessing the land even though the legal procedures are lengthy and cumbersome. This is another factor which militates

TABLE 4.24

Commercial Banks: Breakdown of Collateral by Type, 1965

Type of Collateral	Amount (million baht)		Per Cent of Total	
	May 1965	Oct. 1965	May 1965	Oct. 1965
Land only	1,130.8	1,307.4	29.47	29.33
Land plus inventory	309.6	404.5	8.07	9.07
Land plus buildings	446.9	574.2	11.65	12.88
Land plus notes receivable	205.9	125.6	5.37	2.82
Land plus personal guarantee	339.4	331.3	8.84	7.43
Personal guarantee	1,020.1	1,202.5	26.58	26.97
Business guarantee	308.4	433.6	8.04	9.73
Inventory plus personal guarantee	1.7	3.9	0.04	0.09
Land plus stock	31.1	25.2	0.81	0.57
Time deposit certificate	14.6	15.6	0.38	0.35
Stock plus inventory	8.5	5.9	0.22	0.13
Bonds and gold	20.7	17.7	0.54	0.40
Time deposit certificate plus stock	–	9.8	–	0.22
Time deposit plus bonds	–	0.1	–	0.002
Total	3,837.6	4,457.3	100	100
Total, foreign banks	982.4	1,187.2		
Grand total	4,820.1	5,642.5		
Total outstanding[a]	8,225.1	8,820.9		

aAs shown in Bank of Thailand, Monthly Bulletin. Difference due to fact that the table excludes loans and advances under 500,000 baht and loans to very large borrowers made without collateral.

Source: Compiled from information obtained from the Bank of Thailand.

against putting emphasis on the productive purpose
of the loan.

The reasons for the limited success of the central bank in reducing the cost of borrowing and in
directing more commercial bank resources into development channels are discussed in Chapter 6.

This brief examination of the salient operational characteristics of Thai commercial banks does reveal a number of elements which seem to be consistent
with the "unused capacity" hypothesis. Thai bankers
seem to direct their activities toward trade (and
real estate development) and are less interested in
sectors where those financed by them may be competing
for scarce resources. They can maintain high interest rates rather than vie for additional banking business because they find attractive outlets for their
excess reserves either in the form of government securities or employment outside banking. Finally,
partly because of their contacts and activities outside commercial banking, Thai bankers can resist such
pressures as may be exerted by the central bank to
reorient their activities and reduce the cost of borrowing. The points touched upon in this section will
be more fully elaborated in Chapter 6.

While the preceding discussion and argument was
about Thai commercial banks, in general, a distinction
should perhaps be made between the foreign and the
domestic banks. As a rule, the inability or unwillingness of the foreign banks to expand their loans
and overdrafts to the fullest extent possible stems
from rather different considerations from those already emphasized. By tradition and design, foreign
banks specialize in foreign trade or in trade of
businesses run by the nationals of the countries they
represent. They are also somewhat less well equipped
to go much beyond their traditional lines of activity.
Finally, being guests in Thailand, many of them seem
to feel that any aggressive drive for additional banking business would be out of place. It should be emphasized that the alleged "unwillingness" of Thai bankers to expand their earning assest is closely related
to the real and imaginary difficulties in following an

aggressive lending policy. The scarcity of personnel
was already mentioned. This scarcity is acute in
those professions, such as auditing and loan apprais-
ing, which are key ones.

COMMERCIAL BANKING IN THE
SAVING-INVESTMENT PROCESS

It should be stated at the outset that the findings and conclusions of this section are tentative.
Additional research is needed before the development
planner can, with confidence, attempt to modify the
structure and the operations of commercial banks. In
particular, more information is required about the
breakdown of deposits by origin, size, and possible
motivation. Similarly, more needs to be known about
the primary securities of the business sector and the
way business finances its requirements of both fixed
and working capital. Subject to these and other
qualifications, however, it does appear that the performance of Thai commercial banks as financial intermediaries could be substantially improved. (Many of
the assertions about the behavior of banks and bankers in Thailand appear to be confirmed by the findings
of an urban credit survey which the Bank of Thailand
completed in 1967. See Chapter 7.)·

On the face of it, the banks have done quite
well in getting the households to accept claims
against banks, particularly time deposits. Even so,
it is doubtful whether the increase in commercial
bank deposits over the past decade and more represents
an increase in real saving or merely a shift in the
composition of financial assets, particularly cash into deposits and demand deposits into time deposits.
The latter kind of asset shift would, in itself, be
significant, because it would enable the banks to
lengthen their portfolios, provided one could be con-
fident that time deposits did actually represent the
banks' longer-term liabilities.

But it is in financing deficit spending units,
particularly with regard to investments of a developmental character, that the banks have fallen short
of their potential. This is especially so with

respect to the financing of small and medium manufacturers producing primarily for an export market (see
chapter 7 for some evidence on this point). If the
hypothesis of excess capacity has any validity, it
strongly implies that Thai commercial banks could
have provided more funds to industry, mining, and
agriculture, even at the expense of trade, real estate
development, or sheer speculation.

Here the problem is one of quality as well as
quantity of financing. Not only could commercial
banks have increased the volume of their loans to
sectors other than trade and real estate, but they
could have worked harder to develop the types of
claims which would be attractive to the deficit units
and still satisfy the banks' needs for liquidity and
safety. It would be difficult to finance the fixed
capital requirements of industry, for instance, when,
as suggested earlier, the claims on the banks themselves are of a short-term nature. One would hope
to see the development of term lending or revolving
credit within the Thai banking system as a partial
answer to the dilemma of "lending long and borrowing
short." It is not generally appreciated that term
lending is really quite consistent with liquidity
because term lending may typically contain amortiza-
tion features.[15]

The allegation implicit in the "unused capacity"
hypothesis is that the commercial banks in Thailand
simply did not expand their output sufficiently and,
by failing to compete vigorously for business, helped
to maintain a structure of high interest rates. If
this is true, it has important implications for developmental planning. Prima facie, the type of market behavior in which several firms in an industry
maintain a high price for their product by failing to
expand output sufficiently is characteristic of oli-
gopoly. But the analysis of imperfect competition
does not appear very promising from the standpoint of
the developmental saving-investment process. (See,
however, the discussion of "efficiency" in Chapter 1.)

High interest cost to the would-be investor
means that the payoff cannot be a distant one. The
capital has to be recouped in a very short period when

the annual cost of capital averages 24 per cent.
While the cost of bank credit to sectors other than
foreign trade was until recently only 15 per cent
per annum, many investors without access to bank credit had to pay more. Even in the case of bank credit,
there were in some cases additional costs beyond the
legal maximum rate; see Chapter 7. An industrial
undertaking with a fairly long gestation period will
appear less attractive to the entrepreneur than a
short-term enterprise, frequently of a speculative
character. For many productive undertakings with
good prospects of substantial profits in the future,
there will be the problem of the initial period of
construction, development of markets, and so on, during which there are no revenues but a heavy debt burden to service. In this way, a high cost of borrowing tends to distort the pattern of allocation of
resources, at least from the social, developmental
vantage-point.

The fact that there is substantial spread between the return to the saver and the cost to the
borrower in Thailand means that a "liquidity gap"
exists, indicating the financial markets do not efficiently perform their function of intermediation.
(See Chapter 1.) Increasing the level of interest
rates given to the depositers would, in the absence
of higher rates charged to the borrowers, impinge
on the profits of the banks, and raising the costs
to the investors would further aggravate the problems touched upon in the preceding paragraph. In
order to simultaneously reduce costs to borrowers
and increase returns to savers, the banks would have
to increase their operational efficiency and/or greatly reduce their profits.

As a matter of fact, while the Thai commercial
banks do not show any great drive to expand their
loans and overdrafts to sectors other than trade,
they do seem anxious to attract more deposits, particularly longer-term deposits. One of the banking
community proposals, repeatedly submitted to Thai
authorities, asks the government to allow banks to
pay a higher rate on deposits held for periods longer
than one year.[16] Moreover, while there is little

competition for loans and advances, there seems to
be vigorous competition for time deposits.

This competition for deposits is difficult to
reconcile with alleged disinterest in expanding loans
and advances. It is one thing to argue that Thai
commercial banks do not maximize profits and quite
another to suggest that they deliberately incur costs
of additional deposits without intending to utilize
the proceeds fully. This, indeed, is a challenge to
the "unused capacity" hypothesis. It may mean that
the hypothesis is invalid, or valid only in part
(the banks do lend out a proportion of the funds at
their disposal). Alternatively, it may mean that the
bankers are not fully rational or not very sincere
in their clamor for additional deposits. Finally,
it is possible that they somehow manage to put the
additional funds to use without such flows being
fully reflected in the bank statements.

This last possibility would not only vitiate
the hypothesis but also offer additional support for
it. Yet the point is a very delicate one and is as
strongly suggested by some as it is denied by others.
The question is not so much one of misappropriating
bank funds for private purposes (although an incident
of this sort did come to light a few years ago) but
rather of dividing the banking transaction into two
parts, one of which is effected through the bank itself and the other through a separate, if bogus, entity such as the compradore.

It is this uncertainty about the validity of
the "unused capacity" hypothesis, plus the lack of
information mentioned at the beginning of this section, which make one cautious of suggesting far-
reaching reforms for commercial banking in Thailand.
There is little question that commercial banking
could and should participate more fully in the financing of other sectors of the economy, particularly
manufacturing, mining, and agriculture. Some suggestions as to how this participation could be brought
about will be given in Chapters 5 and 6. In the main,
the suggestions call for strengthening of the moral
suasion exerted by the central bank by other measures.

It is also clear that institutions other than the commercial banks would be needed to provide noncontractual, long-term finance to manufacturing. (See Chapters 8 and 9.)

Within their present structure and functions, however, there is still room for further improvements and modifications which could make the banks more efficient. The need to institutionalize term lending has already been mentioned. Another possibility worth exploring is that of a self-insurance scheme among the Thai banks which would increase the confidence of the public, on the one hand, and help to introduce more uniform and, hopefully, sound practices among the Thai commercial banks, on the other.

Certain changes in existing laws and regulations could also help commercial banks serve the public better and could, in principle, be offered as a quid pro quo against the costs of, say, a self-insurance scheme of the Federal Deposit Insurance Corporation type. For example, simplification of the registration of mortgage deeds, facilitating the pledge against second mortgage, and subdividing one land title into smaller parcels would fall into that category. Legislation of chattel mortgage is now being implemented and should help to remove some of the attachments to land collateral. This could lead eventually to a type of banking operation which analyzes the project rather than the borrower in making loans. The full fruition of project-oriented banking will take some time in Thailand, not only because of ingrained attitudes but also because of the shortage of qualified loan appraisers. Yet there is some evidence that traditionally oriented bankers can sometimes change their attitudes and practices rather quickly and, once having changed them, perceive their merits and attractions.[17]

NOTES

1. See J. G. Gurley and E. S. Shaw, "Financial Aspects of Economic Development," _American Economic Review_ (September, 1955), pp. 219-220.

2. National Economic Development Board, "The
Second Five Year Plan--Preliminary Draft" (Bangkok:
Government of Thailand, 1966), Chapter 5.   (Mimeo.
in Thai.)

3. For a full account of the early history and
development of Thai banking, see Paul Sithi-Amnuai,
Banking and Finance in Thailand: A Study of the Com-
mercial System 1888-1963 (Bangkok: Thai Watana
Panich, 1964), and the sources cited therein, par-
ticularly S. Y. Lee, "Currency, Banking and Foreign
Exchange of Thailand," Far East Economic Review
(October, 1959); and Ravi Amatayakul and S. A. Pandit,
"Financial Institutions in Thailand," IMF Staff Papers
(December, 1961).

4. S. Y. Lee, op. cit. Much of the information
used throughout this chapter was obtained from private and unpublished rather than printed sources.
Statistical information was provided by the Bank of
Thailand under a special arrangement whereby an official of the Bank collaborated with the author in
developing data from confidential sources without ex-
posing or compromising these sources. Even when
available to the public at large, information were
frequently modified for the purposes of this study.
For that reason, unless otherwise indicated, statistical tables in this chapter are to be taken as derived from information provided by the Bank of Thailand.

5. See Charoen Chinalai, "Thailand: Mopping
Up," Far Eastern Economic Review (April 14, 1966).

6. Commercial Banking Act of B. E. 2502
(Bangkok, 1962), Section 10.   (English translation.)

7. Government Gazette, LXXIX, Part 40, Article 4.

8. See P. Sithi-Amnuai, "An Appraisal of the
Commercial Banking Act 1962," Bangkok Bank Monthly
Review (June, 1962), pp. 31-33.

9. See Bank of Thailand, Annual Economic Report,
1964 (Bangkok: Bank of Thailand, 1964), pp. 34-35.

10. See, for example, Antonin Basch, _Financing Economic Development_ (New York: Macmillan, 1964), p. 159.

11. Bank of Thailand, _Annual Economic Report, 1962_ (Bangkok: Bank of Thailand, 1962), p. 27.

12. See, for example, A. Mousny, _The Economy of Thailand: An Appraisal of an Exchange Policy_ (Bangkok: Social Science Association Press, 1964), pp. 192ff. However, this view, with variations, is held by a number of other observers.

13. See H. Peter Gray, "The Effects of Monetary Policy on Rising Costs in Commercial Banks," _Journal of Finance_ (March, 1963), p. 231.

14. Bank of Thailand, _Annual Economic Report, 1968_ (Bangkok, 1969), p. 98.

15. For a fuller discussion of term lending in American practice see Federal Reserve Bank of New York, "Term Lending by New York City Banks," _Monthly Review_ (February, 1961); and Federal Reserve of Chicago, "Term Loans--Big Business for Big Banks," _Business Conditions_ (May, 1968).

16. See, for example, "Draft Submission of the Thai Bankers Association to the Subcommittee on Financial Institutions of the NEDB" (November, 1965). (Mimeo in Thai.) This particular suggestion was incorporated in the official second five-year plan.

17. See David C. McClelland, "Achievement Motivation Can be Developed," _Harvard Business Review_ (November-December, 1965), and example cited therein.

CHAPTER **5** BRANCH BANKING

Relative to its geographic size and its gross national product, Thailand appears to be quite well endowed with respect to branch banking. Compared with its neighbors, the spread of commercial banking throughout the countryside is a significant feature of the Thai financial system. According to available information, the number of branches and/or bank offices in selected countries of Southeast Asia at the end of 1967 was approximately as follows: Singapore 117, Vietnam 36, Malaysia 277, Philippines 215 (in 1962), Indonesia 277. At least 500 private banking offices dot the Thai landscape. Although these offices are concentrated in urban centers, they do provide banking facilities for most of the country's rural population. In the Philippines and elsewhere, semi-official, specialized provincial financial institutions may be more numerous, but no country in the area can boast a better network of private institutions providing general banking facilities outside the capital.

THE EXTENT OF BRANCH BANKING IN THAILAND

Little published data is available regarding commercial bank branches in Thailand.[1] In particular, information regarding individual banks is not generally available to the public (except for location and number) and the author's sources at the Bank of Thailand were constrained with respect to the detail they could release. Thus, information given in this chapter had to be culled from interviews with bankers and from data gathered during field trips, as well as from data made available by the Bank of Thailand. Consequently, the figures are not always strictly comparable, do not always pertain to the same time period, and, on occasion, are not reliable. In general, however, the statistics given in the text

do provide a picture of branch operations which would
not be modified drastically had accurate figures been
available throughout.

The spread of commercial bank branches in Thailand is a comparatively recent phenomenon. At the
end of 1953, there were less than 100 branches. Their
number quadrupled within the next twelve years and
was in excess of 500 at the end of 1966.

The first branch set up by a commercial bank in
Thailand was actually that opened by the Chartered
Bank (itself a branch of a bank with headquarters
abroad) in 1910 in Phuket. If one considers a foreign-
chartered bank to be itself a branch, then the first
branch in Thailand was the Hongkong and Shanghai Bank,
set up in Bangkok in 1888.[2] The first branch established by a locally chartered bank was that opened by
the Siam Commercial Bank in Chiengmai in 1926. At
the time, this was a daring move and hotly argued.
However, events proved its soundness, and in 1930 the
Siam Commercial Bank set up another branch in Lampang.

Very few branches were established during World
War II, but with the advent of the Korean War, branch
banking really got into stride. On the average, 35
branches were set up annually from 1955 to 1965.

Commercial banks in Thailand operate branches in
every province of the Kingdom except Hac Hong Sorn,
a remote northwestern area bordering on Burma. Apart
from the Bangkok-Thonburi area, there is little correlation between the number of persons inhabiting a
province and the number of branches, even though these
branches do tend to be located in the more populous
towns within a province. Thus, Songkla province,
which includes the important mining and plantation
center of Haadyai, has at least 20 banking establishments; Ubol, which has a population of more than twice
that of Songkla, had only 6 branches at the end of
1965. There has been a pronounced tendency in recent
years to establish branches outside the capital, the
ratio running 3:1 in favor of the provinces.[3]

As shown in Table 5.1, even though the marginal
ratio of provincial to capital branches was 3:1 at

the end of 1966, the average ratio was only 2:1. Commercial banks with headquarters abroad are precluded
from setting up branches in the provinces, and several locally chartered banks do business only in the
Bangkok area. Only 20 new branches were founded in
1966, as contrasted with an annual average of 35 in
the preceding decade. This decline does not appear
to stem from any lack of desire on the part of commercial banks to continue expanding their facilities
in the provinces but, rather, from a deliberate policy of the central monetary authorities to control
the indiscriminate spread of branches.

Of the 16 locally chartered banks authorized to
open branches in the provinces, one, the Wang Lee Chan
Bank, is more properly regarded as a family, rather
than a commercial, bank. Four other banks have branches
only in the capital area, and 2 additional banks operate only one provincial branch each. Thus, only 9
or 10 Thai banks can be said to be actively engaged in
the business of branch banking in the provinces.

OPERATIONAL CHARACTERISTICS

Branches of Thai commercial banks fall into two
major categories. On the one hand, the head office
has subsidiary establishments which it fully controls
and supervises, owns and operates, and directs by
placing one of its own paid officials in charge.
These are branches as that term is understood in the
United States. On the other hand, there are a number
of subsidiary establishments which have no exact
counterpart in Western banking. In these establishments, the mother institution lends its name, its
credit status, and other facilities to a local entrepreneuer who, while operating under the formal aegis
of the headquarters, is in fact a partner in the local operation. This is the agency arrangement that,
although decreasing in importance, is still an important part of the branch banking scene in Thailand.
Generally, the manager of an agency has greater latitude and more operational discretion than his branch
counterpart. He can engage in a greater range of
banking functions. He can make more, and more substantial, loans than a branch manager and he shares

TABLE 5.1

Branches of Commercial Banks, December 1966

Bank	Number of Branches		
	In Bangkok & Dhonburi	In Provinces	Total
Siam Commercial Bank Ltd.	7	11	18
Wang Lee Chan Bank Ltd.	1	–	1
Thai Development Bank Ltd.	13	35	48
Bank of Asia Ltd.	4	6	10
Siam City Bank Ltd.	10	54	64
Bangkok Bank of Commerce Ltd.	5	72	77
Bangkok Bank Ltd.	27	28	55
Bank of Ayudhya Lts.	16	16	32
Thai Farmers Bank Ltd.	25	28	53
Leam Thong Bank Ltd.	2	–	2
Union Bank of Bangkok Ltd.	10	1	11
Thai Danu Bank Ltd.	5	1	6
Bangkok Metropolitan Bank Ltd.	13	–	13
Thai Military Bank Ltd.	2	–	2
Asia Trust Bank Ltd.	1	–	1
Krung Thai Bank Ltd.	10	72	82
Hongkong and Shanghai Banking Corp.	2	–	2
Chartered Bank	2	1	3
Banque de L'Indochine	2	–	2
Four Seas Communication Bank Ltd.	1	–	1
Bank of Canton Ltd.	1	–	1
Mercantile Bank	2	–	2
Bank of China	1	–	1
Indian Overseas Bank Ltd.	1	–	1
Chase Manhattan Bank, N.A.	1	–	1
Bank of America NT. & SA.	1	–	1
Mitsui Bank Ltd.	2	–	2
Bank of Tokyo Ltd.	1	–	1
United Malayan Banking Corporation Ltd.	1	–	1
Total	169	325	494

Source: Compiled from information provided by the Bank of Thailand.

in the profits of the local branch, usually fifty-
fifty with the headquarters. At the same time, he
is usually required to post a substantial personal
bond with the mother institution and is, more likely
than not, required to contribute to the cost of operation, if not to the initial capital, of the local
branch.

While the branch manager may or may not be a
local man, the agency manager is almost invariably a
local person, most frequently a prominent merchant
who continues to ply his trade in addition to his
banking activities.

Although the latitude of the agency manager
typically exceeds that of the branch manager, both
are subject to various operational constraints. These
pertain to the types of accommodation, to the maximum size of loan which can be made without prior con-
sent of the headquarters, and to the over-all ratio
of earning assets to deposits.

With respect to types of accommodation, seldom
are these clear or explicit. In one or two cases,
the subsidiary establishments are interdicted from
making "straight" or fixed-term loans and are confined to bills and discounts. In those instances
when loans are allowed, there is a distinct preference for overdrafts over straight loans. Even though
the limitations are not imposed explicitly, there
seems to be a definite preference for granting business accommodation which is in the nature of self-
liquidating paper for the carrying on of trade. On
the other hand, headquarters seems to impose few restrictions or regulations with respect to the type
and size of the collateral. It would appear, however, that, with the exception of certain kinds of
shipping bills, the collateral actually required by
managers is predominantly real estate mortgage instruments, only an occasional personal or business guarantee being accepted in lieu of, or in conjunction
with, a mortgage deed. In any event, the matter of
collateral is handled sooner or later at the headquarters, either when granting prior approval to a
loan application or when confirming smaller loans
made at the discretion of the branch manager.

The amount of an individual loan which the branch manager can make on his own authority varies considerably from bank to bank, from one branch of the same bank to another branch, and from prescribed rules to actual practice. With one exception, mother institutions set a baht limit on the amount of single loan, 150,000 being indicated as the highest amount allowable among Thai banks. The one exception puts the limit on an individual loan at 95 per cent of the borrower's deposit at the branch where the loan is to be made. (There may be a number of reasons why a person would prefer to borrow even though his assets at the bank exceed the amount of the loan. His deposit may be for a fixed period of time, with loss of interest revenue in the event the deposit is reduced to the expiring of that time period. Interest payable on deposit is tax exempt, while that due on bank accommodation is deductible for tax purposes.)

More significant from the standpoint of developmental finance are the restrictions placed on the subsidiaries--both branches and agencies--with respect to the over-all ratio of accommodation to deposits. The earning assets of branches seldom contain much else beyond overdrafts, bills, and discounts. There is only a modicum of straight loans, and there are hardly any investments. Maximum ratios of these assets to deposits liabilities range from a low of 10 per cent to a high of 70 per cent. In actuality, however, there is much greater flexibility than these ratios suggest. Even when they are set out explicitly, a considerable deviation is allowed individual branches at different times. The ratios are set mainly as guidelines, and appear to apply to the entire complex of branches of a given bank rather than to each separate branch in particular. Nevertheless, rigid or not, these prescribed ratios do have the effect of inhibiting the growth of bank accommodation relative to deposits. The implications of this state of affairs will be discussed later.

Tables 5.2 and 5.3 summarize the available information regarding the chief characteristics of Thai branch banks. Much of the contents of the tables have been touched upon in the preceding discussion but

one aspect of Thai branch operations emerging from
Table 5.2 merits a separate discussion. This aspect
has to do with employment of compradores by provincial banks.

TABLE 5.2

Frequency of Agencies and Compradores
in Branch Banks

Group	Total Number of Branches	Number of Branches Operating as Agencies or Employing Compradores
Group A: Banks with agencies		
A_1	76	58
A_2	63	50
A_3	31	3
Group B: Banks employing compradores		
B_1	81	49
B_2	54	17
B_3	47	33
B_4	10	4
B_5	9	5
Group C: Directly con- trolled by head office		
C_1	52	
C_2	17	
C_3	12	

Source: Field interviews and other sources.

There were in the fall of 1966 over 120 compradores attached to commercial banks, and most of them

operated in the provinces. Both agencies and branch-
eas appear to avail themselves of the services of the
compradore, but the latter employ the bulk of them.

TABLE 5.3

Selected Operational Characteristics
of Branch Banks

Individual Loan Limit (baht)	Total Loan Limit (% of branch dep.)	Restriction on Loan Type
10,000	10%	only overdrafts
20,000	30	apparently no fixed-term loans
25,000	25	none
50,000	30	no term loans
50,000	50	none
50,000	50-60	none
100,000	not clear	none
150,000	50-60	none
150,000	70	none
95% of borrowers' deposits	40	not clear
not clear	none	some but not clear

Source: Information obtained from Thai commercial
         banks.

    The position of the compradore in Thai commer-
cial banking is somewhat ambiguous. He is apparently

employed by commercial banks both to bring in additional business and to guarantee the repayment of
advances by customers whose credit status is unknown
to the bank manager. Presumably, the second function
is the more important one, inasmuch as most branches
are not particularly aggressive in seeking out local
borrowers. But even in his capacity of an acceptor
or a guarantor, the exact role played by the compradore is by no means clear, partly because loans
(used in the broad sense to include all kinds of bank
accommodation) are sooner or later reviewed by headquarters. Doubtless the compradore's acceptance is
of importance in determining the headquarters' position with respect to the loan application. But insofar as much of the branch lending is secured either
by commercial paper or by mortgage instrument, the
function performed by the compradore can only occasionally be a truly crucial one.

    Even less clear is the profit nexus in which
the compradore himself operates. In principle, the
compradore is supposed to receive 3 per cent on the
volume of loans made either under his sponsorship or
under his guarantee. Inasmuch as the volume of such
business is limited by the amount of the security
bond that the compradore himself is required to deposit with the headquarters, it is difficult to see,
at first glance, why anyone would want to engage in
the compradore business. After all a return of 3
per cent on assets cannot appear too attractive to
someone well versed in the business affairs of a
town. It is true that the bond which has to be deposited with the mother bank can be concurrently engaged elsewhere. This means, for example, that the
headquarters may accept a lien on the total operating
assets of a well-known local trader as bond which
permits this trader to continue to obtain the usual
rate of return from his business while earning the
compradore's commission from these same assets on a
contingent basis, as it were. Sometimes the compradore's volume of business at the branch may exceed
the amount of his bond, and he, in his capacity as
trader or merchant, may then derive some ancillary
benefits from his compradore activities. Nevertheless, the apparent modesty of the commission paid to
the compradore is one reason why rumors abound that

he supplements that commission with kickbacks from
the branch customers.

Those who take a sinister view of the compradore
and his function as an intermediary in branch banking
operations point to the incidence of postdated checks
among branch banks' assets. (Postdated checks are
written with a date sometime in the future, presumably when the loan becomes due. The presumption is
that the drawer will, at the date written on the
check, deposit sufficient funds to his account at the
branch on which the check was drawn.) This assertion
is very difficult to document for a variety of reasons. Official data on the subject of postdated
checks are not available or, if available, are not
likely to be released. Those branch managers who are
queried on the subject show a marked reluctance to
provide any precise answers. Postdated checks are
not apt to be held prominently among branch assets,
particularly at a time of official audit. To the extent that they are issued to the compradore personally, there is no reason why they should appear in
the branch portfolio at all.

The significant fact about postdated checks is
that their misuse has been liable to criminal penalties since 1954, while with respect to other types
of collateral only civil remedies are available to
creditors. That is, a branch holding a mortgage deed
of a delinquent borrower will have to secure a court
order for eviction, repossession, sale, and so on.
On the other hand, a delinquent borrower who writes
a postdated check and whose deposit is inadequate
at the time his check falls due may find himself in
prison.[4]

At the very worst, an unscrupulous compradore
(or, for that matter, a branch manager or agent) may
accept a postdated check from a hard-pressed borrower, knowing full well that the borrower is unlikely
to make the check good by the date due. The possibility of criminal action is then held over the unfor-
tunate borrower who is thus blackmailed into paying
the lender or the guarantor an extortionate interest.
More often, the postdated check serves as a convenient

device to evade income tax liability or cover up the
use of bank funds for purposes other than those for
which they were intended.[5]

The use of postdated checks, while certainly
quite widespread in Thailand, appears to be concentrated in the unorganized, rather than the organized,
financial markets. Branch managers in the provinces
usually deny strongly that they ever accept them or,
at most, admit that they accept them only occasionally. The anatomy and pathology of the usage of
postdated checks would certainly throw much needed
light on the transition from one type of market to
another. It is the compradore who plays a key role
in this process of transition though, as suggested
above, the use of postdated checks cannot be laid at
the feet of the compradore alone.

Be that as it may, the decline in the relative
importance of the compradore on the Thai banking
scene has been aided and abetted by the monetary
authorities who, whether speaking off the record or
officially, do not conceal their dislike of this intermediary. The decline of the compradore was also
caused by the foreign banks' gradual abandonment of
this intermediary as they developed their own credit
services. It is interesting to note that foreign
banks, the originators of the compradore system, are
using it less and if they have not given it up altogether, they merely have a Chinese manager to help
read Chinese signatures or supply credit information.
On the other hand, it is the Thai local banks who
have recently adopted the compradore system, some of
them, including a government bank, on quite a substantial scale.

Both branches and agencies are subject to periodic internal audit. There is a growing informal
clearing arrangement among branches of various banks
in the same locality and among branches of the same
bank in various localities, but the bulk of interbank
clearing continues to be sent via Bangkok. As a result, a check drawn on a branch will take from one
to three weeks to clear. The delay in clearing is attributable, in part, to the lack of any formal

clearing mechanism in the provinces and, in part, to inadequate postal facilities. It is also possible to argue that some of that delay is is deliberate, and designed to prolong control over funds. Paul Sithi-Amnuai suggests that postdated checks are commonly issued by buyers of commodities, the receipt of which is delayed in the expectation, presumably, that by the time the check is presented for payment at the Bangkok Clearing House, the goods will be sold and the proceeds deposited to the buyer's account.[6] T. H. Silcock, on the other hand, hints that the delay may well be to the advantage of the branch manager or compradore.

THAI BRANCH BANKING IN THE DEVELOPMENT PROCESS

As mentioned above, there is no close correlation between the number of people living in a province and the number of branches operated by Thai commercial banks there. Similarly, there exists no apparent relationship between the over-all size of a bank and the number of branches it operates. Thus, the Thai Development Bank, whose total assets are about half those of the Siam Commercial Bank, has three times its number of branches.

The relative importance of branch banking varies greatly among Thai banks. For demand deposits, the proportion held by branches ranges from a low of 2 per cent to a high of 89 per cent. Similar range obtains with respect to time deposits, from 3 per cent for the Thai Military Bank (which has only one or two Bangkok branches), to over 90 per cent for the Bangkok Bank of Commerce.

For all commercial banks (for which data were available), the ratio of all branch deposits to total deposits hovers around 60 per cent. On the asset side, however, the importance of branch banking diminishes sharply and amounts to less than 40 per cent for all the banks surveyed. This points out the key issue of branch banking in Thailand relative to developmental planning. Commercial banks appear to be less interested in providing accommodation to local business than

in collecting deposits from areas outside the capital. This point emerges with much greater force when
the chief assets and liabilities of commercial banks
are considered with respect only to those branches
which are provincial, i.e., outside the Bangkok-
Thonburi area. As seen in Table 5.4, the proportion
of provincial branch deposits to total deposits is
about twice that of loans and overdrafts.

A closer examination of the behavior of individual banks suggests that while those banks with greater
commitment to provincial branch banking (as measured
by the number of branches and the relative size of
branch deposits) generally shows a greater proportion
of local earning assets relative to total assets, the
correlation is far from perfect. In Table 5.5, the
Bangkok Bank of Commerce is shown to rank highest with
respect to the ratio of its provincial time deposits
to its total time deposits and next to highest both
with respect to demand deposits and with respect to
the relative importance of its provincial earning assets. Such sporadic evidence as is available strongly suggests that the ratio of provincial earning assets to a bank's total assets tends to be greater
for agencies than for branches. Both the Siam City
Bank and the Bangkok Bank of Commerce operate a number of agencies, the former in particular. The middle position of the Bank of Ayudhya, another institution with a significant number of agencies, may be
explained by its modest total of branches, resulting
in moderate rankings with respect to both the deposits and the earning assets ratios.

The tendency for agencies to be somewhat more
involved than branches in the provision of local
credit is not particularly surprising. An agency
manager is given greater latitude with respect to
both individual and over-all loan limits and, like
the local businessmen, tends to be more interested
in developing local trade, especially as he has a
direct stake in the profits of the branch he manages.

The entire question of the incentives of branch
managers is extremely difficult to pin down. In
numerous field interviews, the managers of branches,

TABLE 5.4

Commercial Banks: Activities of Provincial[a] Branches, Fall, 1966
(million baht)

Bank	Time Deposits			Demand Deposits			Loans & Overdrafts		
	Total	Branches	%	Total	Branches	%	Total	Branches	%
Siam Com. Bank	863	–	–	863	–	–	524	–	–
Bank of Asia	124	21	16.94	184	28	15.22	327	51	15.60
Siam City Bank	466	338	72.53	359	211	58.77	589	380	64.52
Krung Thai Bank	1,119	830	74.17	691	444	64.25	1,835	286	15.59
Bangkok Bank	1,414	216	15.28	1,087	247	22.72	1,840	174	9.46
Bangkok Bank of Commerce	554	422	76.17	464	294	63.36	684	408	59.65
Bank of Ayudhya	377	127	33.69	369	79	21.41	1,032	103	9.98
Thai Farmers Bank	424	158	37.26	464	148	31.90	934	69	7.39
Laem Thong Bank	167	–	–	72	–	–	237	–	–
Union Bank of Bangkok	94	7	7.45	293	9	3.07	267	–	–
Thai Danu Bank	195	8	4.10	112	2	1.79	240	6	2.50
Bangkok Metropolitan Bank	416	–	–	230	–	–	431	–	–
Thai Military Bank	72	–	–	67	–	–	400	–	–
Thai Development Bank	281	159	56.58	349	164	46.99	537	104	19.37
Total	6,566	2,286	34.82	5,127	1,626	31.71	9,877	1,581	16.01

[a]Outside the Bangkok-Thonburi area.

Source: Compiled from data obtained from Thai commercial banks.

as distinct from agencies, could not relate their
performance to their rewards in any precise fashion.
This applies to such factors as salaries, promotion,
or the locale of posting. Their salaries were quite
modest, though many of them enjoyed other emoluments
in kind.

TABLE 5.5

Commercial Banks: Activities of Provincial
Branches, Fall, 1966, by Rank

Bank	Rank[a]		
	Time Deposits[b]	Demand Deposits[c]	Loans & Over-drafts[d]
Bank of Asia	4	3	7
Siam City Bank	8	8	10
Krung Thai Bank	9	10	6
Bangkok Bank	3	5	4
Bangkok Bank of Com.	10	9	9
Bank of Ayudhya	5	4	5
Thai Farmers Bank	6	6	3
Union Bank of Bangkok	2	2	1
Thai Danu Bank	1	1	2
Thai Development Bank	7	7	8

[a]Ranked in ascending order (10 is highest). [b]Ratio
of provincial time deposits to total time deposits.
[c]Ratio of provincial demand deposits to total demand
deposits. [d]Ratio of provincial loans and overdrafts
to total loans and overdrafts.

Kendall coefficients
are as follows:

 [b] and [c] : = 0.82222
 [b] and [d] : = 0.57777
 [c] and [d] : = 0.51111

Spearman coefficients
are:

 [b] and [c] : = r_r = 0.9394
 [b] and [d] : = r_r = 0.78182
 [c] and [d] : = r_r = 0.7091

Source: Based on data provided by Thai commercial
         banks.

Insofar as the earning assets are substantially
below deposits, in most subsidiaries operated by commercial banks in the provinces, interest payable by
the branch exceeds substantially the interest received on loans, discounts, and overdrafts. Hence,
provincial operations per se are money-losing propo-
sitions.* At the same time, Thai commercial banks
continue to clamor for the right to establish more
and more branches. The inescapable conclusion is
that provincial subsidiaries are viewed primarily as
a means of collecting resources from the countryside
and transferring them to Bangkok, although the banks,
even at the headquarters level, do not make full use
of their available resources.

This state of affairs is of concern to the development planner for several reasons. The emphasis
on channeling local funds to the capital inhibits the
development of new lines of banking activity in the
provinces and deprives local businessmen of needed
accommodation. The concentration of funds in Bangkok
tends to deflect these funds to purposes other than
those which would be dictated by development priorities. By helping to drain the countryside of investible funds, the branch operations thereby accentuate
further the somewhat lopsided economic growth of the
country and aggravate the kurtosis of the distribution of both regional and personal incomes.

Even though headquarters seldom formally inter-
dicts any particular kind of accommodation, earning
assets of branches usually consists predominantly of
discounts, financing of shipping bills, and overdrafts. In very few cases will the branch make a loan

------

*The accounting device employed in this connec-
tion is that of a "headquarters account." A provincial branch will, typically, list among its assets
such an account which contains the excess of deposits
collected over the loans disbursed. The headquarters
account is supposed to bring interest revenue to the
branch, at about 5 to 6 per cent per annum. The interest is not listed as revenue but is added as principal

to a manufacturing enterprise, or take advantage of
the special rediscounting facilities offered by the
Bank of Thailand, or finance a nascent enterprise
merely on the basis of good prospects for success
rather than land collateral. Only one or two banks
show any interest in expanding their activities in
new directions, such as, for example, the financing
of supervised group credit to farmers. There is
little awareness that one of the key functions of a
commercial bank is to develop economically the area
in which that bank operates.*

When the bank funds are concentrated in Bangkok,
they certainly serve to raise the over-all ratio of
commercial bank earning assets to deposits. But this,
as argued in Chapter 4, does not preclude the Thai
commercial banks from underutilizing their capacity
nor from concentrating their activities on speculation
and the financing of real estate construction. It is
interesting to note that in those areas of the Thai
countryside which are booming under the impact of
defense-oriented construction, the financing does not
come from the local branch but rather from the headquarters, if indeed it comes from the parent bank at
all.

Information on the ownership of deposits in provincial branches is not readily available. But it
would appear that at least 50 per cent of fixed deposits, particularly those lodged with the branch for
twelve months or longer, can be attributed to persons
who are not resident in the urban center in which the
branch is typically located. A substantial proportion
of these depositors appear to be net savers. That is,

_____

*Most of the branch managers interviewed in the
field were keenly aware of the role they have been
assigned to play: that of transmitters of funds to
Bangkok. Many were chafing at the constraints, formal and informal, which inhibited them from opening
new lines of business. Several indicated that they
thought that even relatively risky and complex operations, such as those of agricultural credit, could
and should be undertaken.

they seldom, if ever, borrow and are content to let
their savings accumulate while earning 7 per cent per
annum. To the extent that more precise data on the
distribution of deposits by type and origin could be
developed, the crucial process of transferring resources from agriculture to the rest of the economy
could be better understood and gauged. But there is
little doubt that large resources, with potentially
high net marginal product for regional development,
are diverted to socially less productive ends. If it
were possible to induce the owners of these funds to
invest their resources locally, there is good reason
to believe that the return on their investment would
exceed that payable by the branches. Such an induce-
ment, both in terms of available opportunities and
available instruments, is not currently being offered
by any Thai financial institution, let alone by the
branches of the commercial banks operating in the
provinces.

IMPLICATIONS FOR DEVELOPMENT PLANNING

There is serious question about whether branch
banks in a developing country such as Thailand should
act mainly as depositories and transmitters of provincial funds to the headquarters* or, instead, should
be prodded into participating more actively in the
developmental process. This prodding may well adopt
a dual approach. On the one hand, Thai commercial
banks should be encouraged and given incentives to
participate more actively in developmental financing
on the provincial level. On the other hand, the

---

*Of course, branches do perform functions other
than merely collecting and transmitting deposits.
They provide for safe custody of funds, pass requests
for productive loans on to the headquarters, supervise the existing loans made by the headquarters,
and so on. Nevertheless, the collection and trans-
mission of funds appear to be their chief functions,
and all others are distinctly secondary.

monetary authorities should consider the use of control instruments to insure that the provincial subsidiaries of Thai banks behave as true credit and financing institutions rather than as mere branches of a saving bank or provincial treasury.

Providing incentives and inducements to branch banks so that they will lend to local enterprises more frequently and utilize local resources more productively is a complicated task because, by tradition and training, even the parent institutions are ill equipped to provide the kind of finance which is most desirable for developmental purposes. Under existing circumstances, it is difficult to conceive of the provincial branches doing much balance-sheet term lending to manufacturing or other new enterprises. Moreover, developmental finance often connotes acquisition of relatively illiquid paper which the branches should not be persuaded to hold in large proportion to their total assets. Even after taking into account all qualifications, there seems to be ample opportunity for commercial bank branches to pursue more aggressively business such as agricultural lending, financing the operating capital requirements of local manufactures, and others.

Perhaps the most promising avenue of this kind is that which would link provincial branch operations with those of a specialized developmental institution. For example, a branch could develop its agricultural credit activities in cooperation with the Bank for Agriculture and Agricultural Cooperatives. The Bank would concentrate on training the necessary supervisory personnel, providing the longer-term credit, and handling the other activities which the commercial banks cannot be expected to do profitably.

Another interesting possibility is that which would tie in the provincial activities of the IFCT with those of the branch banks. (The IFCT is discussed in Chapter 8.) Project evaluation, grace period of loan, and, perhaps, contingent liability would be assumed by the IFCT, while the local branch would contribute to the loan and supervise it on the spot.

The second approach, that of having Thai monetary authorities employ control instruments, could
be implemented more promptly. As mentioned previously, Thai commercial banks are anxious to expand their
network of branches for a variety of reasons--not all
of them economic. The Minister of Finance grants the
permit to open a new branch; however, he usually
abides by the recommendation of the Bank of Thailand.
The set of regulations which govern the system of
granting permits is remarkable both for comprehen-
siveness and for vagueness. Whether or not a permit
is granted appears to depend upon a host of considerations, including the applicant's former record,
his competitive position in the past and present,
the economic situation, prospects of the locality,
and so on. But there are no clear-cut rules or criteria which would define these considerations. Perhaps this is as it should be. The power to grant
permits for new branches is a valuable one and, hence,
one which should be used with discretion. That it
has been so used would follow from the fact that,
from 1962 to 1967, the ratio of branch permits granted to the number of applications declined from a high
of 56 per cent to about 30 per cent.

There is, then, a prima facie case for the monetary authorities to intimate to the banks that aggressive development of local business will, henceforth,
become a prime factor in their examination of applications to open branches. Inasumch as the future
conduct of a branch cannot be determined at the time
an application is submitted, it would seem to make
sense to grant permits for a limited number of years,
the continuance of the permit being subject to review
at the end of the stated period. After all, there
is nothing in the law or custom which would compel
the monetary authorities to grant a business privilege in perpetuity. Many such concessions and privi-
leges are now being granted, both in Thailand and
elsewhere, for a limited time only. There are ample
precedents in such fields as taxation, customs,
patents, and copyrights.

It could be argued that it is difficult, if not
impossible, for a commercial bank to make a heavy

investment in a branch operation without knowing
whether such an operation will be allowed to continue
beyond, say, five years. This is a cogent argument,
but the same sort of problem arises in the case of
the tire factory which obtains a special import con-
cession for a limited period of years. Moreover, as
indicated earlier, most branches lose money in their
provincial operations and are profitable only in the
sense that they manage to obtain relatively cheap
funds for use by the headquarters.

Nonetheless, the granting of permits for a limited time only would have to be handled gingerly. It
would probably be inappropriate to lay down specific
rules of good behavior, such as requiring the branch
to have at least 60 per cent of its deposits lent
locally by the end of a five-year period. Rather,
the monetary authorities would reserve the right to
review the entire picture five years hence and, in
the event that external indices suggested that the
branch fell woefully short of desirable performance,
they would invite the branch and the headquarters
representatives to state their positions. Refusal
to renew a permit would be resorted to very rarely
and only in cases of blatant nonadherence to the
guidelines set down by the monetary authorities. After
all, even when such an extreme measure is employed,
it can hardly mean the collapse of the entire bank.

The importance of the suggested control instrument would thus lie not in rigid rules and ruthless
elimination of branches at the expiry of their probationary period but in suasion, guidance, and example, backed, however, by the possibility of a real
sanction in extreme cases.

The commercial banks will be given notice that
provincial branches must serve the developmental interest of the province rather than the interests of
headquarters exclusively. The putting-on-notice
should in itself be instrumental in improving the
operational performance of many branch banks.

Neither the tie-in with developmental institutions nor the probationary granting of branch permits

can be expected to effect drastic changes in the operations of provincial banks in the near future.
Most of the people who run these banks are hard-
working, competent people who have the long-term interests of the country very much at heart and who
honestly believe that they are doing the best they
can. In a sense, they are, indeed. Thai commercial
banking has developed to the point it is at today by
force of circumstances, rather than by any sinister
plot to impede developmental financing. To veer now
toward developmental planning, much effort and patience
must be expended by both the banks and the monetary
authorities.

The one thing which the monetary authorities
ought to reconsider is their decision not to grant
permits for new subsidiaries to agencies, but only
to branches. While there have been occasional abuses
and instances of slack agency management in the past,
such abuses and sloth were not confined to agencies.
In fact, in some parts of the country and for some
banks, the agency record is far superior in almost
every respect to that of competing branches. Moreover, as argued above, agency managers have, prima
facie, greater incentives to develop local business
and greater interest in engaging a higher proportion
of local deposits in earning assets. What is needed
is the removal of the rigid interdiction against agencies and a consideration of each application on its
merits.

It should be noted that the probationary granting of permits suggested is not meant to apply to
branches already established, but only to those which
might be set up after the suggested measure was put
into operation. This arrangement could, however, be
combined with one in which, after a period of years,
a branch could revert to the status of an agency.

More can be lost than gained by drastic measures
and sudden attempts at "fundamental" reform. The
suggestions made here are modest ones and are designed
to insure that the real contribution of Thai banking
to the economic life of the country is enhanced rather
than tampered with.

NOTES

1.   The only published account of commercial
bank branches in Thailand known to the author is contained in Paul Sithi-Amnuai, <u>Finance and Banking in
Thailand: A Study of the Commercial System 1888-1963</u>
(Bangkok: Thai Watan Panich, 1964), Chapter 6. Some
aggregate statistical information is published periodically in the Bank of Thailand annual and monthly
reports and in similar publications of the Bangkok
Bank, Ltd.; see particularly <u>Commercial Banks in
Thailand, 1964</u> (Bangkok, 1965), Part I.

2.   See Sithi-Amnuai, <u>op. cit</u>., pp. 120ff, for
a detailed account of the development of branch banking in Thailand.

3.   Sithi-Amnuai, <u>op. cit</u>., p. 127.

4.   See Sithi-Amnuai, <u>op. cit</u>., pp. 131-132.

5.   See T. H. Silcock, "Thai Money: Review
Article," <u>Malayan Economic Review</u> (April, 1966), p.
109.

6.   Sithi-Amnuai, <u>op. cit</u>., p. 134.

CHAPTER 6 CENTRAL BANKING

Central banks influence the real part of the economy by their decisions affecting savings and investment. These decisions are influenced primarily by the central banks' relations with the commercial banks and, to a lesser extent, by the central banks' dealings with the fisc. In Thailand, at least, the decisions of households to save and of business to invest are, as yet, only marginally affected by the central banks' transactions with financial intermediaries other than the commercial banks. The fact that relations with commercial banks are at the heart of the central bank's influence on the economy is reflected, in this chapter, in frequent references to points touched upon in Chapter 4.

The way in which the financial intermediaries transfer resources from the surplus to the deficit units is influenced by central banks' changes in reserve requirements, rediscount policy, debt management, and by open market operations and selective credit controls, although the last two control instruments play little part in Thailand.

For practical purposes the central bank is here equated with the Bank of Thailand even though, in law, the Ministry of Finance is the supervisory agency and retains the formal overriding power over many decisions routinely made by the Bank of Thailand.

One reason why the control of commercial banking is nominally vested in the Ministry of Finance and why the Minister is, in principle, the supervisor of the Bank of Thailand operation is that the Bank of Thailand is a relatively recent institution, established in 1942. Thus, when after some banking

failures in the first quarter of the century, the
need for some supervisory authority became clear,
this task was entrusted to the Minister of Finance
under the Commercial Banking Act of 1937. The in-
flationary pressures during the war and the occupation led to the passage of the Emergency Control Act
of 1943, under which powers over all credit institutions were given to the Ministry of Finance rather
than to the fledgling Bank of Thailand. Due to circumstances surrounding the establishment of the Bank
of Thailand, the act setting up this institution
dealt primarily with the transfer of the note issue
from the Treasury, and other functions of the bank
were barely outlined in an accompanying Royal Decree.
There is some difference of opinion regarding the
degree of independence that the Bank of Thailand enjoys at present. It would appear that much depends
on the Governor and his deputy, who, unlike other
members of the bank's Council, are appointed by the
Crown. It would seem that especially since 1962 the
effective, operational control of the Bank of Thailand and of commercial credit, in general, has gradually shifted from the Minister of Finance to the
Governor of the bank. This shift was brought about,
in part, by the recognition of the integrity and skill
of the top management of the Bank of Thailand, partly
by the growing complexity of the matters with which
it deals, and partly by the passage of the Commercial
Banking Act of 1962 which gave the Bank of Thailand
some instruments of control. Yet it still remains
true that on many significant matters the ultimate
decision rests with the Minister of Finance and that
he, as a member of the Cabinet, wields political power denied to the Bank of Thailand.[1]

It is interesting to note that the establishment
of a central bank in Thailand followed rather than
preceded the development of a lively and fairly sophisticated commercial banking system and that, unlike
many countries to whom the formation of a central
bank is one of the appurtenances of a newly acquired
independence, Thailand has long resisted the setting
up of a central bank merely as a status symbol. This
resistance was led by three factions which were not
necessarily separate and distince. The British

monetary advisers who long held sway over the financial policies of the country opposed the formation
of a central bank from 1890 on. "Conservatives" at
the Treasury argued against the "nationalists" of the
1930's that a central bank would be both superfluous
and ineffective, inasmuch as the commercial banks
were dominated by branches of foreign banks not easily amenable to central control. The branch managers
of large foreign banks were also lukewarm to the idea
of a central bank. Yet events necessitated the establishment of some institution which could implement
the policy of large-scale public works of the 1930's
which was one aspect of the anti-Chinese, anti-
Western tendencies prevailing in the country under
the Pibul Songram regime. In 1939 the Banking Bureau
was established. Its primary function was to provide
loans to public enterprises, even though, in principle, the bureau was empowered to perform most central
banking functions except that of note issue. In
fact, however, beyond performing the fiscal function
and beyond some clearing for the existing commercial
banks, the bureau did not attempt to act either as a
banker's bank or as the manager of the country's monetary affairs. The bureau was a "marriage of political reason and administrative need."[2] It was not
until 1942, under the pressure of Japanese occupation
authorities and as an alternative Japanese domination
of Thailand's monetary affairs, that the Bank of Thailand at last came into existence.

This sketchy background may help explain some
aspects of Bank of Thailand policies and operations.
From the very outset the Bank was meant to enforce
and continue the tradition of financial independence
of the country and to safeguard the integrity of its
money at home, if possible, but certainly and above
all abroad. The lessons of history as understood by
the Thais are clear. A country whose financial affairs are in disorder, whose currency fluctuates
wildly in the foreign markets, and one which has difficulty in maintaining payments on its external debt
invites the intervention of interested foreign powers
and risks its existence as an independent polity.[3]
The circumstances which attended the formation of the
Bank of Thailand did nothing to lessen the emphasis

on the importance of maintaining financial integrity
in the foreign markets, but they also brought to the
fore the importance of maintaining internal price
stability in the face of wartime inflation, the demands of the occupation authorities, and, later on,
the needs of the Thai government. The point made
here is that by tradition, training, and dictates of
the times, the Bank of Thailand had to be primarily
concerned with the soundness of its currency, and
only incidentally and only in recent times could it
devote much thought and energy to the control of
credit or the structuring of the financial markets
toward developmental needs.[4]

There can be little question that the Bank of
Thailand accomplished what it considered to be its
primary task. By 1955 the external value of the currency was well-nigh stabilized and the multiple exchange rate system eliminated. By 1959 the era of
large budgetary deficits was pretty well brought to
an end; and by the onset of the 1960's the internal
price level had shown remarkable stability, the baht
was firm in world markets, the country possessed a
large stock of foreign exchange reserves, budget deficits were either small or easily managable, the
credit-standing abroad was first-rate, and the rate
of growth of the economy was more than satisfactory.
No small measure of credit must go to the managers
of the Bank of Thailand for bringing about this state
of affairs and for clearing the decks, as it were,
for efforts in the areas of developmental finance
and the control of credit.

In this study, oriented as it is toward developmental strategy, no more than a passing tribute can
be paid to the excellent performance of the Bank of
Thailand in defense of the value of the currency both
internally and externally. Inasmuch as the main interest of developmental finance lies in the very
areas which were, perforce, somewhat neglected in the
past by those at the helm of the Bank of Thailand,
the impression of undue criticism may be obtained.
It behooves the writer, therefore, to reiterate both
his admiration of the way in which the bank has ac-
quitted itself of its tasks in the past and of his

belief that these tasks will have to change their
focus in the future.

ASSETS AND LIABILITIES OF THE BANK OF THAILAND

One convenient way to look at the operations
of the Bank of Thailand is to consider its balance
sheets over a period of time which is long enough to
register significant changes in the composition of
assets and liabilities but short enough to preserve
a modicum of accounting comparability. Table 6.1
gives the baht amounts of the main balance sheet
items.

During the twelve-year period 1955-1967, total
assets of the Bank of Thailand merely doubled, compared with a more than sevenfold increase in the assets of commercial banks. At the same time, the
composition of these assets underwent considerable
change. Up to 1959 the bulk of the bank's assets
was divided about equally among gold, foreign exchange, Treasury bills, and government overdrafts.
By the end of 1967, over two-thirds of the bank's
assets were in the form of gold and foreign exchange,
and the holdings of government bonds became second
in importance. Government overdrafts disappeared
from the balance sheet, and claims on banks and contributions to the IMF made their appearance.[5]

The gradual reduction in the proportion of gold
to total assets represents the desire and the need
to obtain a greater return on foreign assets and was
made possible by an increase in Thailand's holdings of
other foreign securities as well as by its full membership in the IMF. It is also possible that the
country's growing political and economic ties with
the United States have contributed to the policy of
reducing holdings of gold and of increasing holdings
of securities held in, among other places, the United
States.

More important, perhaps, was the elimination of
government overdrafts by 1960. These claims on government came into being in 1952, when the government,

taking advantage of the provision of the Bank of
Thailand Act that enables the government to borrow
up to 25 per cent of ordinary budget expenditures,
without collateral, in the form of an overdraft, began to borrow from the bank without security at an
annual interest rate of 2½ per cent. By November
1960 this claim was eliminated, parallel to the improvement of the budgetary position of the country
and the determination of the bank to reduce infla-
tionary forms of finance. The same considerations
were operative in the sharp reduction of Treasury
bills in the bank portfolio. In 1955 these amounted
to over 30 per cent of total assets, a proportion
which fell to a fraction of 1 per cent by the end of
1967.

Under the Currency Act of 1958, government bonds
designated in local currency could be used as a cover
against the note issue, provided that such bonds (and
Treasury bills) did not constitute more than 40 per
cent of notes issued. (IMF subscription and short-
term commercial bills rediscounted by the Bank of
Thailand can also form a part of the secondary backing of the currency provided that, together with
government securities, they do not exceed 40 per cent
of the note issue.) However, inasmuch as foreign
exchange reserves continued to increase throughout
the period, there was little pressure on the bank to
increase significantly its holdings of government
bonds. These holdings did increase after 1960, but
the increase was moderate; by the end of 1967 the
proportion of government bonds to total assets was
about the same as it was at the end of 1955.

The Bank of Thailand did not actively begin to
provide liquidity to the commercial banks until 1959.
More important than direct loans were rediscounts,
which had increased eightfold by the end of 1967.
Even so, claims against commercial banks totaled
less than 2 per cent of assets at the end of 1967.

The contribution to the IMF did not change very
much until 1965, when it nearly doubled, reflecting
the growth of both the national product and of the
foreign exchange reserves.

TABLE 6.1

Assets and Liabilities of the Bank of Thailand, 1955-1967[a]

(million baht)

	Gold & Foreign Exchange			Claims on Government					Claims on Banks			Contribution to IMF	Other Assets	Total Assets or Liabilities
Year	Gold	Foreign Exchange[b]	Total	Overdrafts	Balance at Provincial Treasuries[c]	Treasury Bills	Bonds[d]	Total	Loans	Rediscounts	Total			
	(1)	(2)	(3)	(4)	(5)	(6)	(7)	(8)	(9)	(10)	(11)	(12)	(13)	(14)
1955	2,246.4	2,452.2	4,698.6	549.8	454.5	3,172.8	1,621.7	5,798.8	3.0	–	3.0	–	5.7	10,506.1
1956	2,246.4	2,799.7	5,046.1	969.7	560.7	3,109.7	1,651.8	6,291.9	–	–	–	–	11.7	11,349.7
1957	2,246.4	3,153.6	5,400.0	1,250.2	413.0	2,966.0	1,925.0	6,554.2	–	–	–	–	15.0	11,969.2
1958	2,246.4	3,056.2	5,302.6	1,412.4	403.7	2,917.7	2,098.0	6,831.8	8.7	–	8.7	–	15.8	12,158.9
1959	2,083.9	3,119.0	5,202.9	1,737.3	614.7	2,944.2	2,037.8	7,334.0	118.1	41.7	159.8	162.5	21.5	12,880.6
1960	2,083.9	3,717.7	5,801.6	–	523.0	2,033.7	2,909.2	5,465.9	130.0	97.2	227.2	162.5	23.1	11,680.3
1961	2,084.1	5,404.5	7,488.6	–	370.0	1,468.8	3,174.7	5,013.5	137.8	86.0	223.8	162.5	21.2	12,909.6
1962	2,084.1	6,791.0	8,875.1	–	403.0	1,348.4	3,299.5	5,050.9	197.0	89.8	286.8	162.5	20.3	14,395.6
1963	2,167.4	8,294.1	10,146.5	–	525.5	180.1	3,267.1	3,972.7	144.8	72.5	217.3	169.0	26.5	14,847.0
1964	2,167.4	9,586.9	11,754.3	–	584.2	356.9	3,237.1	4,178.2	170.5	146.8	317.3	169.0	53.7	16,472.5
1965	2,006.2	11,144.4	13,150.6	–	547.1	482.6	3,201.6	4,231.3	179.4	209.5	388.9	330.2	45.0	18,146.0
1966	1,907.4	14,897.6	16,805.0	–	792.5	451.9	3,075.1	4,319.5	169.6	280.7	450.3	429.0	41.2	22,045.0
1967	1,907.4	16,762.7	18,670.1	–	889.5	33.9	2,796.7	3,720.1	30.0	326.8	356.8	429.0	48.3	23,224.3

194

LIABILITIES

| | | Government & Official Entities | | Deposits | | Private Sector | | | | | | | |
| | Notes in Circula-tion | in National Currency | in Foreign Currency | Commer-cial Banks | Other Banks | in National Currency | in Foreign Currency | Counter-part Funds | Others | Ex-change Differ-ences | Other Liabil-ities | Capital Accounts |
Year	(15)	(16)	(17)	(18)	(19)	(20)	(21)	(22)	(23)	(24)	(25)	(26)
1955	5,542.6	311.8	13.5	320.8	28.2	122.2	–	118.6	0.1	3,201.5	1.2	845.6
1956	5,803.5	435.3	1.9	338.8	14.1	98.8	–	351.8	6.0	3,178.4	1.3	1,119.8
1957	5,993.3	336.5	57.0	398.4	32.6	92.7	3.9	452.7	91.9	3,163.0	0.3	1,346.9
1958	5,863.5	453.9	14.1	358.7	16.6	34.8	1.3	375.5	280.5	3,163.0	0.4	1,596.6
1959	6,248.5	462.6	11.0	503.9	19.3	142.6	–	451.1	170.0	3,163.0	7.6	1,701.1
1960	6,661.0	988.5	4.1	554.8	20.7	96.5	1.6	464.9	0.1	1,004.3	7.0	1,876.8
1961	7,267.9	1,202.6	19.5	645.4	30.4	154.5	1.7	544.0	0.2	–	8.2	3,035.2
1962	7,413.7	2,038.3	76.8	788.0	18.5	245.8	1.7	566.6	2.1	–	7.2	3,236.9
1963	7,741.0	1,489.5	113.7	1,016.7	9.8	260.3	1.1	483.9	3.1	–	10.3	3,717.6
1964	8,474.1	2,448.0	169.5	1,000.5	26.3	201.3	0.5	382.8	0.7	–	10.0	3,758.8
1965	9,379.1	3,221.5	109.5	1,061.7	34.2	149.2	0.1	162.4	1.1	–	16.7	4,010.5
1966	10,570.6	5,573.0	38.7	1,183.2	37.3	154.2	–	53.2	–	–	22.8	4,412.0
1967	11,086.8	5,493.8	59.9	1,401.3	40.3	310.3	–	55.8	1.1	–	20.1	4,754.9

aYear end.
bIncluding foreign treasury bills and bonds.
cBeginning with June 1963, revised to report gross instead of net.
dIncluding Thai government bonds floated abroad.

Source: Bank of Thailand.

195

Other assets, which include real estate and miscellaneous items, increased sharply after 1964 coinciding with the construction of branch premises in the provinces.*

With respect to liabilities, note issue increased somewhat less than total liabilities. This reflects both the growing importance of deposits in the money supply and the prevailing price stability throughout most of the period.** As a percentage of total liabilities, notes in circulation decreased somewhat--from 53 per cent at the beginning of the period to 48 per cent at the end of the thirteen-year period.

Paralleling the drastic shift in the composition of assets after 1959, the composition of liabilities also showed a significant change at about the same year. This was due to the disappearance of the Exchange Stabilization Fund, the proceeds of which were used to retire the government overdrafts outstanding, as well as to retire a good proportion of Treasury bills. This account, set up in 1955, was used to maintain the unofficial parity of the baht in foreign markets and thus to dispense with the multiple exchange rate system in operation up to that date.[6]

The elimination of 30 per cent of total liabilities consequent to the liquidation of the Exchange

---

*By 1969 the Bank of Thailand operated branches in Haadyai in the South, Khonkaen in the Northeast, and Lampang in the North.

**For historical reasons already touched upon, the bank is organized into two departments, the Issue Department and the Banking Department. For a time the balance sheets of these two departments were published separately. This somewhat archaic procedure has given way to a joint balance sheet, published monthly by the Bank of Thailand, even though the official Government Gazette continues to publish two separate sets of financial statements.

Stabilization Fund created a gap which was filled by the growth of deposits and the growth of the bank's capital account. Deposits of government and other official entities were 3 per cent of all liabilities in 1955 and almost 25 per cent by the end of 1967. This spectacular growth was due mainly to the very considerable increase in Treasury balances. Compared with the nearly eighteenfold increase in government balances held in local currency, the less than four-fold increase in commercial bank deposits appears modest indeed. The share of commercial bank deposits rose from slightly over 3 per cent of all liabilities in 1955 to some 6 per cent by the end of 1967.

Over 90 per cent of total liabilities of the Bank of Thailand at the end of 1967 were composed of notes in circulation, government deposits, and capital accounts. Of the remaining, and disregarding the commercial banks' balances, no liability exceeded 1 per cent of the total. Private sector deposits represent, in the main, the holdings of various quasi-official bodies and monopolies; e.g., the tobacco monopoly, the state sugar enterprises, and so on. Counterpart funds which, in principle, arise out of the sale of commodities imported under U.S. aid programs are, at present, simply a budgetary designation of Thai funds used to support U.S. funded projects, where the foreign exchange component is imported free by the United States and the Thais provide the local currency.

This rather cursory look at the changing pattern of assets and liabilities of the bank brings out the crucial significance of the demarcation date, which occurred about midway through the period, when the bank began to turn to the commercial banking system and away from financing the government. Moreover, an examination of the balance sheets reveals that the bank's involvement with the private sector of the economy has not yet reached any significant proportions. Commercial bank deposits at the Bank of Thailand are but a fraction of the total liquid resources of the system, prima facie evidence of the inability of the Bank of Thailand to affect the behavior of the commercial banks by economic pressures alone. The volume of accommodation extended to commercial banks via the Bank of Thailand constitutes a small proportion of the bank's resources and an even smaller proportion of those of the commercial banks themselves. The balance sheets of the bank do not show explicitly the obligations of other financial intermediaries or of specialized development institutions. During 1968 and 1969 the Bank of Thailand did acquire a token amount of the obligations of the IFCT and of the Bank for Agriculture and Agricultural Cooperatives.

Two other aspects of the Bank of Thailand balance sheet are of interest. The first of these is the large stock of foreign exchange held as assets at the bank. In a real sense, the possession of large foreign balances, which yield a return almost certainly below the alternative return these resources could earn if employed internally, represents a rent exacted from owners of the savings incorporated in large foreign exchange reserves.[7]

The accumulation of "treasure" has been one of the characteristics of the growth of the Thai economy in the past and helps explain, in part, why the country has not reached a higher level of development in spite of a high rate of voluntary saving, relative internal stability, and certainly a positive marginal productivity of capital, all of which Thailand has enjoyed for several decades.[8]

The other aspect of the balance sheet which deserves attention is the changing composition and volume of government securities held among its assets, an outward manifestation of debt management.

It will be convenient to analyze the role and the impact of the Bank of Thailand's operations in three parts: the provision of credit by the Bank of Thailand to the commercial banking system, the implications of debt management policies, and the role of the central bank in structuring the financial market in a developing country, its functions in the development process, and its contribution to the financial intermediation between savers and investors.

These three discussions are unequal in both scope and depth. The provision of credit to the commercial banks, which now stands at the center of the Bank of Thailand's operations, is discussed most fully. The analysis of debt management policies, although detailed in some respects, concentrates on selected aspects of the problem and deals only incidentally with budgetary policy or over-all monetary policy. The third subject is discussed largely tentatively and intuitively; the content is seldom rigorously substantiated. This will not necessarily make the subject less inportant from the standpoint of development strategy.

PROVISION OF CREDIT

In general, Bank of Thailand credit is extended in one of two ways. Commercial banks can borrow from the Bank of Thailand, usually against the collateral of government securities, or they may obtain credit against one of the several lines of rediscount made available by the Bank of Thailand. It is the latter form of credit provision which not only shows a more rapid growth but also contains a number of features of special interest. Therefore, it will be discussed first.

Inasmuch as direct borrowing from the Bank of Thailand is done mainly against the security of government bonds in the portfolio of the commercial banks, it will be convenient to discuss this form of credit provision later, under the heading of debt management.

Rediscount Facilities

There are two types of rediscounting facilities made available to the commercial banks and their customers by the Bank of Thailand.* The oldest, and

---

*Rediscounting of promissory notes for the production of rice and maize, briefly mentioned in

still the most important in terms of the value of
paper discounted, is the export rediscounting facility.

Export Rediscounting

Begun in November 1958, the rediscounting of
exporter's paper is the best established, the most
widely used by the commercial banks, and the best
known to the business community. Started in conjunction with the export drive, it was initially confined
only to certain kinds of export transactions and only
to selected types of paper, but its coverage was
gradually extended so that, at the present time, it
embraces most of the important agricultural exports
and covers letters of credit, purchase contracts,
usance bills, bills of exchange, and other documents
used in export finance. The duration of this credit
facility is limited to 90 days, and the Bank of Thailand rediscount rate is 5 per cent per annum, provided the exporter is not charged more than 7 per cent
by the discounting bank.

When the facility was first offered, the rate
charged by the Bank of Thailand for rediscounting
purposes was set at 7 per cent. At that rate there
was little interest in rediscounting on the part of
the commercial banks and the rate was reduced at the
end of the year. Initially the rediscounting facility was confined to rice. A year later it was extended to other crops, but certain important exports
(e.g., tin) remained excluded. With the development
of newer agricultural exports it became necessary to
extend the facility to cover documents other than
those familiar in the traditional export markets,
where bills of exchange and, to a lesser extent, irrevocable letters of credit predominated.

Chapter 3, was begun on a tentative basis in mid-
1968. This line of rediscounting is confined to the
Bank for Agriculture and Agricultural Cooperatives
and is not yet available to commercial banks.

Even so, the existing regulations tend to favor the more established export documents. Thus, the maximum amount of credit granted against bills of exchange is 90 per cent of the face value of the invoice. Against irrevocable letters of credit it is 70 per cent, and the maximum is only 60 per cent against purchase contracts. In every case the foreign documents must be accompanied by the exporter's promissory notes, supporting documents, and a number of requisite statements from the sponsoring bank. These supporting documents include warehouse and godown receipts, invoices and sales slips, bank and special forms, and pledges required by the Bank of Thailand. The maturity of each promissory note cannot exceed 90 days from the date of rediscounting. When export proceeds have been completed before maturity date, the exporter must repay his promissory note in whole or in part.

In the course of time the requisite procedures have been somewhat simplified and adjusted to the needs of the export trade, but they still remain rather complex and time consuming. There are, in fact, two separate aspects in the process of obtaining the rediscounting credit from the Bank of Thailand. The first of these involves the commercial bank and the second, the exporter. Any commercial bank which wishes to avail itself of the facility must first apply for a line of rediscounting to the Bank of Thailand. The approval is by no means automatic, and the pertinent regulations make it clear that the facility is a privilege rather than a right. In fact, while most banks operating in Thailand, whether foreign or domestically chartered, are now eligible, the power to grant and to revoke the privilege of acting as a discount bank under the export rediscounting facility is a significant power of the Bank of Thailand and one which, in principle at least, may be used to achieve objectives other than those directly related to export trade.

The exporter is also not granted the privilege automatically. He must apply to the Bank of Thailand through his commercial bank and must establish, to the satisfaction of the Bank of Thailand, his bona

fides, his standing as an exporter, and his over-all
credit rating. This is so in spite of the fact that
the discounting commercial bank assumes contingent
liability in the event of nonpayment by the exporter
on the date due. Initially, the whole process takes
from two to three months. Once the bank and the exporter have assured themselves of the line of credit
under the rediscounting facility, the release of the
Bank of Thailand funds under a specific transaction
is done promptly and quite efficiently.

Although some commercial bankers still complain
about cumbersomeness and length of the export discounting procedures, an intensive series of field interviews disclosed that these complaints either refer
to the initial establishment of the line of credit or
are due to the shortage at some of the smaller banks
of competent clerks able to prepare the necessary documents promptly and fully. It would appear that once
a line of credit is established and all the documents
sent to the Bank of Thailand, the transfer of funds
to the account of the discounting bank takes no more
than a day or two.

While there is little question that export rediscounting plays a role in sustaining the remarkable
export performance of the Thai economy, its quantitative importance must be kept in perspective. Measured as a proportion of total exports, the value of
rediscounted paper has never exceeded 9 per cent, nor
has there been any discernible upward trend in this
proportion. Export rediscounting continues to be but
a small part of the total value of bank credit extended to the export sector (which, in turn, is only
a fraction of the total value of exports). In recent
years, for example, the value of rediscounted export
paper as a percentage of export credit outstanding
at the commercial banks ranged from 3 to 8 per cent.
Moreover, the availability of the export rediscounting credit facility is far in excess of its actual
utilization. Exact figures are hard to come by, and
they vary considerably from one bank to another.
Each of the discount banks is given a quota, which is
currently 50 per cent of the sum of its cash deposits
at the Bank of Thailand and its unencumbered holdings

of government bonds. The combined quota for all the
commercial banks ranged, in the last four years, between 1 and 1.5 billion baht. The annual value of
discounted paper averaged .75 billion baht. Assuming random distribution of this type of credit over
time, about one-fourth of this amount (360 divided
by 90) should be compared with the total line of
credit available. Thus it would appear that for all
commercial banks, taking the last three or four years
of the 1960's as a whole, the ratio of utilization
to availability did not exceed 20 per cent.

There are several reasons why the export rediscounting facility still constitutes a small fraction
of total export finance. For example, rubber, tin,
and a significant fraction of rice exports do not
come within the purview of this credit facility. Exports of rubber are traditionally conducted on the
basis of sight bills. Tin has special characteristics of trade and financing which make it unsuitable.
Some 40 per cent of rice export is on government-
to-government basis. Bankers may not like the procedural aspects of the credit facility and certainly
do not like the narrow spread of two basic points
between the discount and the rediscount rate. Exporters may have a variety of reasons for financing their
exports in ways not open to rediscounting scrutiny.
But the main reason for the underutilization of export rediscounting facility is simply the considerable
and growing liquidity of the commercial banks in Thailand. So long as their own funds are by and large
abundant, the rediscounting facility will be taken
advantage of only marginally to tide over a temporary
or seasonal tightening of funds or, perhaps more importantly, to enable the commercial banks to engage
in other activities in the comfortable knowledge that
they have a readily available source of funds at their
disposal--a source of funds which not only is costless
but also brings in a modest return. Thus, the commercial banks may still be quite anxious to establish
themselves as discount banks and to present themselves
to exporters as providers of cheap credit, but they do
not necessarily have to exhaust this line of credit.
After all, so long as their own funds are available,
a 7 per cent return is better than a 2 per cent return.

Another reason for the low rate of utilization of the export rediscount facility was the availability of foreign funds to Thai banks engaged in financing foreign trade. Even though foreign credits are used more extensively in financing imports than exports, the amount borrowed from abroad by export-financing Thai banks considerably exceeded the volume of rediscounting, at least until 1968, when a sharp world-wide increase in interest rates made borrowing from abroad too costly.

All this does not, of course, mean that the export rediscounting facility is of no importance or that it does not need to be further improved and streamlined. It may be marginal, but for some exporters at all times and for other exporters at certain times it may make the difference between profit and loss. For the economy as a whole it may mean that, in the absence of this line of credit, certain exports would not have taken place. Export rediscounting appears to be particularly valuable for newer exports, such as shrimp, and for extension of other exports to new markets.

Rediscount to Manufacturers

In line with the growing emphasis on the development of manufacturing capacity in the country, the Bank of Thailand has, since 1963, made available to the commercial banks rediscount facilities to manufacturers. At present these facilities are of two types. The first makes it possible for the domestic manufacturer to obtain cheap funds for the purchase of raw materials. The second provides credit facilities, below the market rate of interest, against sales of manufactured goods on credit. The rediscount rate is 5 per cent provided no more than 7 per cent is charged to the manufacturer. Credit is extended for a maximum of 120 days, and although the maximum amount granted may not exceed 90 per cent of the face value of the invoice, it will not be less than 30,000 baht. The maturity of the promissory note dates from the day of rediscounting.

While, in principle, the procedures for obtaining credit under the two manufacturing lines of

rediscounting are similar to those under export
rediscounting, in practice they appear much more
vexing and cumbersome to the banking community and
their clients. To a large extent this is because
officials at the Bank of Thailand and at the commercial banks are still in the process of evolving
standards and practices which will insure compliance
with the intent of the regulations, on the one hand,
and the needs of the industrial community, on the
other. It does seem, however, that a manufacturer
seeking rediscounting credit must provide a lot of
information, and he must undergo a thorough credit
examination, not once but twice. Moreover, there
are several areas of disagreement as to what constitutes raw material, what is meant by manufacture,
and on other matters on which agreement is difficult
to come by.

The Bank of Thailand stands ready to rediscount
promissory notes issued by the manufacturer and previously discounted by the commercial bank, provided
that the commercial bank submits such notes to the
Bank of Thailand together with documents which must
include, but are not confined to, the following:
balance sheets, operating accounts, profit and loss
statements, and a special lengthy statement by the
manufacturer. In addition, the commercial bank must
certify that the promissory note is bona fide, and
that the face value is not greater than is customary
in trade. Finally, the commercial bank must sign an
authorization to debit its account at the Bank of
Thailand, and it must also authorize that, in the
event the balance in its debit account is insufficient to cover its liability under the promissory
note, the Bank of Thailand may dispose of other assets held. Even then the rediscounting facility may
be refused to the applicant bank, particularly if the
bank has been guilty of contravening the provisions
of the Commercial Banking Act. This sounds reasonable, but the regulations go on to say that when
under its contingent liability the commercial bank
has to dispose of its assets other than cash held at
the Bank of Thailand, it disqualifies itself for the
rediscount facility. The latter provision would suggest that a commercial bank which had once made a
bad credit appraisal will be debarred from the

206 FINANCE AND DEVELOPMENT IN THAILAND

rediscounting facility in the future. This sounds less than reasonable.

Yet, despite shortcomings in procedure and applications, most of which are expected to be reduced or eliminated in the course of time, the provision of credit to manufacturers constitutes the first deliberate step taken by the Bank of Thailand to channel resources in directions deemed critical by the country's planners. Regardless of whether manufacturing represents the truly critical direction from the standpoint of optimal development strategy, the rediscounting facilities offered to manufacturers are highly significant because they demonstrate that the Bank of Thailand now considers it its responsibility to influence the flow of savings and their utilization. The official rationale for offering facilities to manufacturers is that they will reduce the competitive disadvantage of local producers who face rates of interest higher than those obtaining abroad and who suffer from a shortage of working capital.

Insofar as the rediscounting of raw material purchases is concerned, there is another alleged comparative disadvantage in that imported raw materials benefit from cheap financing by foreign suppliers. Accordingly, more lenient treatment is given to those who apply for rediscounting credit for the purchase of local raw materials. Here again the Bank of Thailand deliberately tries to influence the direction of funds and the nature of economic activity.

In terms of value and as a proportion of total credit extended to manufacturing, rediscounting facilities offered by the Bank of Thailand have yet to play a major role. At the end of 1968, the joint total of raw materials and credit sales rediscounting did not exceed 11 per cent of the outstanding total bank credit to manufacturing. Even though the value of raw material rediscounts rose from 70 million baht in 1965 to 239 million in 1968, much of this increase was due to promissory notes against purchases of tin, which were, in turn, due to the

establishment of a major tin smelter on the island
of Phuket.

It is reasonable to expect that credit sales
will continue to be more popular than raw material
rediscounting. Much of Thai industry is of the fin-
ishing and packaging variety, the raw materials being
imported under financial arrangements which compare
favorably with those proffered by the Bank of Thailand. Many established firms can get up to eighteen
months credit abroad. Moreover, many of the manufacturing firms are, in reality, subsidiaries of foreign
manufacturers, and the import of components presents
mainly accounting problems. The Bank of Thailand
has, accordingly, devised strict rules regarding the
physical change in the imported materials to be effected by the local manufacturer before he can qualify for rediscounting. These rules, while well
motivated, create occasional problems. The type of
industry which is based on local raw materials and
which is largely locally financed and managed is not
yet well established in Thailand. There is also the
problem of finding suitable local materials. For
example, the local textile industry finds that only
about one-fifth of its needs can be met with local
cotton and the rest must be imported.

But more disquieting is the apparent tendency
for credit sales residcounting to be preempted by
larger and more established industrial units. There
is a real question whether such units should finance
their distribution costs at a subsidized rate of interest and whether their operations would indeed be cur-
tailed or slowed down if this subsidy were unavailable to them. Yet the small manufacturer may either
be unaware of the facility or be reluctant to provide
all the information required for his eligibility.
Most likely, he simply lacks the necessary documen-
tation. There are also reasons to suspect that bankers are much less eager to endorse the promissory
notes of the small firms than they are of the large
industrial units. Yet, as shown later, it is the
small and medium manufacturer who, in Thailand, has

the most acute need for access to finance at reasonable terms.   (See Chapter 7.)

Three Problems

From the preceding discussion of the Bank of
Thailand's rediscounting facilities, three main problem areas seem to emerge. The first of these has to
do with methods, techniques, and procedures governing the administration of the present facilities.
The second area concerns itself with the possibility
of extending the range and scope of rediscounting,
perhaps by offering similar facilities to other segments of the economy. The last problem area pertains
to the allocation of credit by the Bank of Thailand,
to insure that such credit flows to those who need
it most and that it promotes activities which would
not thrive in its absence.

The administration of currently offered facilities could perhaps be improved by making rediscounting truly what the term connotes. That is, the
commercial banks would be responsible for the discounting process and the Bank of Thailand would provide additional resources to the banking system _para
passu_ with the increase in the volume of discounted
paper submitted to it. This implies that the credit
investigations, certification of documents, and other
procedural aspects should be left to the commercial
banks and not be duplicated by the Bank of Thailand.
The central bank should, however, retain the control
over the direction of the subsidized credit by requiring the commercial banks to abide strictly by
eligibility rules. One way to achieve this would be
for the Bank of Thailand to announce that it stands
ready to rediscount eligible paper whenever submitted
by the commercial bank subject to a formal statement
by a responsible official of that commercial bank
that the discounted paper represents eligible transaction. The Bank of Thailand would retain the right
to postaudit and could take legal action in the advent of fraudulent intent. It might be desirable
to amend the legal code to the effect that such a
fraudulent misrepresentation constitutes a felony,
with prison sentences imposable on the responsible

officer of the commercial bank. Making the provision
of credit at favorable terms to selected areas of the
economy truly a rediscounting activity also implies
the abandonment of the quota system and the relaxa-
tion of the rather extreme provision that a commercial bank is ineligible for rediscounting if it ever
made a bad credit appraisal. It would also seem that
to the extent a quota is necessary, given the limited
resources of the Bank of Thailand, it should be related to the composition of a bank's portfolio rather
than to its liquid assets.

Insofar as extending the range and scope of rediscounting is concerned, by far the most promising
is the scheme outlined in Chapter 3 for refinancing
group loans made to farmers for productive purposes.
There is a possibility that rediscounting could be
broadened to include processing of crops destined
for exports, but the matter requires further study.
There is little to recommend the introduction of rediscounting facilities into construction activity.

In order to insure that the credit provided by
the Bank of Thailand flows to those who need it most
and that such credit adds most to total capital formation, the commercial banks could be offered a
greater spread on discounted promissory notes below
a specified face value. Thus, a small manufacturer
would be able to discount a bill for 7 per cent as
at present but his bank could refinance it at 4 per
cent rather than at 5 per cent, provided the total
discounted to one name does not exceed a specified
sum in any one year. The availability of a greater
spread would provide an incentive to the commercial
banks to go after this type of business.

Debt Management

The ostensible reason advanced by the Bank of
Thailand for entering the area of provision of cheap
credit to selected kinds of borrowers is that these
borrowers face high interest rates in the money market, and this puts them at a competitive disadvantage
vis-á-vis their counterparts abroad. There is little
question that the interest rates in Thailand are high,

both in the organized and the unorganized markets.
As is shown in Chapter 7, the modal rate of interest
for bona fide small or medium-size businessmen was,
prior to 1968, in excess of 20 per cent per annum,
with a range from about 6 per cent to over 30 per
cent per annum.* These rates were certainly higher
than those prevailing in the industrialized countries and almost certainly higher than those available to businessmen in most of the countries of Southeast Asia. Yet the subsidized credit provided by
the Bank of Thailand under the various lines of rediscounting goes, in the main, to those who already
appear to have better than average access to relatively cheaper credit in the Thai financial markets. As
argued above, large exporters and large manufacturers
seem to have been the main beneficiaries of rediscount provisions and it is these two groups whose
credit status within the country is appreciably better than that of many others. Moreover, the experience with rediscounting to 1967 hardly justifies the
hope that the provision of limited quantities of
cheap credit to narrowly selected groups will tend
to depress downward the entire interest rate schedule.

      One reason for the persistence of both actual
and potential high interest rates in Thailand in the
face of large resources of the monetary system in
general and the commercial banks in particular must
be sought in the debt management policies pursued by
the country's monetary authorities. On the one hand,
the availability of government securities provides
the commercial banks with attractive outlets for their
idle funds and, on the other, it inhibits their willingness to seek other, untried, and more risky outlets for these funds.[9]

----

      *The sharp world-wide increase in the level of
interest rates which was most pronounced during 1968
and 1969 has shifted upward the entire schedule of
interest rates in Thailand. The discussion in the
text is based on field research completed in 1967.

Table 6.2 gives the holdings of government securities, classified by principal category of holder,
for the period 1956-1967. These securities are of
two types, long-term bonds, maturing in from 8 to
15 years, and short-term bills, whose currency ranges
from 3 to 4 months. As of the end of 1967, holdings
of bonds far outweigh holdings of bills, on which
the volume outstanding steadily decreased from 1959
through 1966.

Government Bonds

Table 6.2 shows that the composition of bond
holders changed considerably over the years. In
1956, nearly 80 per cent of all bonds outstanding
were held by the Bank of Thailand, other banks (commercial banks and the Government Savings Bank) holding less than 10 per cent of the total. By the end
of 1967 the Bank of Thailand held slightly over 20
per cent of the total, commercial banks held nearly
35 per cent, and the Government Savings Bank held
33 per cent of the amount outstanding. The category
of holders designated as "others" (including eleemosy-
nary and similar institutions, private corporations,
insurance companies, and individuals) held the remaining 12 per cent.

The commercial banks find government bonds attractive for a number of reasons. Not only is return
on them riskless, but it is also substantial in terms
of alternatives. While it is true that commercial
banks can charge up to 14 per cent on commercial accommodation, the process of extending loans, assess-
ing the value of the collateral, and so on imposes
operating costs which are probably in excess of those
associated with the acquisition of government bonds.
Bonds are acceptable as collateral against loans
from the Bank of Thailand, against promissory notes
issued for settlement of rice premium, against imports financed by the Agency for International Development (AID), and other obligations, direct or
contingent, of the banks.

By far the most important attraction of government bonds is that they are now the principal asset

TABLE 6.2

Government Internal Securities Outstanding, by Holder, 1956-1967[a]

(million baht)

	Government Bonds and Holders					Treasury Bills and Holders			
Year	Bank of Thailand	Com. Banks	Govt. Savings Bank	Other	Total	Bank of Thailand	Com. Banks	Other	Total
1956	1,636.2	135.3	56.4	230.4	2,058.4	3,132.8	94.1	39.8	3,266.7
1957	1,934.6	149.1	124.5	257.1	2,465.3	2,988.2	79.8	218.7	3,286.7
1958	2,089.8	198.3	168.7	295.0	2,751.8	2,946.6	43.7	276.4	3,266.7
1959	2,041.2	289.5	267.2	374.1	2,972.0	2,973.8	16.1	276.8	3,266.7
1960	2,920.8	394.8	440.2	516.8	4,272.6	2,057.2	23.5	27.0	2,107.7
1961	3,193.8	531.5	646.3	678.3	5,049.9	1,495.9	80.0	31.8	1,607.7
1962	3,328.3	943.8	981.0	816.3	6,029.4	1,377.0	183.6	46.4	1,607.0
1963	3,287.0	1,379.6	1,324.0	978.8	6,969.4	182.2	304.6	163.2	650.0
1964	3,266.5	1,903.8	1,751.6	1,212.3	8,134.2	361.1	262.1	26.8	650.0
1965	3,237.5	2,342.7	2,405.0	1,372.2	9,357.4	452.4	197.0	0.6	650.0
1966	3,063.0	3,728.7	3,456.4	1,583.2	11,831.3	484.2	391.0	4.8	880.0
1967	2,701.8	4,343.5	4,111.8	1,388.4	12,545.5	34.0	514.7	401.3	950.0

aYear end.

Source: Bank of Thailand.

against which the commercial banks can borrow from
the central bank. The terms on which these loans
are extended are quite lenient and insure that the
banks may regard their portfolio of government securities as almost equivalent to cash reserves in
terms of liquidity and much more rewarding than cash
in terms of return. The interest cost of borrowing
from the Bank of Thailand is equal to the bond coupon; but while the interest received on the bond is
tax exempt, the interest payable on the loan can be
deducted from the commercial bank's gross income for
income tax purposes. Interest income on bonds issued
after January 29, 1969 is not tax exempt to the commercial banks. If the commercial banks were allowed
to borrow the full face value against the security
of the bond, they would actually make money in the
process. In fact, however, the banks cannot borrow
more than from 70 to 90 per cent of the face value
of the bond, depending on the length to maturity.

Even so, the net cost of borrowing is minimal.
A loan from the Bank of Thailand may be obtained
either by spot pledging of government securities or
by an advance pledge of such securities. On the date
due (loans are usually made for 90 days) the commercial bank can, if it wishes, settle its debt by disposing of the bond collateral. This is seldom done,
however, inasmuch as few banks either need or are
willing to accept a reduction in interest return.
Most frequently loans are settled, if need be, by
replenishing the bank's account at the Bank of Thailand which is debited on the date the loan is made.

Thus, there is little wonder that commercial
banks continued to purchase large quantities of government bonds, despite the reduction in the coupon
rate in 1965. What needs explaining, however, is the
fact that the amounts borrowed from the Bank of Thailand remained but a minor source of funds to the Thai
commercial banking system, averaging less than 1 per
cent of its liabilities over the 13 years to 1967.
During 1969 the volume of borrowing from the Bank of
Thailand increased substantially due to the high cost
of borrowing from foreign banks.

As shown in Table 6.3, borrowing from the Bank
of Thailand over the period 1957-1967 averaged substantially less than 10 per cent of all borrowings
of commercial banks even though that proportion has
been increasing over the years. At the end of 1967
total loans outstanding of commercial banks, both
local and foreign, operating in Thailand amounted to
3.4 billion baht, of which only 299 million was owed
to the Bank of Thailand.

The acquisition of bonds by commercial banks
was given another fillip in 1965 when the proportion
of government securities allowed to count as reserves
against deposit liabilities was raised from 25 to 60
per cent. Given the attractions of bonds to the commercial banks, there ensued, in 1965 and 1966, a
shift in the assets of the commercial banks from cash
to securities. Thus, at the end of 1965, the ratio
of cash assets to demand deposits stood at 9.74 per
cent. By the end of 1966 it fell to 8.63 per cent.
On the other hand, the ratio of liquid assets (which
differ from cash assets mainly by the inclusion of
government securities) to deposits rose from 25 per
cent at the end of 1965 to 30 per cent at the end
of 1966. Because of the highly seasonal demand for
bank accommodation, the liquidity ratio tends to
vary considerably from month to month. As shown in
Figure 6.1, however, the liquidity of commercial
banks in 1966 was very high throughout the year.[10]

With commercial bank liquidity assured by recourse, if need be, to foreign credit and by the
rapid growth of deposits, particularly time deposits,
the Thai commercial banks increasingly converted
their excess reserves into government securities.
Demand deposits were 6.4 billion baht at the end of
1965 and 7.5 billion at the end of 1966. Time deposits rose in the same period from 6.8 to 9.3 billion baht. As mentioned previously, most of the increase in time deposits was a result of increased
holdings by private residents. By the end of 1965,
the banks' holdings of government securities were
larger than their excess reserves (see Figure 6.2).

Table 6.4 shows that the policy governing distribution and treatment of government bonds (as well

TABLE 6.3

Commercial Banks: Borrowing by Source, 1957–1967[a]

(million baht)

Year	Borrowing by All Banks				Borrowing by Banks Incorporated in Thailand				Borrowing by Banks Incorporated Abroad			
	From Bank of Thailand	From Banks in Thailand	From Banks Abroad	Total	From Bank of Thailand	From Banks in Thailand	From Banks Abroad	Total	From Bank of Thailand	From Banks in Thailand	From Banks Abroad	Total
1957	–	95.1	543.8	638.9	–	91.5	179.5	271.0	–	3.6	364.3	367.9
1958	8.7	100.9	559.9	669.5	8.7	83.8	202.3	294.8	–	17.1	357.6	374.7
1959	41.9	252.9	738.4	1,033.2	40.1	194.8	353.5	588.4	1.8	58.1	384.9	448.8
1960	109.7	202.2	804.9	1,116.8	104.7	166.5	402.1	673.3	5.0	35.7	402.8	443.5
1961	106.3	243.5	1,065.5	1,415.3	103.0	167.1	549.7	819.8	3.3	76.4	515.8	595.5
1962	103.5	293.1	1,429.8	1,826.4	103.5	141.3	949.6	1,194.4	–	151.9	480.1	632.0
1963	98.0	370.2	1,852.3	2,320.5	91.7	136.4	1,373.1	1,601.2	6.3	233.8	479.2	719.3
1964	164.7	326.4	2,383.9	2,875.0	142.6	96.1	1,665.0	1,903.7	22.1	230.3	718.9	971.3
1965	244.4	241.4	2,727.9	3,213.7	218.6	112.5	1,848.6	2,179.7	25.8	128.9	879.3	1,034.0
1966	336.9	198.5	2,889.4	3,428.8	290.5	92.8	2,053.8	2,437.1	46.4	105.7	835.6	987.7
1967	298.5	154.4	2,901.4	3,354.3	272.9	16.2	1,997.7	2,288.8	25.6	138.2	901.7	1,065.5

[a]Year end.

Source: Bank of Thailand.

FIGURE 6.1

Commercial Banks: Ratio of Liquid Assets to Deposits, 1962-1966

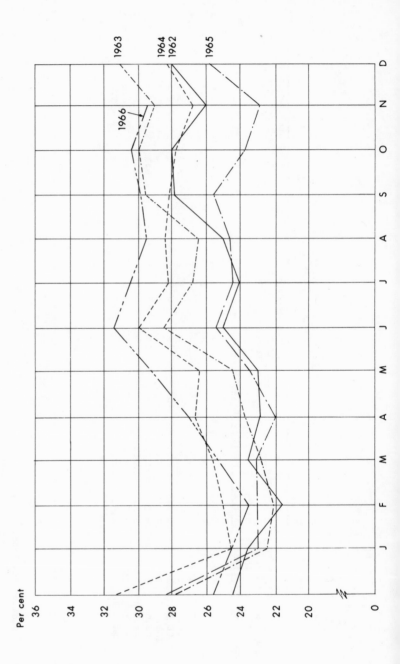

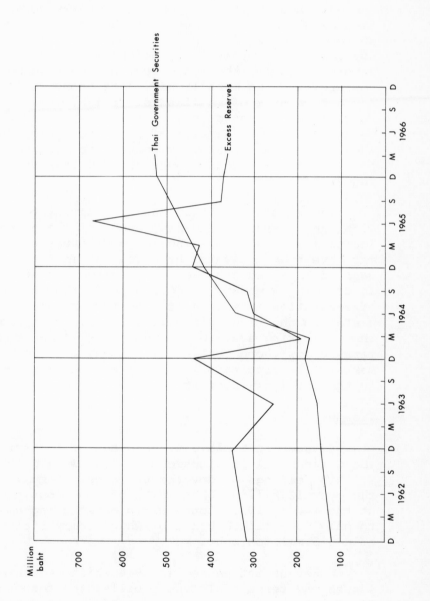

FIGURE 6.2

Commercial Banks: Holdings of Government Securities and Excess Reserves, 1962-1966

as Treasury bills) was not determined by budgetary
needs. Issues of government bonds have been, in
recent years, substantially in excess of deficits
and have been mainly responsible for the accumulation of large cash balances at the Treasury account.
Whatever the exact reasons for making available to
the commercial banks large blocks of bonds at very
favorable terms, the net effect has been to make the
commercial banks more liquid, less economically dependent on Bank of Thailand direction, less anxious
to compete for customers, less likely to reduce interest charges as a means of securing employment of
their idle funds, and more content to continue business as usual instead of seeking new uses for their
funds.

The Bank of Thailand has, of course, to contend
with many pressures and many needs of the economy.
The policy of accumulating large Treasury balances
may have been motivated by a fear of inflation. The
Bank of Thailand has been interested, for some time,
in creating a money market and feels that issuance
of securities in excess of budgetary requirements is
a step in the right direction. Also, it may feel
that by making available bonds and bills at coupon
rates below those obtainable in many parts of the
market, it helps to bring about a general reduction
in the level of interest rates.

Treasury Bills

As seen in Table 6.2, holdings of Treasury bills
among financial institutions in 1967 were much smaller than holdings of government bonds. Compared with
the over 12 billion baht worth of bonds outstanding
at the end of 1967, total bills outstanding amounted
to only 950 million baht, of which commercial banks
held 515 million baht.

Under an act passed in 1944 which regulates the
issues and terms of Treasury bills, the responsibility for their management is vested in the Ministry
of Finance. In practice, however, the management of
bills is now in the hands of the Bank of Thailand.
In fact, until about 1960, the bank was almost the

TABLE 6.4

Government Deficits, Borrowing, and Treasury Balances,
1962-1967[a]
(million baht)

Item	Amount					
	1962	1963	1964	1965	1966	1967
Treasury cash deficit	-1	-358	-555	-240	-668	-1,478
Sale of bonds	576	900	905	1,195	2,302	1,632
Sale of bills	-123	277	-699	-51	145	100
Coin issues	14	48	67	91	77	54
Change of treasury balance	466	867	-282	995	1,856	308
Treasury balance, end of year	1,871	2,738	2,456	3,451	5,307	5,615

[a]Fiscal year.

Source: Bank of Thailand.

sole purchaser of the bills from the Treasury, and
the proceeds of these sales were credited to the
Treasury account to finance operating needs of the
government. The rate of return offered on these
bills, together with other terms of issue, were not
sufficiently attractive to attract other buyers;
the chief holder in the "other" category is the Government Savings Bank. At the outset, when the bills
were first issued by the Ministry of Finance, they
did attract a number of commercial banks as well as
the Government Savings Bank. But the Bank of Thailand, by bidding close to the fixed price, managed
to depress the yield below 1 per cent per annum and
became, after 1947, the sole buyer of bills. After
1948 the yield on the bills continued to increase
but the return on bonds increased even faster, rising
to 8 per cent in 1955. Moreover, until about 1960,
there were no provisions for reselling the bills before maturity. It was not until 1960 that the Bank
of Thailand succeeded in convincing the Ministry of
Finance that it should increase the maximum rate of
interest paid on Treasury bills from 3.0 to 4.5 per
cent and permit their issue on tap as well as on
tender. The Bank of Thailand stood ready to sell
bills from its own portfolio to commercial banks and
others with an option to buy them back before maturity at a penalty rate of one-fourth of 1 per cent.

Parallel to the development of a secondary
market in Treasury bills, the volume of outstanding
bills has gradually been reduced, and the emphasis
in Treasury bill policy has shifted from that of financing government to that of developing a money
market.

Table 6.5 shows the main features of Treasury
bills. The amount of bills outstanding was reduced
from over 3 billion baht in 1959 to about half that
amount in 1961 and to 950 million in 1967.

The maximum rate payable on 90-day Treasury
bills was further increased to 5 per cent in 1961,
leading to increasingly large purchases of bills by
the commercial banks. In 1965, however, the coupon
was reduced to 4.5 per cent. The penalty rate for

TABLE 6.5

Treasury Bills, Selected Characteristics,
1956-1967

(million baht)

Year	Amount Issued	Terms (months)	Average Interest (discount)	Amount Sold	Amount Redeemed	Amount Outstanding
1956	9,801	4	2,260	9,801	9,801	3,267
1957	9,855	4	2,279	9,835	9,835	3,287
1958	9,800	4	2,923	9,800	9,820	3,267
1959	9,853	4	2,990	9,853	9,853	3,267
1960	8,653	3	3,077	8,653	9,812	2,107
1961	4,953	3	4,647	4,953	5,453	1,608
1962	4,493	3	4,978	4,493	4,494	1,607
1963	3,749	3	4,980	3,749	4,706	650
1964	2,900	3	4,994	2,900	2,706	650
1965	3,150	3	4,461	3,150	3,150	650
1966	4,650	2	3,900	4,650	4,450	850
1967	4,750	2	4,042	4,750	4,650	950

Source: Bank of Thailand.

repurchase of bills by the Bank of Thailand was reduced from one-fourth to one-eighth of 1 per cent.
In 1966, the coupon was further reduced to 4 per
cent, the currency of the bills was limited to 60
days and, as a partial compensation, the penalty
rate was cut to one-twelfth of 1 per cent. In 1969
the ceiling on the yield from Treasury bills was
raised to 7 per cent.

In recent years the monetary authorities have
attempted to reduce the proportion of bills bought
on tap in favor of direct tender from the Treasury.
The schedule of maturity dates, penalty rates, and
repurchase prices were so arranged as to provide in-
ducement for holding bills longer and, in consequence,
to buy them on tender basis. The schedule at the end
of 1967 was as follows:

Length of Maturity	Yield	Repurchasing Rate
1-15 days	2.50%	2.63%
16-30 days	3.05%	3.13%
31-45 days	3.34%	3.25%
46-60 days	3.60%	3.88%

These attempts met with some measure of success, as
shown in Table 6.6.

It would seem that the entire policy regarding
Treasury bills has not, as yet, been clarified. There
appears to be some confusion regarding objectives,
methods, and goals. In particular, three aspects of
this policy are, prima facie, inconsistent with the
avowed objectives. In the first place, there seems
to be little justification for reducing the Treasury
bills outstanding to the current low level. Treasury
bills are generally a cheaper means of financing government needs than bonds and, to the extent that borrowing has to be resorted to, reliance on long-term
securities increases the budgetary cost of internal
debt.

In the second place, to the extent that issuance
of bills is motivated by the desire to develop a money

TABLE 6.6

Commercial Banks: Purchases of Treasury Bills, 1960-1967
(value in million baht)

Year	Purchases by Tender		Purchases from Bank of Thailand		Total Purchases	
	Value	% of Total	Value	% of Total	Value	% of Total
1960	13.0	3.8	329.0	96.20	342.0	100
1961	40.0	2.96	1,300.3	97.04	1,340.3	100
1962	125.0	3.51	3,434.2	96.49	3,559.2	100
1963	310.0	8.26	3,442.2	91.74	3,752.2	100
1964	555.2	18.01	2,527.4	81.99	3,082.6	100
1965	724.0	26.67	1,990.3	73.33	2,714.3	100
1966	1,918.0	42.89	2,554.2	57.11	4,472.2	100
1967	1,486.0	36.46	2,589.4	63.54	4,075.4	100

Source: Bank of Thailand.

market in Thailand, over and above budgetary needs,
it is difficult to understand why sales by tender
should be emphasized and encouraged. In a truly competitive market with many buyers of different types
and with many alternative outlets available, tender
bills could be said to reflect market forces. It is
doubtful if this is true in Thailand, where the
ceiling on all bills is set by the Minister of Finance. The tap market at the Bank of Thailand provides a secondary market which the commercial banks
find very useful because it enables them to select
the maturities they need on a day-to-day basis.

Finally, the over-all reduction of interest
yield and reduction of maturities appears inconsistent with specific steps to encourage banks to hold on
to the bills for longer periods so as to receive a
higher yield. In any event, so long as these banks
continue to be very liquid, Treasury bills will play
on a marginal role in their portfolios.

This discussion of debt management as implemented by the Bank of Thailand brings out two factors
which tend to inhibit its ability to direct a greater
volume of savings into developmental channels. The
first of these factors is the existence of only one
type of long-term government security and the second
factor, related to the first, is the absence of any
intermediate-term issues. At present there is nothing available in the market between the 60-day Treasury bill and the eight-year government bond. There
appears to be a clear need for two sets of measures.
One of these sets would attempt to tailor the long-
term government bonds to the different markets. Thus,
for example, the tax exemption feature, while important to the private individual, is of no significance
to a charitable institution. To some segments of the
market the length of the bond to maturity may be more
significant than its coupon. Others would perhaps
be willing to accept a lower rate of interest in exchange for more immediate redeemability.

As things stand at present, to sell a given volume of bonds the monetary authorities are compelled
to offer terms and conditions acceptable to the most

reluctant buyer. There is little doubt that tailoring of bond issues to different markets in terms of
yield, maturity, tax status, and other variables
would not only be more efficient but would also lower their total cost to the Thai government.

But tailoring of bond issues can achieve an effect which is more important than that of efficiency
or lower budgetary costs. Throughout the discussion
much stress has been put on the fact that the availability of high-yielding, tax-exempt government bonds
was instrumental in the apparent reluctance of commercial banks to aggressively seek out additional
business other than that of the financing of trade.
There is thus the possibility that a bond could be
issued, to be sold only to the commercial banks,
which would both insure their liquidity and also provide them with a somewhat greater incentive to compete for additional business. It is difficult to
suggest the specific types of bonds which would
achieve these ends, but the range of possibilities
is rather wide. Two approaches suggest themselves.
One approach would, say, reduce the coupon rate significantly, but keep it above the yield on Treasury
bills. Other attractions of government bonds would
be retained and, if need be, an instant redemption
feature, at par, would be added. The second approach
would provide that additional purchases of bonds
could not be counted as part of the legal reserves,
or could be so counted only to a very limited extent.
In deciding on a specific type of bond it is important to bear in mind the welfare and stability of the
commercial banks and their real need for liquidity
and reasonable profits.

During 1969 the Bank of Thailand took a number
of steps which parallel these suggestions. For example, new issues of government bonds were divided
into those which could and those which could not be
sold back to the Bank of Thailand. Bond interest exemption from tax was removed in the case of corporate
buyers and the yield on Treasury bills was increased.

The adoption of various types of bonds to different segments of the market is closely related to the

the need to provide for an intermediate type of security, say of from one to three years currency. In
fact a three-year, instantly redeemable, 6 per cent
bond may be the type of security which could be re-
served for commercial banks only. Yet other intermediate bonds could have special features which would
make them potentially effective vehicles of developmental finance. Among these are convertibility features. Thus a bond could be convertible into shares
of other undertakings, whether public or private.
Such a bond need not, of course, be of any specific
currency, but it would appear that in Thailand convertible features could well be appended an an
intermediate-term bond.[11]

CENTRAL BANKING AND THE FINANCIAL NEXUS

The effectiveness of central banking operations
in directing the flow of savings and investment into
developmental channels depends on the central bank's
willingness and ability to pursue a growth-oriented
policy. As mentioned previously, throughout most of
its existence the Bank of Thailand has been preoccu-
pied with maintaining the external and internal value
of the baht, and only recently has its leadership
become concerned with economic growth.[12] While its
willingness to channel resources into growth-oriented
activities can be said to have increased somewhat,
its power to do so effectively is yet to be examined.
Willingness and power are, of course, intertwined.
The cognizance of the limits if power affects the
willingness to undertake certain actions. This, in
turn, inhibits the use of power. The reluctance of
the Bank of Thailand to use certain powers formally
vested in it can be traced not so much to its unwillingness to use them as to the recognition that these
formal powers are not always tantamount to real power.

In this section, two aspects of the willingness
and the ability of the central bank to influence the
direction of economic activity are discussed. The
first is central bank relations with commercial banks
and other institutions. The second, more speculative,
is the direction which Bank of Thailand activities

should take, given certain assumptions regarding the
optimal strategy for Thailand's development.

Relations with Financial Institutions

The commercial banks are by far the predominating financial intermediaries on the Thai scene. Their
relations with the central bank are manifold and occasionally complex. Some of these relationships
arose out of the powers and obligations of the Commercial Banking Act of 1962 and subsequent amendments
by the Minister of Finance. Other relationships are
those which, although enabled by pertinent legislation, were more fully developed under various administrative notices and provisions of the bank. Finally,
there are those operations of the bank which affect
the activities of the commercial banks but which have
already been discussed, either in this chapter or in
Chapter 4. Again, it should be noted that many of
the activities of the Bank of Thailand which affect
the commercial banks stem from the powers and obligations formally vested in the Minister of Finance.

For purposes of this discussion the significant
relations with the commercial banks are those which
deal with the ability of the Bank of Thailand to control the behavior of these banks, in general, and
their lending policies, in particular.

Three types of controls can usefully be distinguished. The first set of control instruments
derives from statutory or administrative enactments
but is largely useless. Either these controls are
not implemented or they are not effective. The formal powers from which these control instruments derive are not invoked for a variety of reasons or, in
those rare cases when they are invoked, they are
either bypassed or not pressed with sufficient vigor.

The second set of controls over the behavior of
commercial banks is also based on formal powers, but
these powers are rooted in economic and/or political
realities. The Bank of Thailand can exert some influence over commercial bank portfolios and policies to
the extent that it pushes these instruments vigorously.

Finally, there are those instruments of control which are rooted less in formal powers of the Bank of Thailand than in its standing, integrity, and prestige. It is at least arguable that changes in commercial banking operations have been brought about more by moral suasion than by the exercise of legal powers by the Bank of Thailand.

The formal powers at the disposal of the Bank of Thailand include the power to set maximum interest rates on various types of accommodation, to vary reserve requirements within rather wide margins, to limit the ratio of risk assets to capital, to prescribe the ratios of specified assets to capital, to regulate the proportion of loans to one name, to examine the books of the banks, and many others. (Some of these powers are discussed below; see also Chapter 4.) Many of these provisions, however, remain in abeyance. Thus, even though the Bank of Thailand can set the ratio of cash assets to deposits at a rate as high as 50 per cent, the ratio remained constant at 6 per cent up to the end of 1968. There are many reasons for the reluctance to use these rather standard control instruments, but some of the more telling ones are quite clear. Given the great liquidity of the commercial banking system as a whole, a very sharp increase in the reserve ratio would be needed to put the commercial institutions at the Bank. But such a sharp increase would affect the commercial banks quite unevenly, the smaller banks probably no longer being able to operate. Yet some of the smaller and relatively less liquid banks need to be protected, not only because some of them wield considerable political power, but also because it would be both unfair and unwise to press their backs to the wall. Should it prove politically feasible, the change in reserve requirements could be brought about gradually over a period of time, as has been done in Hong Kong and the Philippines. Such a gradual change may be considered in implementing the scheme for bringing banks into the agricultural credit field spelled out in Chapter 3.[13]

Less clear are the reasons for not exercising some of the other statutory powers which, in principle

at least, could quite considerably affect commercial
bank behavior. Among these are the powers to prescribe the proportion of selected assets to capital
and the maximum proportion of capital which can be
lent to one name. The Bank of Thailand also has the
power of counting unused portions of overdrafts as
deposits. The exercise of this power, however, is
subject to the limitations mentioned in the preceding
paragraph. The power to vary the ratio of assets to
capital has been exercised only negatively by excluding certain assets from the definition of risk assets.

Inasmuch as capital resources of Thai commercial
banks are more of a constraint on their liquidity
than liquid assets, the regulation of commercial bank
behavior via selective control of assets would appear
feasible. In particular, the Bank of Thailand could,
in principle, direct lending activities of the commercial banks into certain directions merely by posting a requisite ratio of a specified asset to total
capital resources. But such forcible direction would
cause more problems than it would solve. Suppose,
for example, that the Bank of Thailand required commercial banks to increase their loans to manufacturers to a much higher proportion of capital than at
present. Without proper safeguards on both sides of
this particular market for lendable funds, and without rather basic changes in the entire credit structure, such requirements could not be implemented or
enforced. The language of the 1962 act is not clear
as to whether the various ratios must apply equally
to all banks or whether the Bank of Thailand may discriminate among banks. It is understood, however,
that these ratios are equally binding on all banks
operating in Thailand.

A bank examination, which is routinely performed
by the Bank of Thailand, is, even when competently
done, a negative instrument of control at best. Certain glaring abuses can be avoided or rectified, but
examination of the books, per se, can do little to
channel bank lending in desired directions. Moreover,
it is very difficult to obtain any information regarding the number of abuses found, their frequency and
distribution among banks, remedial action taken, and

so on. The Bank of Thailand must protect the confidential relationship it enjoys with the commercial
banks, and it would perhaps be improper for it to
divulge to an outsider any more than can be gleaned
from Table 6.7.

TABLE 6.7

Bank of Thailand Operations: Number of
Commercial Bank Examinations, 1962-1967

Commercial Bank Office Examined	1962	1963	1964	1965	1966	1967
Head office	3	4	23	7	16	14
Bangkok branches	12	9	35	78	39	58
Provincial branches	20	130	21	136	98	107
Total	35	143	79	221	153	201

Source: Bank of Thailand.

The purpose of a bank examination is twofold. On the
one hand, it is to insure that the commercial bank
will remain solvent and, on the other, it is to exact compliance with the numerous provisions regarding
lending to directors, purchases of certain assets,
and engaging in certain transactions. When solvency
is in question, the bank, in principle, can be forced
into liquidation. Contraventions of existing rules
may result in up to one year's imprisonment and fines
of up to 20,000 baht.

    The Bank of Thailand does have the power to set
maximum rates on different types of deposit liabilities and on different kinds of loans of the commercial banks. This is an area where the Bank of Thailand
was and is active, but its ability to set effective
ceilings on interest rates is, in some instances, bypassed by the devices employed by certain banks to
exact higher interest rates on loans and/or to pay
higher than the official rates on deposits.[14]

It would thus seem that the formidable arsenal
of control weapons available to the Bank of Thailand
under legislative enactments is seldom used, or used
rather haltingly. The reasons for this are both
economic and political. The economic reasons have
to do with commercial bank liquidity which, however,
is unevenly distributed among the individual banks.[15]
The political reasons have to do with the considerable
political muscle at the disposal of many of the commercial banks incorporated in Thailand. It is a rare
bank which does not have on its board a field marshal,
a general, or a high police officer.[16] Many Thai
banks have close ties with high civil servants, members of the ruling families, or both. No matter how
intrepid the leadership of the Bank of Thailand may
wish to be, it must reckon with political realities.[17]

But the Bank of Thailand does employ control instruments which enable it to affect the flow of funds
through the commercial banks and, hence, the economic
behavior of these banks. Perhaps the most important
of these are related to rediscounting activities and
to granting of permits for new branches. (See Chapter
5.) As mentioned earlier, the bank seems to have a
good deal of discretion in allowing rediscount facilities and there is no reason why elements of these
discretionary powers should not be employed to achieve
certain desired, albeit limited, objectives. The objectives must be limited so long as total volume of
rediscounting remains low relative to the volume of
commercial bank's operations.

The possibility of utilizing the right to grant
permission to commercial banks to open new branches
as a control instrument has already been discussed
(see Chapter 5). Again, its scope can only be a limited one. Perhaps the best way to achieve desired
changes in commercial bank policies would be to com-
bine potentially effective but politically awkward
control instruments with economic benefits which would
accrue to the banks once they adhere to the policy
change. This, of course, is the essence of the
"carrot and stick" approach to the provision of agricultural credit by commercial banks suggested in
Chapter 3.

It may be a truism to say that among the controls available to the Bank of Thailand, the ones
that have the best chance of influencing the policies
of commercial banks are those which promise them direct or indirect benefits. Whenever the aims of the
economy, as interpreted by the Bank of Thailand, coincide with or can be made compatible with those of
the commercial banks, the control instruments can be
made to work. When there is little overlap of economic benefit or a direct conflict emerges, the implementation of legal powers of the Bank of Thailand
will have to contend with the political realities.
Thus, the commercial banks are anxious to have new
branches, and they might be willing to abide to a
limited extent by Bank of Thailand direction in order
to get these branches. On the other hand, they will
resist a straight increase in the cash-deposit ratio
or the substitution of other assets for government
securities in their legal reserves. The Bank of
Thailand, hemmed in as it is by economic and political limitations which restrict its ability to direct
the policies of the commercial banks, is not entirely
without resources. To date, its greatest success in
influencing the behavior of the commercial banks has
derived from moral suasion; i.e., in utilizing its
great prestige in the community to bring about certain changes in commercial bank policies. Moral
suasion takes time to make itself felt, and it is not
always easy to relate the cause and the effect; but
there is little question that the general improvement
in banking practices and the reduction in frequency
of the grosser abuses owes a good deal to the per-
sistent prodding and cajoling of the Bank of Thailand.

In at least one case, that of the reduction of
maximum lending rates in 1966, the tie-in between
moral suasion and acceptance by the banking community
was a direct one. The Bank of Thailand supplements
its moral suasion effort by a range of services to
the banking community which tend to make commercial
banking more professional and more responsible. Among
these should be listed the central clearing of checks,
the central register of credit information (confidential information on individuals who owe in excess of
500,000 baht to more than one bank), statistical and
analytical services.

The prestige of the Bank of Thailand is based, first of all, on the skills and integrity of its governors. The bank has been fortunate in that the persons chosen to lead its affairs have been men of unquestioned probity, whose financial acumen and experience have been widely respected. The bank has also been able to retain a measure of independence, both political and administrative, which has stood it in good stead. The Minister of Finance cannot issue orders to the Governor, and his supervisory sanction can, ultimately, take only the form of removal of the Bank of Thailand's directors, a very drastic step indeed. Unlike most civil servants, directors of the bank are personally liable for any losses of the bank's funds which can be traced back to willful negligence on their part. This unusual provision gives the directors some measure of political status. The fact that the Bank of Thailand is outside civil service rules enables it to recruit and retain superior staffs.

The moral suasion of the bank is exerted in a variety of ways. One of the most popular ones is through the speeches of the Governor and other bank officials given at formal occasions. These speeches are widely reported in the press and are frequently reprinted and published.

Membership in the IMF and in the World Bank is said to give a good deal of weight to the pronouncements of the high officers of the Bank of Thailand. The bank is the primary point of contact for the missions of the IMF and its regular annual consultations.

Apart from its close cooperation with the Treasury, the Bank of Thailand has very few transactions with other financial intermediaries operating in the Thai financial nexus. This itself is symptomatic of the past preoccupation of the Bank of Thailand with the control of money supply and with financing government. Only very recently did the bank begin to concern itself with provision of credit to institutions other than the commercial banks. Its assistance to the newly created Bank for Agriculture and Agricultural Cooperatives and to the Industrial Finance Corporation of Thailand has already been mentioned. There are, as yet, no direct financial dealings between the Bank of Thailand and life insurance companies, provident and pension funds, mutual funds, and other institutions of the fledgling capital market. As suggested above, the absence of direct financial dealings does not preclude the bank from being involved in discussions, debates, and deliberations affecting a number of financial institutions. In fact, the officers and staff of the bank play an important part on many official and unofficial committees concerned with development.

Central Banking in the Development Process

The preceding section described in some detail the means at the disposal of the Bank of Thailand for influencing the direction of economic activity, primarily via the commercial banks.* But in order for the Bank of Thailand to channel resources into developmental needs intelligently, it must know what these needs are, what their ordering relation is, and what kind of policy can be expected to bring the desired directional change.

In Chapter 1 it was suggested that one area where there is presumed need to increase the flow of finance, both absolutely and relative to other segments of the economy, is small and medium-scale manufacturing primarily for export markets. So far, little has been done to stimulate the export-promotion type of manufacturing which, in Thailand, appears to possess a comparative cost advantage (i.e., seafood processing and packaging, fruit canning, teak

---

*Bank of Thailand operations do affect households' decisions to save, both directly and indirectly. The direct effects flow from the offerings of government bonds, and the indirect effects from the terms at which the commercial banks accept deposits. As yet, there are not sufficient data available to permit any conclusions, let alone suggestions, with respect to the impact of the Bank of Thailand on household savings, their level, composition, and form.

manufacture, and others). The experience of Taiwan is instructive in this connection. In 1965 Taiwan did not export canned asparagus at all. Three years later it sold $11 million worth abroad. Exports of canned mushrooms rose from nothing in 1951 to $32 million in 1966. Exports of canned pineapple increased from less than $2 million in 1958 to $20 million in 1969. At present Taiwan is the world's largest exporter of canned pineapples and mushrooms, and second largest in asparagus.[18]

A part of the blame for the state of affairs in export-promotion manufacturing must be put on the existing financial structure, which has mirrored the country's economic development and which has helped Thailand achieve its remarkable growth record to date. If it is true, however, that the continuing growth of the Thai economy will hinge on its ability to develop export-promotion manufacturing capacity, then it behooves the Bank of Thailand to redirect the activities of the financial markets away from their emphasis on foreign trade toward the financing of nascent processing industry based on local resources.

While the emphasis on exports and imports is primarily responsible for the dearth of institutions and instruments for financing locally based manufactures, the heavy reliance on unorganized financial markets for the provision of capital to medium-scale and small manufacturers must also bear a part of the responsibility. (For evidence, see Chapter 7.) Hence, it would seem that the Bank of Thailand should promote the development of capital market institutions and instruments capable of providing finance to fledgling Thai industrialists rather than further enhance the ease and convenience of foreign trade financing. Thus, for example, the current policy of providing encouragement to manufacturers using local raw materials is consistent with that objective.[19]

On the other hand, the exclusion of much foreign trade paper from the definition of risk assets tends to make that form of activity even more attractive to the commercial banks. It will be recalled that even though the commercial banks charge

lower interest rates to exporters and importers than
to manufacturers, especially small and medium manufacturers, foreign trade financing is very profitable.
In addition to the interest charges, the banks collect fees for a variety of documents, commissions on
exchange transactions, and other charges.

In 1967, over 47 per cent of commercial bank
loans went to finance domestic and foreign trade and
only 16 per cent to manufacturing, much of it to rice
milling, which accounts for about a third of value
added in manufacturing.

As should be clear from the preceding discussion, the ability of the central bank to channel
economic activities in directions conducive to economic growth will remain limited by the extent of its
economic and political sway over financial institutions. Yet within these constraints a number of
things can and should be done. Some have been suggested in the preceding pages. Other suggestions
will be made in Chapter 9. The bank is, of course,
aware of some of these possibilities; witness its
interest in some of the capital market institutions,
its participation in official committess on financial
institutions, its advisory functions in the prepara-
tion of the five-year plan, and its cooperation with
other bodies concerned with Thai economic growth.[20]

NOTES

1. See Rak Chareonaksorn, "Control of Commercial Banks in Thailand" (Unpublished Master's thesis,
Chulalongkorn University, 1966).

2. The quotation is from the memoirs of H. H.
Prince Viwat Viwar Chai, first Governor of the Bank
of Thailand, in Memorial to Prince Viwat Viwar Chai
(Bangkok: Bank of Thailand, 1961); for events leading to the establishment of the Bank of Thailand,
this is one of the primary sources (in Thai). For
other sources see James C. Ingram, Economic Change in
Thailand Since 1850 (Stanford: Stanford University
Press, 1955), especially pp. 17ff; Paul Sithi-Amnuai,

Finance and Banking in Thailand: A Study of The
Commercial System 1888-1963 (Bangkok: Thai Watana
Panich, 1964), Chapter 3; Ravi Amatayakul and
S. R. A. Pandit, "Financial Institutions in Thai-
land," IMF Staff Papers (December, 1966); and S. Y.
Lee, "Currency, Banking and Foreign Exchange of
Thailand," Far Eastern Economic Review (October,
1960).

3.   "The chief aim of monetary policy has been
to safeguard the international position of the baht
and the government seems to have put this aim above
such national interests as economic development and
stability of prices and income": Ingram, op. cit.,
p. 17.

4.   See T. H. Silcock, "Thai Money: Review
Article," Malayan Economic Review (April, 1966).

5.   All statistical data in this chapter were
obtained from the Bank of Thailand, either directly
from published sources or through the courtesy of
responsible officials.

6.   See Andre Mousny, The Economy of Thailand
(Bangkok: Social Science Council, 1964) for details.

7.   I am indebted to Professor Edward Shaw for
bringing this to my attention. On the other hand,
the existence of large foreign exchange reserves has
played an important part in attracting foreign capital to Thailand and in enhancing the confidence in
the economy of other foreign and local investors.

8.   See Robert Muscat, Thailand, A Strategy for
Development (New York: Frederick A. Praeger, Inc.,
1965), pp. 29ff.

9.   For a discussion of the circumstances and
conditions under which commercial bankers will compete for business by lowering the interest rate
charged, see Marshall Freimer and Myron J. Gordon,
"Why Bankers Ration Credit," Quarterly Journal of
Economics (August, 1965), especially p. 416.

10.　See Bank of Thailand, Monthly Report (June, 1965), p. 7.

11.　See Robert F. Emery, "The Successful Development of the Philippine Treasury Bill Market" (Board of Governors of the Federal Reserve System, March, 1967).　(Mimeo.)

12.　"There is considerable doubt whether macroeconomic factors related to the money supply as a whole are as important for growth as redirection of the energies of the financial institutions into growth-promoting activities": T. H. Silcock, ed., Thailand--Social and Economic Studies in Development (Durham:　Duke University Press, 1967), p. 197.

13.　I am indebted to Robert Emery of the Board of Governors of the Federal Reserve System for bringing the Hong Kong and Philippine experience to my attention.

14.　Concern with this situation is reflected in numerous speeches made by the Bank of Thailand Governor; see Puey Ungphakorn, Speeches, Articles, and Addresses (Bangkok:　Bank of Thailand, 1964).

15.　On the economic limitations of central bank power under conditions resembling those of Thailand, see R. S. Sayers, Modern Banking (London: Clarendon Press, 1951), especially pp. 282ff.

16.　In April 1966 three field marshals were on the boards of ten banks.　Four army generals served on the boards of fifteen banks.　An army lieutenant-general was a board member of three banks.　An air marshal was on the boards of three banks and three police generals served as board members of seven banks. Apart from the special case of the Thai Military Bank, one commercial bank counted among its board members three army generals, a lieutenant-general, and a police general.

17.　For a discussion of the political powers of Thai commercial banks and of the political constraints within which the Bank of Thailand operates,

see T. H. Silcock, "Money and Banking," in Thailand:
Social and Economic Studies in Development, op. cit.,
pp. 182-185.

18.   See "Taiwan's Food Industry and IFC Economic Importance," Industry of Free China, XXXII,
3 (Taipei: C.I.E.C.D., September, 1969).

19.   According to Muscat, among the obstacles
to industrialization are "no commercial bank interest in financing industrial investment, absence of
capital market or the suitable instruments for mobilizing savings and channeling them into the hands
of entrepreneurs looking for capital availability of
industrial credit where it can be obtained only at
very onerous interest rates and for short periods":
Thailand, A Strategy for Development, op. cit., p.
208.

20.   See Puey Ungphakorn, op. cit., pp. 82-84.

CHAPTER **7** FINANCING URBAN
BUSINESS ENTERPRISE

It was shown in Chapter 2 that much of the
financial resources required to start or operate a
business in Thailand comes from outside the organized
institutions of the money and capital markets. (For
information regarding the organized institutions of
the capital market, see Chapter 8.) The sources and
uses of funds emanating from the unorganized markets
and financing agriculture were discussed in Chapter
3. In this chapter the nature and extent of the
unorganized markets in financing "urban," or nonagri-
cultural, enterprise will be examined.

Strictly speaking, it is probably true that the
ultimate financing of capital formation is done chiefly via the organized financial markets. Probably no
more than a fifth of aggregate capital formation is
financed through the activities of the unorganized
sector. But the importance of unorganized markets
extends beyond that suggested by this modest proportion. For example, an importer who obtains resources
from abroad through the use of banking channels may
dispose of a portion of these resources through unorganized markets. Other inputs from abroad may be
acquired by financial techniques outside any commercial banking connection. The farmer who uses a cooperative loan to buy fertilizer, for example, may
have to borrow from a moneylender for his living expenses when the payment falls due. Much of the business funds eventually channeled through organized
financial institutions may have been acquired from
unorganized markets. In any event, the bulk of the
financial transactions affecting business enterprise
flow through the unorganized markets.

NATURE AND SCOPE OF UNORGANIZED MARKETS

Because of the nature of unorganized financial markets, their amorphous structure, their often clandestine operations and high degree of fragmentation, it is neither possible nor desirable to provide a rigorous definition of their extent and scope.

The approach adopted here is to examine the existing links between savers and investors and to group these institutionalized and/or informal links into two separate if not always very distinct categories, i.e., organized and unorganized markets. In some cases no neat distinction pertaining to an entire link can be made. Thus, commercial banks are organized links between savers (depositors) and investors (borrowers). But there are cases where a prospective borrower needs the intermediary of a somewhat shadowy figure to obtain the bank loan. The shadowy aspect of the link belongs to the unorganized markets.

The criterion employed in deciding whether a given arrangement falls into one or another category is whether it is actually or potentially amenable to control and direction by developmental authority. For example, at present no Thai developmental authority exerts any supervision or control over the Bangkok Stock Exchange. But because the exchange has made its records and so on available to the public, and the existing legal framework provides for a measure of control to be exercised by the Bank of Thailand, for example, the operations on the Bangkok Stock Exchange would be classed as those of the organized financial markets. (See Chapter 8.)

Similarly, while the Ministry of Finance and the Bank of Thailand have control powers over the commercial banks, banks which certainly make their official records available to the public, so far little of this existing power of scrutiny and control has been used for strictly developmental ends. In the case of commercial banks, however, both the power and the awareness of the need to orient their operations to societal development goals exist; therefore, their operations fall clearly into the organized financial markets category. (See Chapters 4 and 6.)

One can envisage an almost infinite range of relationships linking the saver to the ultimate investor. It would be almost impossible to describe these links in all their ramifications and complexities. Instead, only a simplified outline will be given below, and the number of links will be confined to those which appear to be significant in present-day Thailand.*

The most common type of relationship between the saver and the investor is one in which they are one and the same person. But because this type of relationship does not involve going through a financial market and because there is no "link," properly speaking, between the saver and the investor, it will not be discussed here.

Much of the financing of investment is of a direct type. The simplest link exists between the saver and the borrower who maintain face-to-face contact without any intermediary. The saver acquires an asset which is at the same time a liability of the investor, and the exchange of claims takes place directly between the parties concerned.

A farmer who borrows from the village moneylender or the businessman who obtains funds from a friend or relative engages in direct financing of this type. The assets and liabilities exchanged need not be formal instruments, nor does the contract need to be an explicit one. Indeed, in most financing of this type, especially in the less developed countries,

---

*The discussion is based on numerous conversations held with bankers, moneylenders, compradores, businessmen, government officials, and many others, as well as on personal observations and contacts made during two years of field work in Thailand.

the respective claims of the parties tend to be customary and implicit rather than formalized and explicit. It is not unusual, for example, for a small
shopkeeper to obtain funds from a kinship or ethnic
group against only vaguely defined liability in terms
of the rate of return, the currency of the loan, the
collateral, and so forth. A farmer who obtains seed
on credit from the village shopkeeper may be under
no obligation to the lender other than that of selling him his crop at the time of the harvest.

This simplest of all links between the saver
and the investor is entirely within the unorganized
financial sector. No institution participates in the
dealings between the parties, and no regulations of
the state are abiding. It is difficult to conceive
of a mechanism of supervision and control of this
type of direct financing. Strictly speaking, the
statutes are full of regulations purporting to set
maximum interest rates, prescribing and proscribing
moneylenders, and so on. But these are unenforce-
able and unenforced.

Direct financing is, of course, important even
in highly developed countries, and even in highly
developed countries much of it takes place outside
the orbit of official control and scrutiny. There
is little doubt that in the less developed countries
such financing is both relatively more significant
and also less conducive to economic growth. This
is true for at least two reasons. First, the claims
exchanged between the saver and the investor tend,
in the more developed countries, to be more formal
and, hence, less liable to abuse. They are more
amenable to legal and other redress. Second, for
many of these claims there exist secondary markets
which have many of the characteristics of the organized markets. Presumably, these secondary markets
actually or potentially influence the nature of the
primary direct transactions. Thus, secondary markets
in accounts receivable, or in individual farm mortgages, remove from the unorganized markets in the
more developed countries some of the impediments to
economic growth. This is not to say that direct financing in the less developed countries is invariably

misdirected from the standpoint of social, developmental goals, or that it should be institutionalized in its entirety. On the contrary, the bulk of its transactions (other than those that serve to satisfy consumption needs and, hence, can hardly be termed links between the saver and the investor) are as necessary and as efficient as they could be in a country where there is little in the way of capital markets, where primary securities issued by business units are primitive with respect to underlying accounting procedures, and where the farmer and the small businessman can only seldom deal with a commercial bank.

While much of the business of unorganized markets in the less developed countries has to do with consumption loans, which from a development standpoint are hardly relevant, involving as they do merely interpersonal transfers, note must be taken of the fact that often a consumption loan allows direct investment outlay. The farmer who is anxious to obtain cheap fertilizer from his cooperative may have to borrow from a moneylender for clothing, for example, to tide himself over until after the harvest. A small shopkeeper will finance the acquisition of his stock through the organized financial market (or trade credit) but may be forced, in part because of that, to go to a usurer for cash to give to his children at the beginning of the school year.

A type of link between saver and investor which is both peculiar to and prevalent in the less developed countries is one that has some of the aspects of direct financing but also takes on characteristics of an institution. This is the rotating credit society, which, in Thailand, is best known as the _pia huey_. In this very informal type of institution, savers and investors interchange their functions intermittently. Though they negotiate face-to-face, the directness of the financing arrangements is circumvented by the rotating system. At any given time all members of the society but one are savers, and this single investor will become a saver at the next meeting. The _pia huey_ is an important segment of business finance in Thailand and merits a more

extended discussion. (See below. Contrary to the
impression given in the limited literature on the
subject, the rotating credit society, in Thailand at
least, is not confined to financing consumption ex-
penditure.) It is, of course, an institution of the
unorganized market.

Of those links which reside firmly in the organized financial markets, the most important is that
between the saver and the investor through the intermediary of a commercial bank. The saver deposits
money in a fixed deposit account, and the bank lends
it to an investor who acquires assets with it. This
simple picture is, in fact, much more complex, even
in Thailand. For example, the owner of a deposit
account may borrow from the bank himself; borrowing,
as in the case of a postdated check, may antedate the
deposit of funds; and bank lending may finance consumption as well as capital formation. But, basically, the relationship between the saver and investor
takes place in two steps, the second step being the
intermediary of a financing institution. This institution, the commercial bank, clearly belongs to
the organized financial markets on the basis of the
criteria set out above.

The situation becomes less clear and the classification more difficult where the intermediation
between the saver and the investor extends beyond
the commercial bank itself and requires additional
intermediation. For example, it is alleged that for
some borrowers to obtain any funds at all it may be
necessary for them to engage in shady dealings with
a person close to, yet separate from, the bank. Similarly, it is said that some savers may obtain particularly favorable terms on their deposits if they
are willing to deal with somebody connected with the
bank, yet acting independently of it. Whether this
shadowy intermediary is a compradore, an agency manager, or an officer at the headquarters is immater-
ial. The penumbra of commercial bank operations
must be classed as belonging to the unorganized markets. More important, according to reliable accounts
this penumbra is quite significant on the Thai financial scene. An agency manager, for example, may make

little distinction in his own business dealings between his own funds and those of a bank. A provincial bank manager will, on occasion, attract deposits
by paying "extra" interest. He will obtain funds for
this purpose by requiring borrowers to pay, in addition to maximum interest charges, a fee for contribution to a "welfare fund" or some other such designation. A compradore may charge both the employer and
the client, and so on. It is alleged that in some
banks a loan will be made on condition that the lender will be allowed to participate in the profits of
the enterprise. Should the enterprise fail, the bank
may have to write off the loss; should it succeed,
the lender may profit over and above the interest
payment to the bank. It seems that this kind of participation is not uncommon in real estate development. For example, on occasion a real estate devel-
oper, a person of some credit standing, manages to
create a shopping center on a remarkably small equity
base. He will approach the owner of suitable land
and obtain a fifteen-year or twenty-year lease from
him, either against payment of a fee or a promise
to share in the profits. Armed with such a lease,
he will secure funds from the commercial banks sufficient to cover about 20 per cent of the costs of
the construction of building shells. As soon as
these shells are erected, they will be sold to prospective tenants (so as to minimize taxable income).
The cash so obtained will be used to make payments
to creditors and to garner a tidy capital profit.
After the expiry of the lease period the buildings
revert to the landlord.

All these and similar dealings are illegal, and
their frequency is strenuously denied by the chief
executive of all the commercial banks. Yet they exist, even though it is difficult to assess their incidence and quantitative importance. (See below for
quantitative information.)

Stretching from the penumbra of commercial bank
operations deep into the heart of the unorganized
markets is the "wholesaling" of credit. The links
here are as follows: The bank obtains deposits from
savers and then lends them to a "wholesaler" of credit.

The wholesaler then distributes the funds to others,
who may or may not be the ultimate investors (or
consumers). The wholesaler is usually a person who
has easy access to commercial bank credit because of
his credit standing or because of the availability
of acceptable collateral or for some other reason.
His customers are those who lack these attributes.
The number of steps leading from the wholesaler to
the ultimate user of funds may vary from one to five
or more. At each descending step the terms at which
the funds are acquired become steeper. The larger
the number of steps, the less it is likely that the
ultimate user of the funds obtains them for investment purposes. In fact, in the next, even darker
layer of the unorganized markets where the "retailers" of credit operate, the connection of the financial transactions with investment and capital formation becomes very tenuous. As stated earlier, for
the small shopkeeper or farmer the distinction between his personal needs and his business needs is
an uncertain one at best.

Finally, at the bottom of the unorganized financial markets, the small "retailers" operate. These
are small operators, frequently night watchmen
(babus), and the like, who are not beyond lending 100
baht to a person in desperate straits but at an extremely high price. The loan may be repaid in a
month or through daily payments of 1 baht or less.
In the same category, one will find "unofficial"
pawnships, and gold shops operating as fronts for
usurious lending organizations. Official pawnshops
are, however, a part of the organized market, inasmuch as they are controlled and supervised by authorities (by municipalities in Thailand). The lending
rate of official pawnshops is limited to 2 per cent
per month.

An important area of the unorganized financial
markets in Thailand, but one which lends itself only
uneasily to an analysis in terms of links between
the saver and the investor, is that of trade credit.
As is true of all other aspects of the unorganized
markets, little is known about magnitudes and practices of trade credit, but some information about

this important form of financing business is presented below.

As might be expected, the terms at which financing takes place become steeper the more one pene-
trates into the unorganized markets. The interest
rates on loans made in the penumbra of the commercial
banking system will range from 1.5 per cent to 2 per
cent per month, while at the bottom of the scale a
consumption or emergency loan to someone in dire
straits may reach a monthly rate of 20 per cent or
more. Other terms of loans, such as the type of
security, the currency of the loan, and so on, do
not follow an equally neat gradation (for some of
the details see below).

Table 7.1 summarizes the preceding discussion.
It should be emphasized that both the composition
of the markets and the range of prices prevailing in
each are approximate and illustrative. In particular, great variations exist with respect to implicit
cost of borrowing in the rotating societies and in
trade credit.

The division of the unorganized markets into
six categories is arbitrary because each market
shades almost imperceptibly into an adjacent category
above and below it. Nevertheless, the division is
useful if only because it focuses attention on the
suppliers of credit in each market, who, as opposed
to borrowers, are a much more distinctive group.
Little more can be said about the borrowers beyond
the rather obvious fact that they are businessmen
first and householders second at the top of the scale,
and householders first and businessmen second at the
bottom of the scale--the scale being, in this context, that of interest charges. What is significant
with respect to borrowers is that they are frequently
active in both the organized and the unorganized
markets. On the supply side this, too, is frequent,
if rather obvious for such persons as bank officers.
The reasons why a businessman of good credit status
and with access to bank credit should go to a moneylender are discussed below.

TABLE 7.1

Unorganized Financial Markets in Thailand

Type of Market	Supply	Demand	Monthly Rate of Interest (%)
"Penumbra" of commercial bank	Compradores, bank officers, branch managers, agency partners	Businessmen	$1\frac{1}{2}$-2
Wholesalers	Landlords, rich merchants, highly placed individuals	Traders	2-3
Trade credit	Foreign exporters, large corporations, and others	Manufacturers	1-4
Rotating credit societies	Various		3-5
Retailers	Individuals (often wives of officials and traders)	Small businessmen	5-10
Small	"Unofficial" pawnshops, gold shops, night watchmen	Households	10 and over

The composition of the supply side of the penumbra type of market has already been touched on. The wholesalers include landlords who, profiting from the boom in land values, have acquired large amounts of cash. Though they are not interested in going into business themselves, they are interested in obtaining a return on their capital in excess of the maximum interest rate payable on fixed deposits. The fact that interest on bank deposits is tax exempt,

while interest on private loans is not, is of relevance to those engaging in operations through the
unorganized channels.

Apparently there are a large number of reliable,
well-connected retailers who are willing to offer
their own guarantees to these landlords, as well as
to other highly placed individuals or merchants with
idle funds on their hands, and to pay up to 3 per
cent per month for capital. The retailers, in turn,
distribute these funds to smaller businessmen and
householders in need of money, who are prepared to
pay up to 5 per cent per month for its use. It appears that a large fraction of this retail business
is in the hands of wives of officials, a circumstance
which facilitates collection of debts and compliance
with the sometimes onerous terms of the loan.

Those who supply credit to the rotating credit
societies are also those who demand credit from them,
as implicit in the very concept of rotating credit.
However, there apparently exists a group of profes-
sionals in this branch of the financial market who
belong to several pia hueys at once, frequently or-
ganize new ones, and occasionally cover their liabilities in one society by drawing on the facilities of
another.

The suppliers of trade credit are primarily foreign exporters. Under practices prevailing in Thailand today, the importer has some 90 days to pay for
the cost of imports, and within this time limit he
can extend credit to others down the distribution
ladder. Trade credit is a subject which will only
be touched upon in this chapter, but its importance
will become apparent even from the modest quantitative information gleaned.

An allegedly important source of funds to the
unorganized markets, related to trade credit, is the
supposed practice of selling standardized imports
(i.e., condensed milk, tires) at cost or even at a
slight loss upon arrival and using the cash proceeds
in a fashion presumably more lucrative than straight
trading. It is possible, however, that to the extent

that such sales take place, they are motivated by considerations other than the lure of high return on cash in the unorganized markets. Sometimes such sales are merely the means to raise cash to meet urgent debts.

In addition to foreign exporters, the main suppliers of trade credit are large manufacturers with branches or subsidiaries in Thailand who use trade credit in the same way it is used in the industrial countries. There is also a small number of specialized financial firms who deal in receivables.

Small retailers include pawnshops, gold shops, night watchmen, and possibly remittance shops. The importance of remittance shops has declined considerably as fewer persons transmit funds to families in mainland China; however, it is believed that the resources of these formerly important intermediaries still find their way into the internal unorganized financial markets.

SAMPLE SURVEY OF URBAN CREDIT

The preceding discussion provides an over-all view of the unorganized financial markets in Thailand, with a somewhat arbitrary division of these markets from the standpoint of suppliers of credit. In attempting to fill in the picture of these markets which began to emerge from discussions with traders, bankers, moneylenders, and others, it soon became clear that any quantification or precision would not be obtained from the supply side. Many of the practices involved, many of the terms at which funds are advanced, and many of the relationships between the lender and the borrower are not of a nature susceptible to any inquiry, no matter how academic or how detached from tax and judicial authorities. Yet it was felt that an attempt should be made to verify empirically the allegations and assertions made with respect to unorganized markets and to substitute quantitative data for hunches and informed guesses. The decision to undertake a sample survey of credit in urban areas was made with full realization that

the results of such a survey would be doubtful at
best. Even though the respondents would be the de-
manders rather than the suppliers of credit, victims
rather than beneficiaries of any abuses which might
exist, the prevailing ethos rules against disclosure
of information to third parties--quite apart from
the fact that the victims, too, may be held to engage in illegal practices. Although every effort
was made to reassure the respondents that their names
and identities would not be made available to any
authority, the majority of the respondents probably
remained rather skeptical. Nevertheless, the survey
was undertaken in the belief that the resulting information, however scanty and unreliable, would constitute a net addition to knowledge on an important
subject.

The survey was administered by the Bank of Thailand with the cooperation of the Thai National Statistical Office and the Department of Economics of
Thammasat University, under the over-all guidance of
the writer.

The results of the survey turned out to be only
of limited usefulness. Aside from expected shortcomings, due to the reluctance of respondents to dis-
close information, there arose innumerable problems
due to the language barrier, to the lack of experience of the personnel involved, and to the lack of
sophistication on the part of the bulk of those ques-
tioned. Perhaps the most damaging was the language
problem. It proved almost impossible to translate
terms drawn from Western usage into acceptable Thai
in a way that imparted identical meaning to the interviewer, to the respondent, and to the supervisors.
When viewed as a pilot project, however, the survey can
hardly be termed a failure. It did provide a host of
useful data, and it confirmed a number of assertions
and allegations regarding the operations of the unorganized financial markets in Thailand. Last, but
not least, it did bring to light some of the obstacles
which would face another, more rigirous inquiry into
the problem.[1]

Scope of the Survey

After initial discussions with experts at the National Statistical Office, it was agreed to confine the survey to businesses located in the metropolitan area of Bangkok-Thonburi, with subsequent checks to be made of preselected businesses in Chiengmai and Haadyai, the two other important urban centers in Thailand. Given the census data available, the sampling frame was confined to industrial enterprises and trading establishments only. Transport, mining, contracting, and other areas of business activity were excluded. Budgetary and manpower limitations made it necessary to hold the total number of firms in the sample to about 1,000 establishments.

The 1,070 completed questionnaires represent, when the resulting figures are multiplied by the sampling fractions, some 65,000 business establishments in the metropolitan area. Because of the concentration of business units in the Bangkok-Thonburi area, the results of the survey may be said to be quite representative of industry and trade in Thailand. In any event, the tables which follow give data adjusted to the total business population rather than to merely businesses of the sample itself. This proviso will apply to the absolute figures as well as to the percentages given in the tables and in the accompanying text. Reference to the actual number of sample respondents is made only when the number is other than 1,070. It should be noted that extrapolating the universe from the sample is subject to a sampling error of approximately $\pm$ 3 per cent. Consequently, caution should be used in interpreting the absolute (as distinct from the percentage) figures from the sample which are said to represent the universe. Thus, a figure of 42 may, in actual fact, mean that the number in that category may range from 0 to 180.

Tables 7.2 and 7.3 give details of the composition sample. As was to be expected, most establishments were in existence for over five years. The growth of the luxury service-type of business in very

TABLE 7.2

Urban Credit Survey: Number of Firms by Type
and Length of Time in Business

Length of Time in Business	Total	Number of Firms Supplying Urban Credit						
		Big Indus-try	Medium Indus-try	Small Indus-try	Whole-sale	Big Retail	Small Retail	Luxury
Total	64,828	84	793	5,200	2,650	9,950	45,500	650
Less than 1 year	1,402	2	–	325	50	250	750	25
1–5 years	22,885	10	75	1,200	1,100	3,300	17,000	200
Over 5 years	40,541	73	718	3,675	1,500	6,400	27,750	425

TABLE 7.3

Urban Credit Survey: Percentage Distribution of Firms
by Type and Length of Time in Business

Length of Time in Business	Total	Big Indus- try	Medium Indus- try	Small Indus- try	Whole sale	Big Retail	Small Retail	Luxury
				Percentage of Urban Credit Firms				
Total	100	0.13	1.22	8.02	4.09	15.35	70.19	1.00
Less than 1 year	100	0.14	–	23.18	3.57	17.83	53.50	1.78
1-5 years	100	0.04	0.33	5.24	4.81	14.42	74.28	0.87
Over 5 years	100	0.18	1.77	9.06	3.70	15.79	68.45	1.05

255

recent times is indicated by the fact that the luxury
service proportion of businesses in operation less
than one year is nearly double that of its proportion
of total business units. Even more startling is the
relatively high proportion of small industrial establishments in existence less than one year, as compared to their proportion of the over-all total.
Small industrial establishments account for 8 per
cent of the total business units but make up over 23
per cent of those in existence under one year. This
high proportion is probably only partially due to the
boom conditions in the country. It also indicates
that the mortality of small industrial establishments
in Thailand is rather high. On the other hand, the
formation of big industrial units shows little acceleration over time, relative to other types of business. For example, large industrial establishments
comprise 0.18 per cent of all businesses in existence
over five years, but their proportion of all business
units, regardless of length of time in operation, is
only 0.13 per cent. Eighty-six per cent of all large
industrial firms were in existence for more than five
years, and only slightly more than 2 per cent were
formed in the year preceding the field phase of the
survey. By contrast, over 6 per cent of all small
industrial firms were formed during that same year.

Of the 64,828 firms represented by the sample,
small retail establishments are the most important,
accounting for over 70 per cent of all firms.

It is the small retail firm which is also invariably a single proprietorship, as only one large
industrial firm was found to be owned by a single
person or family. Table 7.3 suggests that wholesale
establishments are the predominant type of firm using
the corporate form of business organization. But
this seems so only because wholesalers are a much
more numerous component of the sample than are large
industrial firms. Limited companies account for only
26 per cent of all wholesalers but for 74 per cent
of all large industrial firms. For all firms in the
sample, corporations comprise 3 per cent, and pro-
prietorships 91 per cent, of the total. Limited

partnerships are the most popular type of business
organization among wholesalers. Ordinary partnerships appear to be the least popular form of doing
business among Thai firms.

While the above data appear to be quite reliable,
information gathered from the survey regarding balance sheet items leaves much to be desired. In the
first place, the total of assets does not fit with the
total of liabilities. This embarrassing result came
about despite the determination of interviewers to
reconcile the respective answers, even going so far
as to make estimates of the value of intangibles such
as good will. Moreover, cross check questions, such
as an estimate of the market value of the business,
yielded results vastly different from those of net
asset valuation or net worth. In fact, the answers
to these last two questions were so implausible that
they were not even tabulated. It may be of some interest, however, to give the data regarding the composition and the totals of main assets and liabilities, bearing in mind the caution which should attach
to any interpretation of these particular results.
Assets are given in Table 7.4 and capital and other
liabilities in Table 7.5.

Even with their severe limitations, these tables
indicate one or two things of interest. One is the
importance of trade credit among the liabilities of
the business firms represented in the sample. Twenty-
one per cent of all the liabilities are of this type,
and, not surprisingly, this proportion reaches 39
per cent in the case of wholesale firms. Trade credit
is, of course, also represented on the asset side;
however, its importance is overshadowed there by that
of fixed assets. Indeed, the asset data given in
Table 7.4 appear rather startling. It is difficult
to believe that 64 per cent of all assets of small
retail establishments are in fixed form unless the
cost of the often rickety structure exceeds that of
the meager stock. Equally unexpected is the indication that fixed assets of small industrial firms are
relatively more important than those of medium-size
industrial establishments.

TABLE 7.4

Urban Credit Survey: Type of Assets by Type of Firm
(million baht)

Type of Firm	Total	Cash	Type of Assets			
			Trade Credit	Stock in Trade	Fixed Assets	Others
Total	28,818	2,874	3,239	6,839	13,083	2,783
Big industry	5,967	365	428	635	2,331	1,708
Medium industry	2,483	182	277	608	1,267	149
Small industry	2,881	302	202	296	1,827	254
Wholesale	6,580	981	1,802	2,968	674	155
Big retail	6,390	557	439	1,770	3,405	219
Small retail	3,251	386	65	546	2,074	180
Luxury service	1,266	101	26	16	1,005	118

TABLE 7.5

Urban Credit Survey: Capital and Liabilities by Type of Firm
(million baht)

| Type of Firm | Total | Type of Capital and Liabilities | | | |
		Net Worth	Loans	Trade Credit	Other Liabilities
Total	28,627	17,909	3,487	6,003	1,228
Big industry	5,964	4,205	619	606	534
Medium industry	2,485	1,287	545	453	200
Small industry	2,861	2,031	421	342	67
Wholesale	6,583	3,137	791	2,555	100
Big retail	6,353	3,642	762	1,854	95
Small retail	3,115	2,741	143	172	59
Luxury	1,266	866	206	21	173

Sources of Initial Capital

There are prima facie reasons to believe that
the initial capital of a business undertaking does
not come from the same sources as capital that is
obtained to finance ongoing operations and/or expansion and that it is different in extent and nature.
This seems to be especially true in a country such
as Thailand, where the capital market is not well-
developed, where there are no venture companies, and
where the existing financial institutions rely primarily on the past record and current credit standing
of the would-be borrower of investible funds. For
these and other reasons the questionnaire split the
series of questions dealing with sources of funds
into three categories: questions pertaining to initial capital, those relating to operations of existing firms in the past year, and those concerned with
future financing plans. Another reason for splitting
the series of questions was to minimize the possibility that the respondent, by answering "no" to the
first question as to whether he borrows, does away
with the entire questionnaire. As the interview proceeds, there is a tendency to open up and to answer
affirmatively similar questions later on.

The questions relating to initial sources of
funds were confined to those firms which were in existence less than five years at the time of the survey. There was little likelihood that meaningful
answers to this set of questions could be obtained
from old, established firms if back records are lost
or nonexistent, if the respondent is a person other
than the original entrepreneur, or if the firm has
substantially changed its identity over time. The
answers are summarized in Table 7.6.

Of the 3.3 billion baht of initial capital indicated by the sample, 2.9 billion, or 88 per cent, was
obtained from the personal resources of an entrepreneur's own capital. (Even though the questionnaire
asked for sources of an entrepreneur's own capital--
i.e., savings, inheritance--the responses were not
of a nature which would warrant machine coding.) Less
than 6 per cent of initial capital was obtained from

TABLE 7.6

Urban Credit Survey: Initial Capital by Type of Firm
and Source of Funds[a]

(million baht)

Type of Firm	Total	Entrepreneur	Family or Friend	Commercial Bank	Share Society	Noncommercial Bank	Other
			Initial Capital and Source of Funds				
Big industry	252.4	141.4	1.7	51.0	-	2.0	56.3
Medium industry	46.4	37.6	2.5	5.7	0.6	-	-
Small industry	997.6	963.1	13.8	16.3	4.4	-	-
Wholesale	699.1	583.5	9.8	105.8	-	-	-
Big retail	436.1	384.9	29.4	9.5	12.3	-	-
Small retail	679.7	606.7	42.3	-	30.7	-	-
Luxury service	167.0	154.5	12.5	-	-	-	-
Total	3,278.3	2,871.7	112.0	188.3	48.0	2.0	56.3

[a]Number of answers is greater than number of firms because respondents indicated more than one source of funds.

commercial banks, and family and friends provided a
scant 3 per cent. While the high proportion of funds
from an entrepreneur's own capital is hardly surprising, one would expect a higher proportion than that
indicated, less than 1 per cent, to come from nonbanking sources. These include not only such non-
bank financial institutions as life insurance companies and the Industrial Finance Corporation of
Thailand but also private individuals, both those in
the penumbra of commercial banking and other moneylenders. In fact, no respondents indicated that
their initial capital came from private individuals,
a most unexpected result in a country where moneylending is a thriving profession and where moneylenders are known to be very active in financing
certain business needs. This was perhaps the most
disappointing outcome of the survey, which was designed, in large part, in the hope of eliciting quantitative information about moneylenders and their
practices. With respect to initial capital at least,
it would seem that resort to moneylenders is the exception rather than the rule. It is also quite certain, however, that many respondents are reluctant
to admit borrowing, in general, and borrowing from
moneylenders, in particular. As will be seen below,
a more significant response as regards borrowing from
moneylenders was given with respect to operating funds
during the previous year. For initial capital, only
one firm indicated borrowing from "private individuals" but failed to check either the "moneylender"
or "connected with bank" slots. Only one firm in the
sample borrowed from the Industrial Finance Corporation of Thailand.

Finally, there are good reasons to believe that
many of the relatives or friends are, in fact, moneylenders, or acting as such. Table 7.7 indicates that
a substantial proportion of the firms that borrow from
family or friends pay an annual rate of interest in
excess of 24 per cent, the rate which is considered
to be the prime "market" (i.e., unorganized market)
rate for secured business loans. Over 40 per cent of
all firms that obtain funds from family or friends
pay more than 24 per cent per annum for such funds,
and they account for 16 per cent of all funds obtained

from this source. The high number of firms in the over-all total is primarily due to the high proportion of retail businesses. Because high interest rates charged by moneylenders are illegal and because their place of operation is not advertised, contact with the moneylender is usually on the basis of kinship or personal knowledge, direct or indirect, of the borrower. Under these circumstances a moneylender, naturally, is either a relative or becomes a friend.

TABLE 7.7

Urban Credit Survey: Level of Interest
Rate on Initial Funds Obtained from Friends
and Relatives, by Type of Business,
Percentage Distribution

Type of Business	Interest Rate on Initial Funds from Friends and Relatives			
	Under 24% p.a.		Over 24% p.a.	
	% of Firms	% of Amt. Borrowed	% of Firms	% of Amt. Borrowed
Total	58.39	84.43	41.61	15.57
Big industry	100.00	100.00	-	-
Medium industry	84.00	82.14	16.00	17.86
Small industry	85.00	84.55	15.00	15.45
Wholesale	66.67	97.44	33.33	2.56
Big retail	51.72	61.40	48.28	38.60
Small retail	57.14	93.68	42.86	6.32
Luxury service	100.00	100.00	-	-

"Other" sources provided only 2 per cent of total capital requirements to all the firms represented by the sample. The entire amount was obtained by large industrial establishments, and it represented 22 per cent of their initial capital requirements. These sources included funds obtained from the government, from abroad, and from the sale of securities to the public, all of which are not readily available to smaller businesses. Five large industry firms in the sample borrowed a total of 56 million baht from these "other" sources. Two firms obtained 28 million

baht from government enterprises; two firms obtained
some 21 million from abroad; and one got 7.5 million
from unspecified sources.

As seen in Table 7.6, the amount of initial capital obtained from any one particular source varies
significantly with the type of firm involved. Large
industrial firms, for example, rely much more on bank
credit than do other types of businesses. The amount
of funds obtained from the rotating credit arrangement (pia huey) is greatest for small retail firms,
and that obtained from family and friends is greatest
in the case of luxury service firms. This last type
of business relies for its initial capital on only
two sources: its own capital and family/friends.
It is alleged that much of this type of business is
in the hands of one ethnic group in the metropolitan
area, the members of which frequently band together
for the purpose of starting a new hotel, restaurant,
or similar enterprise. It is said that each member
contributes not only his own capital but his skills
and labor as well.

As was to be expected, initial capital requirements vary in amount between different types of firms.
Large industrial establishments lead the list with
over 21 million baht of initial capital per firm;
whereas a small retail business needed only 38 thous-
and baht to get started within the five-year period
preceding the survey. What is rather unexpected,
however, is the finding, indicated in Table 7.8, that
the initial capital of small industrial establishments
is greater than that of medium-scale industrial firms.
One may be tempted to seek explanations in the nature
of the sample, in the possibility that somehow small
industrial firms (with less than 10 workers) use
high-cost capital equipment, and so on. It is more
likely, however, that the survey is not reliable when
it comes to the consistency of responses pertaining
to specific business operating quantities. This was
found to be true with respect to data on assets and
liabilities above and is true here. Note, however,
that fixed capital bore a higher proportion of total
assets in the case of small industrial firms than in
the case of medium-size industrial firms. (See Table
4.4.)

TABLE 7.8

Urban Credit Survey:
Initial Capital per Firm, by Type of Firm
(baht)

Type of Firm	Initial Capital per Firm
Big industry	21,033,333
Medium industry	618,666
Small industry	654,098
Wholesale	607,913
Big retail	122,845
Small retail	38,287
Luxury service	782,222

Sources of Current Funds

The results of the survey with respect to
sources of capital for ongoing operations and expansion appear to be quite plausible. In part, this
is true because most respondents are more certain and
clear about their financial operations of the past
twelve months than they are about those of several
years before. Furthermore, the questions relating
to sources of funds during the past year appeared to
be less ambiguous than those relating to original
capital. With respect to the latter, vexing problems
of interpretation, translation, and comprehension of
such terms as "own" funds, borrowed capital, and
equity participation plagued the survey from its inception, through the construction of the questionnaire,
and right up to the coding of field-work responses.

As seen from Table 7.9, some 45,000 firms provided usable answers regarding their financial operations in the past year. The number of respondents
differs from the total number of firms represented
by the sample because a number of firms did not seek
additional funds during the past year. Table 7.10
gives a breakdown, by type of firms, of the sources
of funds obtained by the respondents for purposes of
financing ongoing operations and/or expansion of
their business activities.

TABLE 7.9

Urban Credit Survey: Source of Ongoing Funds,
Number of Firms by Type of Firm

Type of Firm	Total	Entre-preneur	Source of Ongoing Funds				
			Family or Friend	Commer-cial Bank Credit	Share Society	Noncom-mercial Bank	Other
Big industry	61	14	8	30	–	3	6
Medium industry	656	65	237	185	135	17	17
Small industry	4,100	125	1,800	375	1,775	–	25
Wholesale	1,550	50	550	550	200	200	–
Big retail	7,000	200	3,050	1,150	2,450	150	–
Small retail	31,310	1,500	14,500	–	13,750	1,560	–
Luxury	300	75	150	25	50	–	–
Total	44,977	2,029	20,295	2,315	18,360	1,930	48

TABLE 7.10

Urban Credit Survey: Amount and Source of Ongoing Funds by Type of Firm
(million baht)

Type of Firm	Total	Amount and Source of Ongoing Funds					
		Entre-preneur	Family or Friend	Commer-cial Credit	Share Society	Non-Bank	Other
Total	3,895	228	684	1,543	162	27	1,251
Big industry	1,472	19	13	303	–	3	1,134
Medium industry	605	10	37	379	60	2	117
Small industry	134	8	58	46	22	–	0.25
Wholesale	699	31	30	625	4	9	–
Big retail	760	153	420	172	15	0.11	–
Small retail	194	4	116	–	61	13	–
Luxury service	31	3	10	18	0.45	–	–

The total amount borrowed for annual operations was 3.9 billion baht, of which 1.5 billion baht was borrowed from commercial banks. During 1966, total commercial bank accommodation to Thai business was slightly over 1.8 billion baht. Inasmuch as the survey sample excludes certain segments of Thai business, such as transport, the amount given in the table is not implausible.

In addition to the 40 per cent of total requirements obtained from commercial banks, the sample firms obtained over 32 per cent from "other" sources (i.e., from government funds, from the issue of securities, or from abroad), about 18 per cent from friends or relatives, over 4 per cent from pia huey, and less than 6 per cent from their own resources. Thus, there is a drastic difference between the sources of funds obtained to start a business and those obtained to carry on with an existing enterprise. Whereas the vast bulk of initial funds comes from the entrepreneur's own resources and/or capital, these provide but a minor part of the funds required for ongoing operations. Commercial banks, official and foreign sources, and family/friends loom much more importantly as sources of ongoing funds.

As was true with respect to initial capital, the proportion of total needs obtained from different sources varies considerably among different types of firms. The high proportion of funds in the overall total obtained from "other" sources, therefore, is due to the practices of big-industry firms which obtain considerable amounts from this source. Of special interest is the fact that small retail firms apparently get no operating funds from commercial banks and rely heavily on family and friends for their funds. Luxury firms, which relied mainly on the funds of the entrepreneurial and kinship groups for their initial capital, here resort heavily to bank accommodation, even though they still remain the type of firm which uses outside sources for funds less than any other.

Some of the findings of Table 7.10 are not unexpected. Once a business is operating and has

acquired some earning assets, it is easier for it to
obtain bank credit, for example, and lesser reliance
needs to be put on insiders, relatives, friends, or
the entrepreneur's own resources.

Of the total amount obtained by the sample firms
to finance their annual requirements, the greatest
proportion of the total was required by large industrial firms. Luxury service firms accounted for less
than 1 per cent of the nearly 4 billion baht. Of the
total amount borrowed from commercial banks, the
greatest share went to wholesalers. Over 90 per cent
of all funds obtained from "other" sources went to
large industrial firms. Even though family and
friends are the principal contributors to the operating requirements of small retail firms, it is the
big retail establishments which account for the bulk
of funds from this source.

The rotating credit society, or pia huey, is of
special interest in any analysis of unorganized money
markets and how these markets are used as sources of
funds to finance Thai business enterprise. Basically, the rotating credit society is a device whereby
persons obtain funds on an intermittent basis from
other persons similarly situated. Credit society
members make periodic contributions to a revolving
fund, and at regular intervals disbursements are made
from this fund to one of the participating group.
Said to be of Chinese origin, the rotating credit
society is found throughout most of the preindustrial
societies in Asia as well as in Africa. Even though
the methods differ, as do the names by which these
methods are known, the basic principles are remarkably similar throughout most of the world.[2]

In Thailand, however, the rotating credit societies appear to have two distinguishing characteristics not usually found elsewhere. In the first place,
the Thai pia huey (literally, "share") seems to be
an exclusively urban phenomenon. It is different
from the Vietnamese ho and the Korean Kye, which are
both rural and urban, and it is certainly unlike the
Indonesian arisan, which is almost entirely rural.
In the second place, while most of the rotating credit

societies discussed in the sparse literature on the subject seem to be designed to provide ad hoc funds for consumption needs, the pia huey does provide a significant amount of funds for ongoing business operations. Whether this second distinguishing feature of the pia huey is related to the first is difficult to say. In any event, even though the pia huey accounted for less than 5 per cent of all ongoing funds needed by the firms represented in the sample, nearly 30 per cent of all the firms did obtain some money from this source.

The information available from the survey on pia huey is summarized in Table 7.11. It indicates that the vast majority of these rotating credit societies meet monthly. The number of members in the society determines the number of meetings; i.e., if the society has 12 members, it will meet monthly for 12 months. At each meeting a sum of money is paid into a pool by all members except one; the nonpaying member, or beneficiary, receives the entire proceeds of the pool. The identity of the beneficiary is determined by one of several methods. In Thailand, the method most commonly employed is that of tender. At each meeting all those members who have not yet received the monthly pool will tender bids, and the successful bidder will receive all contributions paid at that meeting. The bids are made in terms of discount from the agreed value of contributions. For example, if the monthly value of each member's contribution is set at 1,000 baht, the successful bidder may be the one who will accept only 960 baht from each of the other members. Having received the contributions of all other members, the successful bidder is then obligated to pay in, at every one of the remaining meetings, the sum of 1,000 baht less such discount as is determined by the successful bidders at each subsequent meeting. Discounts from the agreed-upon amount of the periodic contributions depend on the type of rotation used. In addition to the periodic tender, the rotation may be determined by lottery drawing or may be set in advance for the duration of the pia huey. An analysis of interest rates payable by members of pia huey indicates that the modal rates range from 3-5 per cent per month.

TABLE 7.11

Urban Credit Survey: Characteristics of
Share Society (Pia Huey) Credit

Type of Firm Drawing on Share Society Credit

Frequency and Method	All Firms		Big Industry		Medium Industry		Small Industry		Wholesale		Big Retail & Service		Small Retail & Service		Luxury Service Establishments	
	No.	%	No.	%	No.	%	No.	%	No.	%	No.	%	No.	%	No.	%
Weekly	35	100	–	–	10	28.57	–	–	–	–	–	–	–	–	25	71.43
Monthly	18,295	100	–	–	120	0.66	1,775	9.70	200	1.09	2,400	13.12	13,750	75.16	50	0.27
Other	75	100	–	–	–	–	25	33.33	–	–	50	66.67	–	–	–	–
Total by frequency	18,405	100	–	–	130	0.71	1,800	9.78	200	1.09	2,450	13.31	13,750	74.71	75	0.40
By tender	15,808	100	–	–	108	0.68	1,750	11.07	200	1.27	2,450	15.50	11,250	71.17	50	0.31
By drawing	2,540	100	–	–	15	0.59	25	0.98	–	–	–	–	2,500	98.43	–	–
By rotation	27	100	–	–	2	7.41	25	92.59	–	–	–	–	–	–	–	–
Other	2	100	–	–	2	100.0	–	–	–	–	–	–	–	–	–	–
Total by method	18,377	100	–	–	127	0.69	1,800	9.79	200	1.09	2,450	13.33	13,750	74.82	50	0.28

Details may not add to total because of rounding.

As seen in Table 7.11, the relative importance of pia huey varies enormously among different types of firms. No big industrial firms seek operating funds from this source, but three-fourths of small retail establishments do, and nearly 10 per cent of small industrial firms.

Even less quantitatively important than pia huey as a source of funds to Thai business firms are non-bank commercial sources. These, it will be recalled, include specialized financial institutions as well as individuals.

Only slightly over 1,000 of the 65,000 firms represented in the sample conceded that they had obtained funds for ongoing purposes from moneylenders or others. Rather surprisingly, no small manufacturers or luxury service firms were in that category.

These results were so unexpected and so much at variance with the observed practices of Thai business that an effort was made to determine the reasons for the poor showing of moneylending in the survey returns. This effort took the following form: first, practicing or, allegedly, recently retired moneylenders were approached and, second, those businessmen who had experiences with private individuals as sources of funds were deliberately sought out. In order not to upset the randomness of the sample, the latter aspect of this effort was conducted during field trips to Chiengmai and Haadyai, where the smallness of the business community and the availability of reliable and informed contacts made it possible to pinpoint the desired kind of respondents.

The emerging picture fails to provide a quantative estimate of the real importance of private individuals as suppliers of business funds. It does, however, provide some insight into the reasons why the survey returns failed to indicate the true dimensions of moneylending in financing Thai business.

In the first place, as asserted previously, many friends and relatives are actually moneylenders or persons connected with commercial banks. The Thai

business community is densely intertwined with kinship ties, and many of the bankers retain active and
varied interests in many businesses. There is also
little doubt that most Thai businessmen are reluctant
to admit that they borrow from anyone, especially
from moneylenders. Indeed, the very fact that they
prefer to refer to such lenders as relatives or
friends underlines this reluctance. The reasons for
this go beyond the fear of criminal or administrative
responsibility and have to do with "face." It is
still true that having to borrow is, for many businessmen, an admission of weakness or dependence. It
is also interpreted by many as an indication that
support from the immediate family is lacking or that
a decline in former wealth and status has taken place.
This consideration of face may in many cases actually
force a businessman of good credit standing, one who
is potentially a welcome bank customer, to go to a
moneylender. He does this because he does not want
the world to know that he has to borrow. The bank
may require a registration of mortgage, a visit or
two to the bank's premises, or an inspection of his
warehouse, all steps not calculated to keep his need
for funds a secret.

Besides reasons of relative intimacy of secrecy
of transactions, there are, of course, other reasons
why a Thai businessman might resort to private individuals for financing. Indeed, the mere listing
of these other reasons suggest their likely frequency
and thus casts further doubt on the validity of the
sample survey in this respect.

A businessman will go to a moneylender when he
is unwilling to pledge his land. Sometimes his need
for funds may be only a fraction of the value of his
land. Land titles cannot be subdivided in Thailand,
and it is understandable that a person may be unwilling to pledge a million baht to secure the use of
50,000. A businessman may also be compelled to resort to moneylenders when and if the branch of the
bank where he does business has gone over the limit
of individual loans allowed it or when the bank feels
that it has advanced him enough for the time being.
Another businessman may already have pledged

his available collateral, other than operating assets
to secure additional accommodation. Finally, and
perhaps most importantly, there are many businessmen
perfectly able to obtain funds from the bank who,
nevertheless, go to moneylenders whenever time is of
the essence. In the course of their normal business
operations, especially when these are predominantly
trading operations, most businessmen will occasionally come across an opportunity which requires quick
and substantial cash for its fruition. It is a rare
bank which can make a substantial loan, even to its
best customer, in a matter of minutes. Most large
moneylenders can and do. This last point acquires
special validity in the provinces, where most large
loans require prior permission from Bangkok headquarters. To the extent, therefore, that the need
for quick cash explains a large proportion of business borrowing from moneylenders, one would expect
them to be underrepresented in a survey of metropolitan businesses.

Many of the above considerations which apply to
independent moneylenders apply equally as well to
those individuals who operate in the penumbra of the
commercial banking system in Thailand. With respect to
the latter, there are other constraints which militate against their being fully reflected in the urban credit survey results. There is, first of all,
the need to protect such sources of funds, a need
which is greater than the one to protect the moneylenders. Both types of lenders act outside the law,
but the bank-connected individuals also act against
the bank. In the second place, extra-bank financial
dealings with bank officials are never simple,
straightforward loan transactions. A bank borrower
may be told, for instance, that he will obtain the
loan from the bank on regular terms but that he must
pay a commission to the compradore or that he may
have to accept "temporarily" a slight cash discount
from the face value of the loan. He may also be
told that he is expected to contribute a sum of money
to a "welfare" fund or that it would be appreciated
if he were to remember the official in question at
Christmas or on his birthday, and so on. Another
reason why businessmen may, on occasion, shy away

from the banks is that a good opportunity, requiring
ready and substantial cash, may need to be hidden
from bank officials, compradores, and others who are
themselves interested in such opportunities.

In addition to private individuals, nonbanking
sources of funds include those obtained from specialized financial institutions. Only very few firms in
the sample resorted to this type of credit. Several
larger firms obtained funds from the Industrial
Finance Corporation of Thailand and one or two from
the Small Industry Loan Funds. No firm in the sample
indicated that it obtained funds from life insurance
companies.

What is amazing is that apparently no firm obtained funds from the sale of securities, such as
debentures, to the public. Inasmuch as the survey
purports to include most large firms in the metropolitan area, some of which are known to have issued
securities in the period covered by the survey, the
results are clearly at variance with facts. Apart
from the possibility that the exact date of issue
cannot be remembered, the main reason for the omis-
sion of this source of funds can be explained by the
way the questionnaire was constructed. When a respondent failed to check any of the alternatives
indicated under a given question, the interviewer was
instructed to mark the "no code" line. The number
of these "no code" markings with respect to the question of issuance of securities was especially large,
reflecting to an unknown extent the ambiguity of the
Thai equivalents of the English designations of the
various types of securities.

One source of funds not reflected in the tables
so far is that of trade credit. Only peripheral attention can be given to this type of credit here, but
its importance is illustrated by the data in Table
7.12. The annual amount borrowed by sample firms in
the form of stock, machinery, and equipment is about
three times the amount of cash. As was to be expected, it is the wholesalers who rely most on this
source for their operations.

TABLE 7.12

Urban Credit Survey:
Trade Credit by Type and Number of Firms

Type of Firms	1965 Trade Credit				1966 Trade Credit			
	Number of Firms		Amount		Number of Firms		Amount	
	Number	%	Amount Million	%	Number	%	Amount Million	%
All firms	31,416	100	9,252	100	32,852	100	9,564	100
Big industry	66	0.21	468	5.06	65	0.20	510	5.33
Medium industry	575	1.83	1,116	12.06	562	1.71	1,090	11.40
Small industry	3,050	9.71	252	2.72	3,125	9.52	254	2.66
Wholesale	1,950	6.21	5,255	56.80	1,750	5.33	5,785	60.49
Big retail	4,900	15.60	1,822	19.69	5,200	15.83	1,664	17.40
Small retail	20,500	65.25	247	2.67	21,750	66.21	202	2.11
Luxury service	375	1.19	91	0.98	400	1.22	59	0.62

Details may not add up to total because of rounding.

Terms of Loans

The analysis of survey results indicates that,
with the possible exception of the funds obtained
from relatives and friends and the possible exception
of some security issuers hidden behind the "no code"
designation, outside financing of Thai business is
done on a contractual basis. Funds obtained are
loans, or at least are shown as such; they require
certain stated obligations on the part of the borrowers; and they are advanced by the lenders subject to
certain conditions.

Even though the greatest proportion of initial
capital comes from "inside," i.e., from an entrepreneur's own funds, outside sources of funds to start
a business are mainly contractual obligations no different in kind from those obtained to finance ongoing
operations. In this section the terms at which these
contractual obligations are made will be discussed
in the light of the findings of the urban credit survey.

The most important of these terms is the interest
rate. Table 7.13 gives the modal rates on initial
capital by sources of funds and type of firm. The
modal rates were determined by two criteria: the
number of firms and the amount borrowed. For example,
the modal interest rate for medium industrial firms
on funds obtained from commercial banks is 14 per
cent per annum when the greatest number of firms in
that category is considered. The modal interest rate
is 6 per cent when the greatest amount borrowed from
this source is taken into account. Table 7.13 suggests that there are significant variations with respect to the source of funds and the type of borrower. Moreover, the modal rate changes significantly
according to whether the criterion used is the number
of firms or the amount borrowed. Small industrial
establishments, for example, can in most cases obtain
funds from relatives and friends at no explicit interest charge. However, whenever the amounts required
are large, they must typically pay 24 per cent per
annum. On the other hand, small retail firms apparently do better with friends and relative in terms of

TABLE 7.13

Urban Credit Survey:
Modal Annual Interest Rates on Initial Capital, by Source of Funds
and Type of Firm
(%)

Type of Firm	Modal Annual Interest Rate[a] by Source							
	Family/Friends		Commercial Banks		Nonbank		Other	
	Mode A	Mode B	Mode A	Mode B	Mode A	Mode B	Mode A	Mode B
Big industry	24	24	6	6	9	9	6	6
Medium industry	0	24	14	6	–	–	–	–
Small industry	0	24	15	15	+	–	–	–
Wholesale	18	18	12	12	–	–	–	–
Big retail	30+	30	12	15	–	–	–	–
Small retail	30+	12	–	–	–	–	–	–
Luxury service	24	24	–	–	–	–	–	–
All firms	30+	24	12	12	9	9	6	6

[a]Two modal rates were compiled: Mode A, the rate paid by the greatest number of firms in each category of firm, and Mode B, the rate at which the greatest amount was borrowed in each category of firm. Plus sign means "over."

the amounts borrowed than they do with respect to
number of units. For all firms, relatives and friends
are the most costly source of initial outside capital
by either criterion. Nonbanking and other sources,
available only to large firms, are the cheapest source.

Of greater significance is the information given
in Table 7.14, which, while constructed on the same
principles as Table 7.13, pertains to funds for ongoing operations. The greater significance derives
from two circumstances. First, as mentioned above,
survey results relating to funds for ongoing operations appear to be more reliable than those for starting capital and, second, the former funds rely more
on outside capital than do the latter.

In Table 7.14, nonbank and "other" are no longer
the cheapest sources of funds, nor are they confined
to large industrial firms. With respect to nonbank
sources, some firms obtained funds from private individuals, notoriously expensive providers of funds.
With respect to "other" sources, a number of small
industrial firms were forced to borrow, abroad most
likely, and at high interest rates.

The modal rates of interest payable to commercial banks are within the formal limits prescribed
by the Bank of Thailand. For the period covered by
the table, these ranged from 7 per cent for an importer's accommodation to 15 per cent for loans to
local entrepreneurs. For each category of loan these
rates are maximum rates, i.e., a customer can get an
import loan at less than 7 per cent but cannot pay
more than that, legally. These modal rates mask,
however, the actual dispersion which is shown in Table
7.15 and which is of interest in the light of these
legal maxima. Table 7.15 shows that 39 per cent of
small industrial firms and 8 per cent of medium-size
industrial firms were required to pay more than the
maximum legal rates to banks for their initial capital.

Table 7.16 shows that the dispersion of costs
of bank loans exists also with respect to capital for
ongoing purposes. While only 2 per cent of the total

TABLE 7.14

Urban Credit Survey:
Modal Annual Interest Rates on Ongoing Funds,
by Source of Funds and Type of Firm
(%)

Type of Firm	Modal Annual Interest Rate[a] by Source							
	Family/Friends		Commercial Banks		Nonbank		Other	
	Mode A	Mode B	Mode A	Mode B	Mode A	Mode B	Mode A	Mode B
Big industry	0	0	-	10	9	9	8	8
Medium industry	24	24	15	15	30	30	8	8
Small industry	24	24	24	12	-	-	24	24
Wholesale	0	-6	15	10	-6	-6	-	-
Big retail	30+	0	15	12	30+	30+	-	-
Small retail	30+	24	-	-	24	24	-	-
Luxury service	12	12	-	-	-	-	-	-
All firms	30+	0	15	10	15	15	24	8

[a]Two modal rates were compiled: Mode A, the rate paid by the greatest number of firms in each category of firm, and Mode B, the rate at which the greatest amount was borrowed in each category of firm. Plus sign means "over," minus sign means "under."

TABLE 7.15

Urban Credit Survey:

Interest Rates on Initial Capital from Commercial Banks, by Type of Firm

Type of Firm	Interest Rates on Initial Capital from Commercial Banks							
	Total		Under 7%		7-15%		Over 15%	
	Amount	%	Amount	%	Amount	%	Amount	%
Big industry	51,000,000	100	42,000,000	82.34	9,000,000	17.65	-	-
Medium industry	5,188,000	100	2,500,000	48.19	2,687,500	51.80	500,000	0.01
Small industry	16,250,000	100	-	-	10,000,000	61.54	6,250,000	38.46
Wholesale	105,800,000	100	-	-	105,800,000	100.00	-	-
Big retail	27,500,000	100	-	-	27,500,000	100.00	-	-
Small retail	-	-	-	-	-	-	-	-
Luxury service	-	-	-	-	-	-	-	-
All firms	205,738,000	100	44,500,000	21.63	154,987,500	75.33	6,250,500	3.04

Details may not add up to total because of rounding.

TABLE 7.16

Urban Credit Survey:
Interest Rates on Additional Funds from Commercial Banks, by Type of Firm

| Type of Firm | Total | | Interest Rates on Additional Funds from Commercial Banks | | | | | |
| | | | Under 7% | | 7-15% | | Over 15% | |
	Amount	%	Amount	%	Amount	%	Amount	%
Big industry	302,724,315	100	–	–	302,724,315	100.0	–	–
Medium industry	374,003,874	100	9,617,300	2.57	359,724,074	96.18	4,662,500	1.25
Small industry	46,050,000	100	–	–	37,000,000	80.35	9,050,000	19.65
Wholesale	625,232,300	100	–	–	615,232,300	98.40	10,000,000	1.60
Big retail	164,755,000	100	–	–	159,755,000	96.97	5,000,000	3.03
Small retail	–	–	–	–	–	–	–	–
Luxury service	–	–	–	–	–	–	–	–
All firms	1,512,765,489	100	9,617,300	0.64	1,474,435,689	97.47	28,712,500	1.90

amount borrowed from commercial banks bore an interest cost above the legal maximum rate, it affected
a broader array of firms than was the case with initial capital.

The interest rates paid to private individuals
ranged from 15 per cent per annum to over 30 per
cent. Most of the firms that obtained funds from
this source were required to pay in excess of 30 per
cent, with no appreciable differentiation among types
of firms except that medium-size industrial concerns
paid considerably less than the small and large retail concerns. "Over 30 per cent" was the highest
category in the questionnaire. Presumably, additional classes would have indicated a greater differentiation among types of firms.

Tables 7.17 and 7.18 summarize the available
information regarding terms of loans other than interest. These tables should be viewed with caution,
however. Because of the technical nature of the
terms employed, it is hard to know to what extent
the answers given reflect real understanding on the
part of the respondents. These typical (that is,
covering the greatest number of firms represented in
the sample) loan conditions were confined to three
aspects of the terms, other than interest, on which
these loans were granted.

These three aspects consist of an extra fee,
collateral, and the duration of the loan. The extra
fee refers to payments that, allegedly, must be made
to certain intermediaries in order to gain access to
the actual lender, as well as secure a loan from him.
The other aspects were intended to have the same
meaning they have in Western usage. Information
garnered from the survey regarding future financing
plans does not appear either meaningful or reliable.
Some 17,000 firms represented in the sample indicated
that they planned to obtain slightly over 2,000 million baht in the twelve-month period after the survey
but stated that these funds would come from their own
resources.

TABLE 7.17

Urban Credit Survey:
Initial Capital, Typical[a] Loan Conditions,
by Source and Type of Firm

| | Initial Capital Loan Conditions and Sources | | | | | | | | | | | |
| Type of Firm | Family and Friends | | | Commercial Banks | | | Nonbank Sources | | | Other Sources | | |
	Extra Fee	Collateral[b]	Duration	Extra Fee	Collateral[b]	Duration	Extra Fee	Collateral[b]	Duration	Extra Fee	Collateral[b]	Duration
All firms	6%	other	no limit	0	sale/right	no limit	0	title deed	over 1 yr.	0	other	over 1 yr.
Big industry	-	-	under 3 mos.	0	title deed	over 1 yr.	0	-	over 1 yr.	0	other	over 1 yr.
Medium industry	0	other	no limit	0	sale/right	3-6 mos.	-	title deed	-	-	-	-
Small industry	0	other	under 3 mos.	0	mortgage	3-6 mos.	-	-	-	-	-	-
Wholesale	0	sale/right	7-12 mos.	0	mortgage	3-6 mos.	-	-	-	-	-	-
Big retail	-	other	no limit	0	sale/right	under 3 mos.	-	-	-	-	-	-
Small retail	6%	other	under 3 mos.	-	-	no limit	-	-	-	-	-	-
Luxury service	-	-	-	-	-	-	-	-	-	-	-	-

[a] Whenever data were available with respect to modality both for numbers of firms and the amounts involved, the modal number of firms was chosen as typical.

[b] "Other" refers to other than pledge, mortgage, sale with right of redemption guarantee (sale/right), title deed, or securities.

TABLE 7.18

Urban Credit Survey: Funds for Ongoing Purposes
Typical Loan Conditions, by Source and Type of Firm

Type of Firm	Family and Friends			Commercial Banks			Nonbank Sources			Other Sources		
	Extra Fee	Collat- eral[a]	Dura- tion	Extra Fee	Collat- eral[b]	Dura- tion	Extra Fee	Collat- eral	Dura- tion	Extra Fee	Collat- eral[a]	Dura- tion
All firms	0	other	no limit	under 5%	guaran- tee	3-6 mos.	0	other	under 3 mos.	0	other	no limit
Big industry	0	guaran- tee	no limit	0	guaran- tee	7-12 mos.	0	title deed	over 1 yr.	0	guaran- tee	over 1 yr.
Medium industry	0	other	no limit	0	guaran- tee	3-6 mos.	under 5%	other	no limit	0	other	over 1 yr.
Small industry	0	other	no limit	under 5%	guaran- tee	3-6 mos.	under 5%	other	no limit	0	other	no limit
Whole- sale	0	other	no limit	under 5%	guaran- tee	3-6 mos.	0	other	no limit	-	-	7-12 mos.
Big retail	-5	other	no limit	under 5%	guaran- tee	3-6 mos.	0	pledge	under 3 mos.	-	-	-
Small retail	0	other	no limit	-	-	-	-	other	under 3 mos.	-	-	-
Luxury service	0	other	no limit	-	-	-	-	-	-	-	-	-

[a]"other" refers to other than pledge, mortgage, sale with right of redemption guarantee, title deed, or securities.

[b]"guarantee" refers to third party guarantor who assumes contingent liability.

URBAN CREDIT SURVEY AND UNORGANIZED MARKETS

The sample survey lends some credence to the
contention that financial markets in Thailand are
layered, both with respect to the predominant type
of supplier of credit and with respect to the gradation of interest rates and other terms of loans. It
provides some evidence that there is, in fact, a
penumbra of the commercial banking system in which
a significant proportion of borrowers must pay interest rates higher than the maximum rates set by the
authorities. It also suggests that some 40 per cent
of business firms probably resort to moneylenders,
however disguised these may be as friends or relatives.

The survey amply confirms the proposition that
sources of initial capital are quite different from
those which provide for the ongoing needs of business. Nearly nine-tenths of initial capital needs
come from personal sources, i.e., an entrepreneur's
own funds, compared with 6 per cent of ongoing capital coming from this source. Commercial banks,
which provide a negligible proportion of initial
funds, account for 40 per cent of ongoing funds, even
though most small-scale establishments do not have
access to commercial bank accommodation.

Four findings of the sample survey are of particular significance for Thai developmental planning
in the area of finance. The first of these is the
revealed importance of trade credit, which, for ongoing capital needs, appears to be about three times
as important as borrowed funds. Even in the developed
countries, trade credit is an important source of operating capital. In the developed countries, however,
it is partly institutionalized, and discount companies, agents, and other institutions retain some relation to the organized money market. In Thailand,
trade credit remains largely outside the control of
developmental authorities, and its relationship to
the organized money market is tenuous at best.

The second significant finding of the survey is
the importance of the rotating credit society as a

source of ongoing capital for Thai business. While
in value terms the Thai <u>pia huey</u> accounts for less
than 5 per cent of ongoing funds, some 30 per cent
of all business firms rely on this form of finance.

The third finding of significance, one which is
probably especially relevant for Thailand, is the
very minor role played by specialized financial institutions in financing Thai business needs. In addition, there are very few public institutions
designed to provide developmental finance. The proportion of funds provided by the IFCT and the Loan
Office for Small Industries is very small indeed,
and neither life insurance companies nor other financial institutions play any significant part in financing business. (For further evidence regarding this
point see Chapter 8.)

The last and perhaps the most important finding
of the survey from the standpoint of developmental
finance is the almost exclusively contractual nature
of borrowing by Thai business establishments. There
is little indication of equity financing, no evidence
of funds being provided in exchange for participation
in profits, and no sign of venture companies or other
similar institutions of capital markets. It is, of
course, possible that part of the allegedly personal
entrepreneur-owned funds connote some participation
in profits on the part of close kin, but external
funds are obtained against a promise of payment of
fixed amounts in the future. In a country where the
level of interest rates is high, this excessive reliance on contractual finance militates against the
formation of sizable manufacturing units, against
productive enterprise with a long gestation period,
and in favor of undertakings which tend to promise a
quick pay-off.

As is true for most market surveys, the reliability of the survey of urban credit appears to be
much greater with respect to prices than with respect
to quantities. That is, the data on the cost of loans
seem more reliable than the figures on their amounts
or information on the way in which they were utilized.
In general, the information on prices (i.e., interest

rates on various sources of loans) is consistent with the qualitative information derived from field research unconnected with statistics.

For reasons touched on in several parts of the preceding discussion, the role of unorganized markets in financing Thai business appears understated by the results of the survey. Even so, the role of unorganized markets in the day-to-day financing of Thai business (as distinct from initial capital financing), even in metropolitan areas, is not negligible. If one includes relatives and friends, private individuals, pia huey, and at least a portion of personal, or "own," resources as deriving from unorganized markets, then up to one-fourth of the total ongoing funds of Thai business comes from outside the organized markets.

It is difficult to assess the plausibility of the above estimate because there is so little comparative data to go by. Measurements of unorganized markets in other countries have typically concentrated on markets for rural credit, and very little quantitative information is available on financing sources of business outside the organized markets. The one striking exception to the above statement is Korea, a country which may serve as a comparison with Thailand. In 1965, 80 per cent of all manufacturing establishments in Korea were said to resort to the unorganized money markets (defined somewhat differently than in here), and one-third of those establishments in debt owed moneylenders between 40 and 80 per cent of their liabilities.[3]

The astonishing fact about these findings is that they were obtained from a mail questionnaire sent quarterly to some 600 manufacturing enterprises in 10 major cities. The response rate is said to be in the neighborhood of 55 per cent.

It is said that 16 per cent of total borrowing by Korean businesses, including manufacturing, was from unorganized financial markets in 1962.[4] Even though Korea has had much less price stability than Thailand, it does have a much greater number of specialized credit institutions and it makes a much greater effort to limit borrowing from the unorganized markets.[5]

The general picture of unorganized financial markets developed early in this chapter, a picture only moderately filled in and supported by quantitative data from the sample survey, is consistent with what is known about these markets in other parts of Asia. While unorganized financial markets in various countries differ quite appreciably with respect to structure and composition and have very different proportions of rural versus urban or consumption versus business credit, they do share a number of operational aspects. Such characteristics as rather high and freely fluctuating lending rates, the absence of cumbersome lending procedures, lesser reliance on formal collateral, and the dispersion of lending centers may be cited as examples.[6] In addition, several studies of unorganized markets in Asian countries have noted the preponderance of relatives and friends as sources of funds. The fact that these funds are often rather costly implies the existence of risks not usually associated with true kinship ties or genuine friendships. The prevalence of rotating credit societies has already been mentioned.

In a number of studies of unorganized markets, the inference is drawn that their spread and development is a direct function of the inadequacies of existing financing institutions, as well as the inability or unwillingness of commercial banks to provide sufficient funds for the legitimate needs of the smaller trader or manufacturer.[7] In particular, a number of studies conclude that unorganized financial markets are not compatible with societal developmental needs, despite their merits or virtues in satisfying needs not elsewhere provided for. Their lending priorities run counter to developmental priorities. The lenders in unorganized markets are typically interested in assets maintenance of their borrowers rather than in the continuing growth of these assets. The very existence of these markets inhibits an effective strategy of developmental financing and of an effective credit and monetary policy. While these markets may

be quite efficient from an operational, microeconomic
point of view, they are inefficient from the standpoint of social macroeconomic policy. From the standpoint of developmental strategy the implications for
policy measures are quite simple. The existing institutions of the capital market must be made more
efficient. The commercial banking system should be
induced to direct a greater proportion of its resources into financing of small and medium-scale non-
trading enterprises. Additional study and research
should be made of arrangements such as pia huey and
trade credit to see if they can be replaced or supported by similar institutions in the organized market, with the aim of making them more amenable to
social goals. But the main thrust of this chapter
is that the primary reason for the financing of business needs outside the organized markets in the urban
areas is the lack of equity finance in those markets.
To start a business, in particular, the Thai entrepreneur has to fall back on his own resources and
those of his friends and relatives. Not only the
volume but the distribution of investment is strongly
affected by the unavailability of finance on participation basis. The existing complex of laws, customs, and trading tends to favor trade, construction,
and "packaging" of imports and the lack of noncontractual equity funds militates against the formation
of manufacturing businesses utilizing local resources
of raw material and personnel. While the analysis
of the tax structure is outside the scope of this
study, the lack of a tax on transfers of property,
and so on, makes trading deals more attractive than
they would be under a more balanced tax and legal
structure.

Thus, the most important single measure calculated to enhance the scope of financing through the
unorganized markets would be the establishment within the organized markets of institutions and instruments which could provide, to some extent at least,
equity funds to actual and would-be entrepreneurs;
specific suggestions are made to that effect in Chapter 9.

NOTES

1.   It will be recalled that the analysis of
the unorganized markets in financing agriculture was
based, to a large extent, on the survey of agricultural credit conducted in 1962/63 by Katsetsart University, with the cooperation of an American scholar.
No comparable information existed with respect to
"urban" finance. Additional information on the survey of urban credit, including a specimen of the
English translation of the questionnaire, is given
in Alek A. Rozental, "Draft of Final Report: Finance
and Development in Thailand" (Washington, D.C.:
Center for Development Planning, National Planning
Association, 1968). (Mimeo.)

2.   For a comprehensive account of the various
practices, see Clifford Geertz, "The Rotating Credit
Society: A Middle Rung in Development," Economic
Development and Cultural Change (April, 1962); for
a detailed account of Vietnamese no, see Nguyen Van
Vinh, "Savings and Mutual Lending Societies," Yale
University, Southeast Asia Studies (Ann Arbor: Uni-
versity Microfilms, 1949); for an account of the Kye,
see Le Duc Soo, "Study of Unorganized Money Market"
(Seoul, Korea: n.d.). (Mimeo.)

3.   See Bank of Korea, Survey of Enterprise
Finance, Private Finance, and Business Prospects
(Seoul: Bank of Korea, 3rd Quarter, 1965).

4.   See Kwang Suk Kim, "Unofficial Money Market
in Korea" (Seoul, 1964). (Mimeo.)

5.   See Chang-Nyul Lee, "Financing and Capital
Formation in Korea" (Seoul, 1966); this work is
written in Korean and was not read by the author,
but the author did benefit from personal discussions
with Kwang Suk Kim, who was attached to the ECAFE in
1967.

6.   In addition to the sources cited above, the
following contain material on the unorganized markets
in the countries of Asia: Government of India,

Directorate of Economics and Statistics, <u>Agricultural</u>
<u>Legislation in India</u>, Vol. I, especially "Regulation
of Money Lending" (Delhi: Manager of Publications,
1956); Reserve Bank of India, <u>Report on Rural Credit</u>
<u>Follow-up Survey 1959-60</u> (Bombay: Reserve Bank of
India, 1962); Dacca University Socio-economic Survey
Board, <u>Report on the Survey of Rural Credit and Rural</u>
<u>Unemployment in East Pakistan, 1956</u> (Dacca, East
Pakistan: Dacca University, 1958); Central Bank of
Ceylon, <u>Survey of Ceylon's Consumer Finances, 1963</u>
(Colombo: Bank of Ceylon, 1964); Central Bank of
China, <u>Financial Statistics Monthly</u> (Taipei: Central
Bank of China, July, 1966); Central Bank of the Phil-
ippines, <u>Seventeenth Annual Report</u> (Manila: Central
Bank of the Philippines, 1965); J. G. Gurley, H. T.
Patrick, and E. S. Shaw, <u>The Financial Structure of</u>
<u>Korea</u> (Seoul: U.S. Operations Mission/Korea, 1965).

7.   "The role and lending behavior of commercial banks in many Asian countries which favor individuals and firms on economically irrelevant grounds
give rise to a class of intermediaries": from an
unpublished paper, "Unorganized Credit Markets: Features and Policies," prepared by the Survey Section
of ECAFE, November, 1966.

CHAPTER **8** THE CAPITAL MARKET

The market for long-term funds is, in Thailand, a
highly imperfect one. This situation is not unique
to Thailand and indeed is not confined to the developing countries. In fact, in very few countries in
the world can it be said that there exist institutions and instruments which are fully adequate to
finance the needs of industry (including the construction and transportation industries) on terms which
are acceptable to both borrowers and lenders.[1] But
it is in the less developed countries where the need
for provision of long-term capital to industry is
more acute and immediate, and where the scope for improvement is perhaps greater.[2]

In Thailand, in addition to the imperfections of
capital markets, common to most developing countries,
there are other peculiarities due to the past history
of the Kingdom. There is, first of all, a paucity
of institutional arrangements and a corresponding
shortage of financial instruments. Compared with,
say, Indonesia or the Philippines, there is rather a
small number of specialized institutions dealing with
long-term finance. This is strikingly true in the
public sector. Apart from the Bank for Agriculture
and Agricultural Cooperatives, there is the Government Savings Bank (GSB), LOSID, and the Government
Provident Fund. With one exception, that of LOSID,
none of these institutions are specifically designed
for development finance, are for the most part very
recent in origin, and dispose of very limited funds,
the supply of which is not likely to increase in the
near future.

All these institutions of the public sector are
discussed in this chapter, except for the Bank for

Agriculture and Agricultural Cooperatives which was
referred to in Chapter 3. In addition, there has
been in operation, since 1953, a Housing Bank in the
Ministry of Finance which uses public funds to buy
land and construct dwellings for lower income groups
in the metropolitan area. Some 60 million baht was
used for this purpose from 1953 to about 1967. The
Housing Bank's resources come from the budget and
from the Government Savings Bank. Its total assets
showed a decline from some 150 million baht in 1965
to 125 million at the end of 1967. The government
also operates municipal pawnshops alongside private
ones. In 1967, there were some 150 pawnshops in operation, of which 90 were privately operated but
licensed by central or local government. In 1967,
all pawnshops accepted pledges to the value of 147
million baht, about triple the level of 1959. The
resources of government pawnshops are not, as yet,
available for developmental finance. Their profits
are low and they have no significant accumulation of
reserves. Those operated by the private sector are
chiefly ancillary to other interests of their owners,
many of whom graduate into commercial banking. In
addition to these private and municipal pawnshops,
there are allegedly "unofficial" pawnshops which make
"consumption" loans at exorbitant rates of interest.

In the private sector the dearth of capital
market institutions is even more pronounced. Only
the IFCT can be said to have the provision of long-
term finance as its main task, and, so far, the scope
of its operations remains a very limited one. Thai
life insurance companies are yet to play a role in
long-term financing, and this applies with even greater force to pension and provident funds. Thailand
has no building societies, no comprehensive welfare
schemes, no national compulsory insurance schemes, a
stock market which is still in its infancy, and an
almost complete lack of any institutions and instruments for equity finance. In brief, unlike its money
market which is relatively sophisticated, the Thai
capital market appears to be much more primitive than
would seem to be warranted by the country's stage of
economic growth. The succeeding sections give a brief
discussion of the institutions and instruments in that

market. The discussion is largely descriptive. It
is designed to substantiate the assertions made in
Chapter 7 that it is in the area of provision of
long-term finance to industry that the organized
markets fall woefully short of developmental needs.

THE GOVERNMENT SAVINGS BANK

Next to commercial banks, the GSB is by far the
most important collector of household savings in
Thailand and, when measured in terms of its assets,
is the most important component of the Thai capital
market. On the other hand, the GSB makes available
the bulk of its resources to the government, participates very little in the provision of funds for
long-term finance, and makes very little contribution
to the private sector. In brief, while the Savings
Bank is a very large financial institution, its importance as a developmental financial intermediary
is much more limited and is not likely to increase
in the future.[3]

The Government Savings Bank came into operation
in 1946 under the Government Savings Bank Act. It
replaced the Postal Savings Bank system which was
set up in 1913, and it still uses a number of country post offices as its agencies or branches. The
Savings Bank, in addition to performing the standard
functions of a savings institution, i.e., accepting
savings deposits from individuals and groups, is also
engaged in a rather bewildering array of other activities which include some commercial banking functions,
selling of insurance, issuance of bonds, and others.
The bank is managed by a board of directors who have
prior approval on any major transaction of the bank
and all of whom are appointed by the Minister of
Finance.

In its years of operation, the Savings Bank has
been remarkably successful in attracting small savings. Its deposits have been growing at an annual
compound rate of more than 15 per cent since 1962, a
rate of growth exceeded only by that of fixed deposits at the commercial banks. At the end of 1967,

total assets of the Government Savings Bank were
5.0 billion baht, and some 4.4 billion of its liabilities were in savings deposits (see Tables 8.1 and
8.2). Government Savings Bonds and Premium Savings
Bonds are essentially a form of savings liability.
They are issued by the Government Savings Bank and
are subject to withdrawal on demand. They represent
household savings and are claims against the bank
analogous to savings deposits.

What makes the record of the Bank a remarkable
one, however, is the fact that even though its deposits are only about one-fourth of those held at the
commercial banks, they represent an aggregate of very
small amounts saved by individuals, many of whom are
in the lower income groups and many of whom reside in
the villages. At the end of 1967, the number of depositors at the Government Savings Bank was over 6
million, compared to slightly over 1 million at the
end of 1947.

To be able to tap the savings of 6 million individuals in a country of some 30 million is no mean
achievement, particularly in view of the fact that
throughout most of its existence the rates of interest paid by the GSB were considerably below those
obtaintable elsewhere. These rates differ according
to the type of deposit and have undergone many changes
over time. The highest rate payable in 1967 was 5
per cent, which compares with the 7 per cent maximum
rate of commercial bank deposits held for 12 months
or longer. The rate on demand deposits is now 3 per
cent; on savings deposits, 5 per cent; and 1 per cent
on premium savings bonds which, however, have an added lottery feature.

It would seem that, in attracting small savings,
availability of saving outlets and an aggressive marketing policy are of prime importance. The GSB has
some 300 branches and agencies outside the metropolitan areas, compared with 50 branches in the Bangkok-
Thonburi region, and its country deposits exceed
those gathered from the metropolitan area by some 50
cent.

TABLE 8.1

Government Savings Bank Assets, 1956-1967[a]

(million baht)

| Year | Cash | | | | Loans and Overdrafts | | | | Bills Dis-counted | Thai Govt. Securities | Other Assets | Total Assets |
	Notes & Coins	Balances at Banks Bank of Thailand	Others	Total	Private	Govt.	Banks	Total				
1956	13	20	35	68	137	281	169	587	97	56	77	885
1957	15	37	48	100	136	328	169	633	113	125	91	1,062
1958	18	21	75	114	165	368	165	698	112	169	115	1,208
1959	19	22	103	144	198	356	266	820	86	267	139	1,456
1960	24	18	145	187	159	403	257	819	113	440	157	1,716
1961	25	30	163	218	158	390	256	804	103	646	178	1,949
1962	35	18	170	223	224	368	248	840	71	940	201	2,275
1963	36	9	149	194	165	368	235	768	43	1,324	218	2,547
1964	36	20	152	208	142	336	210	688	13	1,752	272	2,933
1965	40	34	160	234	137	250	192	579	11	2,405	281	3,510
1966	46	37	148	232	139	65	171	375	12	3,456	238	4,313
1967	50	40	120	210	154	67	69	290	15	4,288	237	5,040

[a]Year end.
Source: Government Savings Bank.

297

TABLE 8.2

Government Savings Bank Liabilities, 1956-1967[a]

(million baht)

| Year | Private Sector Deposits | | | | Govt. Demand Deposits | Bank Demand Deposits | Govt. and Premium Savings Bonds | Insur- ance | Other Liabilities | Capital Accounts |
| | Savings Deposits | Other Deposits | | Total | | | | | | |
		Demand	Time							
1956	657	59	2	718	20	1	71	5	65	5
1957	779	69	1	849	15	2	87	6	85	18
1958	843	93	1	937	20	1	105	7	100	38
1959	888	144	1	1,033	14	-	134	7	215	53
1960	1,057	187	23	1,267	12	2	168	7	192	68
1961	1,232	186	2	1,420	8	6	214	9	214	78
1962	1,387	156	9	1,552	5	14	302	10	297	95
1963	1,531	179	13	1,723	5	7	431	13	255	113
1964	1,683	185	16	1,884	5	8	591	15	290	140
1965	2,031	176	29	2,236	12	8	713	17	351	173
1966	2,573	183	29	2,785	15	9	846	20	428	209
1967	3,108	193	92	3,393	19	5	978	23	367	255

[a]Year end.

Source: Government Savings Bank.

Many of the "countryside depositors" are not members of rural households. Available data suggest, however, that at least a quarter of all deposits originate from rural households. GSB depositors indicate their occupation when making a deposit. In 1964, about 20 per cent of deposits came from farmers and fishermen, and it is reasonable to assume that at least an additional 6 per cent came from those classed as soldiers, rentiers, and others. It is estimated that, in contrast to 6 million depositors in the GSB, the number of those entrusting their savings to the commercial banks is less than 400,000.

In addition, the Savings Bank resorts to such devices as mobile vans sent to remote villages, children's savings plans, and others. Even so, in the opinion of qualified observers, the potential for mobilizing small savings through the efforts of the GSB is far from being exhausted. Apart from internal administrative improvements, it would seem that GSB success in attracting small savings could be further enhanced by abandoning a number of functions which are either marginal or inappropriate to a savings institution, such as selling traveler's checks, endowment insurance, and educational annuities, or discounting bills of exchange. These functions drain personnel resources, are a net loss administratively and financially, and/or could be performed more efficiently by other financial institutions. As seen in Table 8.1, the asset composition of the GSB has changed considerably over time. In 1956, two-thirds of total assets consisted of loans and overdrafts. Eleven years later these assets shrank to less than 6 per cent of the total, while government securities rose from less than 7 per cent to 85 per cent of total assets. Bills discounted, which in 1956 were a significant component of total assets, drastically diminished in importance by 1967 and constituted less than one-third of 1 per cent of all assets. In the twelve-year period, while total assets increased sixfold, government securities rose nearly eightyfold.

There were also significant changes in the composition and the pattern of growth of the Savings

Bank liabilities. Savings deposits decreased in relative importance, but savings bonds and premium savings bonds became a higher proportion of total assets.
These bonds, together with capital and reserves, show
a rate of growth which is a multiple of the rate of
all liabilities.

The rate of growth of premium savings bonds
which contain a lottery feature exceeded that of ordinary savings bonds. It was not possible to obtain
the absolute figures for ordinary bonds and lottery
bonds separately. In 1966, the composite of bonds
accounted for less than 20 per cent of all liabilities, but savings bonds endowed with the lottery
feature amounted to 22 per cent. Other information
confirms the allegation that, except for the capital
account, lottery bonds grew faster than any other
liability of the GSB.

The fact that lottery bonds grew much faster
than any other liability to depositors is of significance for mobilization of voluntary savings in Thailand. The contractual interest rate on these bonds
is only 1 per cent per annum compared to 3, 4, or 5
per cent payable, within the period, on savings deposits, banking deposits, and ordinary savings bonds.

The principal difference between savings deposits and fixed deposits at the banking department of
GSB lies in the acceptable ceiling on deposits. Savings deposits had a much lower ceiling because they
were meant principally for the small saver. Demand
deposits in the banking department paid a rate of
return ranking from 2 to 3 per cent per annum, but
had legal advantage over checking accounts in that
they could be drawn upon more quickly than the demand
deposits at the commercial banks which yield little
or no interest. However, in spite of a high rate of
increase over time, these deposits at the GSB have
not increased very much either absolutely or in relation to other liabilities.

The attraction of lottery bonds must be sought
in their mystique and in the lure of a high pay-off
rather than in their intrinsic superiority over other

savings instruments. The total cost to the Savings
Bank of the interest payments on these bonds is 3
per cent, which is below the return payable on other
deposits. This amount, however, instead of being
evenly distributed to all bondholders, is paid only
to those fortunate enough to draw the lucky lots at
periodic drawings. These lottery bonds have the
added attractive feature that their holders may hope
to win several times during the currency of the bond.
Moreover, this feature induces savers to hold their
bonds to maturity in the hope of being lucky the next
time a drawing is held. The prizes range up to 5,000
baht and more. The inference is strong that the small
saver in Thailand is not so much interested in small
differentials in the rate of return at the margin as
he is in the prospects of a large windfall, when such
windfall is accompanied by little or no risk of the
loss of principal.

There are reasons to believe that, even though
the appeal of the lottery bonds has quickly become
apparent to the directors of the GSB, less than a full
effort has been directed to the promotion and marketing of this type of instrument. The reasons for this
are complex and not entirely clear. In part, they
relate to the reluctance to weaken the acceptance of
other types of deposits and, in part, to the suspi-
cion that large-scale marketing of this type of security may interfere with the proceeds from the
national lottery.

Be that as it may, the experience of the Government Savings Bank has demonstrated that small savings
can be successfully tapped by an institution which,
first of all, provides widespread and convenient outlets to the savers and, secondly, provides savings
instruments which appeal to their prejudices, imagi-
nation, and preferences.

But the success of the GSB in attracting small
savings has not been paralleled by an effort to channel these savings into developmental priorities. The
blame for this can hardly attach to the management of
the GSB. As a government institution it was increasingly called upon to provide funds to the government

TABLE 8.3

Amount of Government Savings Bank Loans by Purpose, 1957-67
(thousand baht)

Purpose of Loan	Amount of Government Savings Bank Loans										
	1957	1958	1959	1960	1961	1962	1963	1964	1965	1966	1967
Housing	97,456	108,484	113,080	122,730	131,561	132,086	132,429	119,382	104,838	102,557	97,212
Education	5,649	5,390	4,738	4,161	3,490	2,748	1,804	2,121	1,314	1,012	8,021
Employee welfare	169	492	315	501	366	467	461	317	163	13	--
Public welfare	224,360	248,429	251,371	250,053	245,253	238,322	235,193	206,732	142,413	2,008	110
Cooperatives	113,650	110,000	112,050	103,875	103,275	95,725	84,682	72,315	60,338	47,440	33,507
Transportation	69,427	71,336	71,042	72,053	56,612	46,815	45,415	28,570	10,809	7,374	2,104
Industry	60,500	89,665	99,526	100,066	90,412	140,861	95,447	73,301	58,000	17,497	8,479
Oil Distribution	--	--	--	370	8,063	9,890	--	--	--	--	--
Hotels	--	--	--	33,000	30,000	25,000	14,000	10,000	7,000	-151	13
Pawn shops	--	--	--	12,000	12,000	12,063	7,584	8,040	8,578	7,324	13,112
Ship repair	--	--	--	3,015	236	248	77	407	-345	-1,668	708
Banking	--	--	--	98,874	98,874	98,874	98,574	91,254	90,150	84,998	--
Broadcasting	--	--	--	--	1,600	1,100	1,100	1,000	750	300	300
Lottery	--	--	--	16,956	21,150	33,819	49,274	73,474	91,775	102,710	123,249
Family annuity	--	--	--	1,141	1,331	1,618	2,043	2,523	2,823	3,197	3,483
Educational annuity	--	--	--	--	--	--	--	--	100	325	611
Other	61,852	63,823	167,944	--	--	--	--	--	--	--	--
Total	633,063	697,619	820,066	818,795	804,223	839,636	768,083	689,436	578,706	374,936	289,469

Source: Compiled from information obtained from Government Savings Bank.

and, of late, primarily to provide a market for government securities. As shown in Table 8.3, loans
have been decreasing in recent years, and less and
less of the reduced volume has been channeled to the
private sector for developmental purposes. In 1958
loans classified as being those to the private sector
were estimated at some 112 million baht. This modest
total shrank to about 10 million baht by the end of
1967. In any event, loans are now a minor component
of total assets of the Government Savings Bank.

THE LOAN OFFICE FOR SMALL INDUSTRIES DEVELOPMENT

LOSID was established within the Ministry of Industry in 1964 to assist small-scale enterprise in
obtaining finance on reasonable terms. It is the
first deliberate governmental attempt to use public
funds for the purpose of channeling private savings
into developmental priorities. The Industrial Finance
Corporation is an institution of the private sector.
The Bank for Agriculture and Agricultural Cooperatives
has functions other than developmental finance. In
the past, the Thai Government has attempted to promote
developmental projects through direct operation of
industrial and commercial enterprises, but LOSID remains the first institution of the public sector designed to promote development through financing,
without control, of private enterprises.

The loan program to small industries is administered jointly with the Krung Thai Bank, the only
deposit institution entirely controlled by the government. Initially two commercial banks cooperated
with LOSID, only one of which was government controlled. In 1966 these two banks merged to become
the Krung Thai Bank. LOSID is responsible for the
technical and economic evaluation of loan applications,
while the Krung Thai Bank appraises the collateral
and handles the procedural aspects. The credit risk
is assumed by the bank. The loan fund resources come
from budgetary appropriatons and from contributions
of the bank deposited to the special account. The
government matches the amounts earmarked by the bank

for LOSID purposes. (See Table 8.4.)* The bank
charges 9 per cent on the loans under the program
and pays the Loan Office 3 per cent of the monies
contributed by the Ministry of Finance. Thus the
bank obtains a 15 per cent gross return on the loan
disbursements.

The deliberate, developmental character of the
loan program lies in its emphasis on manufacturing
facilities and on confining the financial assistance
to "promotable industries." In addition to manufacturing and service industries (mainly repair shops),
handicrafts and cottage industries are also eligible.
But a long list of enterprises is excluded, among
them state enterprises, industries assisted from other
sources, hotels, tourist agencies, transport, dis-
tilleries and breweries, tobacco factories, slaughter
houses, printing presses, soap factories, spinneries,
food preservatives, plywood, cement factories, pharmaceuticals (except those processing local materials),
batteries and dry-cell factories, cold-storage
plants, paper mills, automobile assembly plants., and
the film industry. No enterprise with a capital of
over 2 million baht is eligible, and no loan can be
made for more than 500,000 baht. The applicant must
supply at least 50 per cent of equity in the project,
and he must provide a property collateral.

In 1966, over 80 per cent of all loans were made
to manufacturing enterprises. Up to the end of 1967,
219 loans were approved, with the average size of
the loan at about 200,000 baht (Table 8.4).

While LOSID grants loans for working capital
purposes, an effort has been made to stress loans for
plant and equipment. The proportion of loans made
for working capital decreased from nearly half in
1964 to less than one-fourth in 1967.

---

*Statistical information in this section was
compiled from the data obtained from LOSID and from
interviews with its principal personnel.

TABLE 8.4

LOSID Sources of Funds, 1964-1967
(million baht)

Year	LOSID Budget	Krung Thai Bank	Amount Available[a]
1964	10	5	10
1965	20	10	20
1966	25	15	30
1967	30	25	50

[a]Differs from the sum of the two preceding columns
  because a part of budgetary appropriations is kept
  at the Ministry of Finance and the amount released
  does not exceed the contribution of Krung Thai Bank.

Source: Compiled from data provided by LOSID.

As shown in Tables 8.4 and 8.5, only about one-
half of available resources were actually committed.
But this hardly suggests that the supply of lendable
funds is greater than the demand for them. Only a
fraction of loan applications pass muster and, even
more importantly, there are good reasons to believe
that the number of applicants is but a very small
part of those who could usefully avail themselves
of this facility. In addition to the usual impediments of lack of knowledge, the inability to prepare
an acceptable proposal, and the reluctance to dis-
close information or to deal with a governmental institution, there is the requirement that a property
collateral be offered, which, more often than not,
means land. For a variety of reasons, some of which
have been discussed earlier, the insistence on land
collateral is a serious obstacle to sound finance of
manufacturing enterprise. Moreover, the financing
facilities offered by LOSID are exclusively contractual in character. Loans are granted for periods of
from three to ten years, with, usually, one year of
grace. Although the interest rate charged is below
the market rate, the obligation to pay interest and
amortize the principal before the enterprise shows

any earnings is a serious deterrent to many would-be
applicants. Finally, according to the managers of
LOSID, the very limited scope of operations, circum-
scribed as they are by budgetary limitations, means
that the facility is ignored or disregarded by many
who otherwise could benefit from the program. The
management makes every effort to propagate the cause
of LOSID and is particularly anxious to reach enterprises outside the metropolitan area. It initiated
the changwad program, under which one or more LOSID
officers visit outlying provinces and try to canvass
would-be applicants. In 40 changwads (provinces) at
least one loan has been made.

TABLE 8.5

LOSID Loan History, 1964-1967
(amount in million baht)

Year	Loans Applied for		Loans Approved		Loans Dis- bursed	Loans Outstanding Amt. (end of period)
	No.	Amt.	No.	Amt.		
1964	121	36	12	2	1.3	1.3
1965	123	39	49	11	9.3	10.5
1966	131	45	70	16	11.0	19.9
1967	153	44	88	22	n.a.	n.a.

Source: Compiled from data provided by LOSID.

     There can be little question that provision of
financial assistance to small-scale manufacturing
enterprise, of the type being promoted by LOSID,
should have high priority among the developmental
goals of the country. As shown elsewhere, this is
the type of enterprise that encounters the greatest
difficulty in obtaining finance, pays the highest
rate for the limited amount it can obtain, and is
subject to the most onerous terms in general. (See
Chapter 7.) But LOSID's scale and scope of operations would need to be considerably expanded if it

were to make a significant contribution. Its record
is a good one. Only about 10 per cent of its loans
have gone sour. The 3 per cent return on budgetary
funds which accrues to LOSID was apparently adequate
to cover its operating expenses; after deficits in
1964 and 1965, the return on the loan portfolio exceeded its costs by about one-third. It pursues a
vigorous follow-up program and, in general, its leaders have an awareness of the needs and the means of
meeting them. It is those who run the affairs of
LOSID who feel that the office should make itself
independent of the government budget and should try
to obtain funds from the market at large. To do so,
it may have to revise its present loan policy. More
particularly, there seems to be less need to charge
a rate of interest below the market than to extend
the duration of the loan and to extend the grace period. There is no particular reason why LOSID should
subsidize the provision of working capital at the
expense of commercial banks, but there are good reasons for it to charge more for genuinely long-term
capital and so, in turn, attract savings to that purpose.

THE INDUSTRIAL FINANCE CORPORATION OF THAILAND

Of all the institutions of the Thai capital market, the IFCT is perhaps the most interesting from a
developmental standpoint. This is so for a number of
reasons. IFCT is the first, if not the only, financial institution deliberately set up to "assist in
the establishment, expansion or modernization of private industrial enterprises" and to "encourage the
participation of private capital, both internal and
external, in such enterprises."[4] Unlike other
publicly sponsored institutions in the Thai capital
market, IFCT is intended to operate predominantly in
the private sector, under private management, and re-
lying primarily on private funds; under the act, IFCT
cannot finance firms where more than 10 per cent of
capital stock is owned by government. Under its
statutes and regulations the Corporation has broad
operational latitude and can engage in all forms of
financing, with or without collateral, on contractual

or on equity basis, directly or indirectly. Because
of its scope and also because of its origins, IFCT
has had relatively easy access to foreign venture
capital and to foreign long-term loans. Finally,
even though its performance to date has fallen short
of expectations, IFCT has the potential, either alone
or in conjunction with a sister institution, to play
an important part in financing the industrial development of Thailand. This potential, however, is not
likely to be realized unless IFCT has access to new
and as yet untried modes of operation and financing
and unless it works in much closer cooperation with
other bodies concerned with industrialization of the
country. Until 1966, for example, for over six years
of its existence, there were no formal channels of
communication between the IFCT and the Board of Investments, the official body entrusted with the task
of stimulating industrial investment via such incentives as tax and customs exemptions. In 1966 the
Managing Director of the IFCT was made a member of
the Board of Investments.

The IFCT came into existence in 1959, when it
replaced the Industrial Bank set up in 1952. The Industrial Bank, which was a creature of the public
sector and whose directors were all appointed by the
Cabinet, proved a failure.[5] On its liquidation, some
14 million baht of its assets were converted into an
interest-free loan to the IFCT, whose own capital
was authorized at 100 million baht, of which 30 million was paid in by the end of 1966. In mid-1967, 20
million baht worth of shares were offered for subscription to stockholders. In spite of some problems
in selling the offered shares, all 20 million were
taken up.

The IFCT is controlled by a Board of Directors
which consists of eight men elected by the stockholders and one, usually the Chairman, appointed by the
government. Much of the actual operation of the Corporation is, however, performed by the staff under a
General Manager appointed by the Directors. In recent
years the Corporation has also evolved the practice
of an Executive Committee, composed of five members
of the Board of Directors who have the power to make

decisions within certain limits. In addition to the
general provisions of the act of 1959, as amended in
1962 and 1963, the operational policies of IFCT are
regulated by a set of provisions prescribed by the
Board.

Even though it was intended that IFCT act as a
catalyst to generate private capital financing of a
medium-term and long-term nature to Thai industry,
throughout its entire history the Corporation has
been forced to fall back on public funds to carry
out its functions. In addition to a long-term,
interest-free loan of 15 million dollars obtained
from U.S. counterpart aid funds, IFCT secured a loan
of 20 million baht from the Thai Government in 1962,
another loan of 30 million in 1965, and yet another
of 20 million in 1967. The 15 million dollar loan
from the International Cooperation Administration,
a U.S. aid agency, was for a 30-year period. The
Thai Government loan of 20 million baht in 1962 was
for a period of 50 years, with no interest payable
for the first 20 years, 3 per cent payable in the
next 20 years, and 5 per cent on the remainder of
the currency of the loan. The 1965 loan of 30 million was for 15 years at 6 per cent per annum. Exact
terms of the 1967 loan of 20 million baht were not
available at the time of writing. Even with these
loans, its resources, particularly those in local
currency, proved inadequate to meet the demand for
finance, and during 1967 and 1968 IFCT had to sell
its debentures to the Bank of Thailand and to the
Government Savings Bank.

In addition to baht loans, IFCT obtained loans
from foreign sources. In 1963 it negotiated a loan
agreement with the German Kreditanstalt fur Wiederauf-
brau for 11 million marks (about 54 million baht
equivalent), and in 1964 it obtained a credit of 2.5
million dollars (about 50 million baht equivalent)
from the International Bank for Reconstruction and
Development. These two lines of credit were to be
used up before December 1968 and April 1967 respectively. The loan agreement with the World Bank was
terminated in 1967, with slightly over 1 million
dollars of credit unspent.[6] In 1968, IFCT signed a

loan agreement with the Asian Development Bank for
a sum equivalent to 5 million dollars for a period
of 15 years at an interest rate of 6-7/8 per cent
per annum.

IFCT borrowing history up to the end of 1967 is
summarized in Table 8.6. The table gives the amounts
available for lending rather than the actual amount
borrowed, as the sums available under the various
loan agreements were not necessarily drawn in the
year in which an agreement was signed.

As shown in Table 8.7, it was not until 1966
that the volume of loans made by the Corporation
showed a sharp increase from the rather low levels
of the earlier years. Approved loans are those approved in principle by the Board. Committed loans
are those where signed agreements between the parties
have been completed. Disbursed loans occur when
funds have been released, and loans outstanding are
the balances due on loans committed.

While the volume of loans has shown a sharp
increase in recent years, financing on an equity
basis has remained virtually nil. This is so, even
though regulations have provided, from the very outset, for a broad range of equity participation by
the Corporation, including direct purchase of shares,
underwriting, and other forms of equity participation. A 1.5 million baht equity investment was acquired by IFCT in the course of liquidating a bad
debt. The equity was dissolved in 1967 by a sale of
the assets. Although local currency resources have
proved inadequate to meet the demand for loans, foreign currency funds obtained from the foreign institutions have not yet been used to capacity. This is
somewhat surprising inasmuch as industrial establishments in Thailand may be expected to require a good
deal of imported equipment. There is a good deal of
evidence, however, that borrowers, even when they
require imported capital goods, often choose to borrow local currency and to purchase the needed equipment from a dealer on the spot rather than import the
equipment themselves. This practice meant that the
meager baht resources of the IFCT were unnecessarily

TABLE 8.6

Industrial Finance Corporation of Thailand:
Summary of Lendable Funds, 1960-1967

Type of Funds	Amount							
	1960	1961	1962	1963	1964	1965	1966	1967
Share Capital[a]	6,100,000	6,100,000	6,100,000	18,687,000	30,000,000	30,000,000	30,000,000	46,756,000
Reserves	0	1,700,000	2,550,000	3,550,000	4,850,000	6,500,000	8,330,000	11,045,000
Borrowings								
Baht currency	28,126,691	23,126,691	48,126,691	48,661,184	48,732,684	78,802,684	78,857,684	83,858,000
Foreign currency[b]	0	0	0	55,000,000	105,000,000	105,000,000	105,000,000	93,928,000
Total Funds (baht)	34,226,691	35,926,691	56,776,691	125,898,184	188,582,684	220,302,684	222,187,684	235,587,000
Baht Currency Funds	100%	100%	100%	56.31%	44.32%	52.34%	52.74%	60.13%
Foreign Currency Funds	0%	0%	0%	43.69%	55.68%	47.66%	47.26%	39.7%
Total Funds	100%	100%	100%	100%	100%	100%	100%	100%

[a]Paid up; authorized capital; baht 100,000,000.

[b]In baht equivalent.

Source: Compiled from data by the IFCT.

TABLE 8.7

Industrial Finance Corporation of Thailand: Loan History, 1960-1967

Year	Approved Amount (million baht)	No.	Committed Amount (million baht)	No.	Disbursed (million baht)	No.	Outstanding (million baht)
1960	2,000	1	2,000	1	2,000	1	2,000
1961	11,300	8	9,800	8	6,000	7	8,000
1962	21,800	16	11,400	16	12,004	11	19,754
1963	33,555	15	18,300	15	13,879	13	31,212
1964	48,128	11	19,105	11	13,347	6	40,559
1965	32,680	13	47,498	13	32,434	12	64,208
1966	103,407	32	99,450	32	77,088	29	131,405
1967	102,845	25	96,579	25	96,716	18	209,075
Total	355,215	121	304,132	121	253,468	97	--

Source: Compiled from data provided by the IFCT.

312

depleted while the lenders of foreign exchange found
the rate of utilization of the line of credit they
provided to have been exasperatingly slow.   IFCT has
benefited from the encouragement and advice of the
International Finance Corporation, a subsidiary of
the World Bank.   IFC acquired 4,000 shares of the
30,000 shares of IFCT capital stock, and the World
Bank provided a line of credit in 1964.   One reason
for the dissatisfaction of these organizations with
the operating practices of the IFCT was the slow
drawing of the line of credit.   In April of 1967 the
credit was terminated.

The shortage of local funds now emerges as the
principal operating problem of the IFCT.   From slow
beginnings in the early years, when the supply of
these funds exceeded demand, the Corporation now
faces a continuing problem of finding new means of
financing industrial enterprise.   It is reluctant to
seek additional funds from public sources, and, indeed, it does not find it too easy to obtain such
funds.   The terms at which government funds have been
provided in recent years have become stiffer both in
terms of length of loan and in terms of the interest
cost.   Devices such as the sale of debentures to the
Bank of Thailand or to the Government Savings Bank
do not appear to be the proper means of replenishing
the funds of an institution which was created to tap
private, voluntary savings.

One way to relieve the pressure on scarce baht
resources would be to increase the utilization of
foreign exchange funds.   As suggested above, these
funds have not been utilized fully in the past and
yet their supply seems to be assured by the willingness of various foreign institutions to provide a
line of credit.

Of the 94 loan agreements signed up to mid-1967,
only 11 were made in foreign currency, even though
the annual interest charge on these loans was 7.5 per
cent compared with the standard 9 per cent on baht
loans.   In 1968 the interest rates charged by IFCT
were increased slightly, from 9 to 9.5 per cent per
annum for local currency loans and from 7.5 to 8.6

per cent for foreign currency loans. The interest differential between these two types of loans was thus, if anything, reduced. However, IFCT does not assume the exchange risk on its foreign currency loans and, in fact, charges a fee of 1.5 per cent for insurance against exchange risk, which it farms out to commercial banks. IFCT itself pays a fee of one-quarter of 1 per cent to the government to insure itself against exchange fluctuations. This practice not only eliminates the interest differential incentive to borrow foreign exchange but has the effect of discouraging such borrowing. The industrial borrower prefers to buy his import requirements locally so as to avoid complicated and sometimes costly import procedures and requirements. There seems to be little reason for not assuming exchange risk by the IFCT under the circumstances prevailing in Thailand, and there seems to be a great need to simplify import procedures for industrial borrowers. The management of the IFCT is aware of the need to do something about the exchange risk and to simplify the import procedures. A number of possibilities are being explored. One possibility would be to eliminate the letter of credit procedure and to pay the exporter directly against shipping documents out of funds available abroad.

Another important reason for the relatively feeble demand for IFCT foreign exchange funds is that many of the borrowers, particularly the larger ones, are in one way or another associated with foreign firms. In many cases these variously disguised foreign joint ventures find means of obtaining import components of their product outside the normal import procedures. Moreover, IFCT has only limited discretion in making loans out of foreign lines of credit. In general, for loans in excess of 1 million baht, the prior approval of the foreign lender has to be obtained.

But measures to increase the utilization of foreign exchange funds will not take the IFCT very far. While these funds are currently more readily available than baht finance, their total availability will remain limited. IFCT must find ways and means to

replenish its local currency resources and to do so
without recurrent resort to public funds.

Viewed against the total volume of bank financing
of manufacturing activity, let alone as a proportion
of total value added in manufacture, the volume of
finance provided by the IFCT is puny indeed. In 1966,
value added in manufacturing was about 12,000 million
baht, and the volume of bank loans and advances designated as made to manufactures was in the neighborhood of 1,600 million baht. Against this, the IFCT
is expected to provide, at best, some 200 million
baht annually to industrial undertakings.

As Table 8.8 shows, of the approximately 220
million baht in industrial credit provided by IFCT
from its inception up to September 1967, over 150
million came from borrowed funds. To continue its
operations at that level, let alone to substantially
expand its activities, IFCT must explore other means
of financing its operations. The Corporation
broadened the self-imposed constraints on its activities in 1967; previously, the debt incurred by IFCT
could not exceed three times its equity (including
quasi-equity). This was raised to six times its
equity in 1967, thus enabling the Corporation to borrow additionally at least 500 million baht. The exact figure is difficult to come by. The sum of
capital accounts and quasi-equity was, at mid-1967,
about 130 million baht, but there was some doubt
whether all items classed as semi-equity would qualify. Similarly, the limit of IFCT commitment to any
single enterprise was raised from 15 to 20 per cent
of its equity. More importantly, in 1967 the IFCT
Board consented to set aside only 30 per cent of annual earnings as reserves, instead of 50 per cent,
so as to enable the Corporation to pay a higher div-
idend to its stockholders. The first of these steps
did not, in itself, provide any additional resources,
but it has opened the door to the employment of such
devices as sale of debentures.

Other limits on the operational freedom of the
IFCT were also revised. Thus, equity participation
of IFCT in any single enterprise was increased from

TABLE 8.8

Industrial Finance Corporation of Thailand: Cumulative Sources
and Uses of Funds from Inception to September 30, 1967
(thousand baht)

Sources of Funds

Share Capital	40,257	
Borrowed—AID	15,000	
Government	83,858	
IBRD	20,768	
KFW	36,669	
Loan Repayment—Local	35,882	
IBRD	940	
KFW	1,655	38,477
Interest Income 1960–66	21,155	
Sept. 1967	9,495	30,650
Income from Investment		
1960–66	12,539	
Sept. 1967	707	13,245
Other Income 1960–66	707	
Sept. 1967	107	814
Profit from Sale of Land	868	
	280,606	

Uses of Funds

Loans Disbursement—Local	160,171	
IBRD	21,726	
KFW	38,324	220,221
Reserves		9,198
Dividend Payment 1960–66		6,416
Expenses 1960–66	19,625	
Sept. 1967	7,246	26,871
Cash and Other Balance	27,117	
Minus Reserves	9,198	17,919
		280,625

Total uses and sources may not be exactly equal because of rounding.

Source: Compiled from data provided by IFCT.

10 to 15 per cent of its new worth. Other limitations remained unchanged. These include the provisions that no loans under 500,000 baht be made and
that financing provided by the IFCT be confined to
medium-term and long-term loans. The exclusion of
short-term and working capital finance from the purview of the IFCT is not provided for specifically in
the act, however; and some opponents of the IFCT insist that the Corporation did, in fact, make some
loans the proceeds of which, in whole or in part,
were used by the borrowers for working capital.

The second measure taken in 1967 may actually
increase the drain on baht resources, as it would enable the Corporation to make larger loans. The third
measure does, however, address itself to one of the
major impediments to the ability of the IFCT to raise
additional capital in the private financial markets.
Up to 1966 the IFCT paid 5 or 6 per cent to its stockholders. The rate of dividends was raised to 7 per
cent in 1966, and the debentures carry a 7 per cent
coupon. This is the rate of return that conservative
investors get from fixed bank deposits. Moreover,
the interest income on IFCT stock is taxable, while
bank interest is tax exempt. Thus, neither the stock
of the Corporation nor its debentures are enthusi-
astically received in the private market.* It would
seem that within its current operational structure
and policies, the ability of the IFCT to raise substantial amounts of capital from private domestic
sources will continue to be severely limited. In
part, and perhaps in largest part, this is due to the
availability of more attractive investment outlets in
the private financial markets. But to some extent
which is difficult to gauge with precision, the limi-
tation is a result of the fact that the IFCT is not
exactly beloved by the financial community in Thailand,
even though it is the financial and primarily the

---

*One source of public funds which could be tapped
by the IFCT in preference to budgetary loans may be
the large amounts of government provident funds which
currently earn no interest at all (see below).

banking community which owns the capital stock of
the Corporation and whose creature the IFCT formally
remains. Rightly or wrongly, there is a strong feeling that, in some instances, the IFCT competes un-
fairly with the commercial banks, either by granting
funds on more favorable terms or by performing activities which it was not meant to perform.

One indication of the prevailing sentiment was
given by the response of Thai banks to the 20 million
baht of additional stock offered to existing stockholders in 1967. Thai banks took up much less of the
issue than they were entitled to, and the regulations
regarding the relative proportions held by local and
foreign interests had to be changed substantially
as a result.

Irrespective of the extent to which these allegations are justified, they have to be contended
with. It may be very difficult, if not impossible,
for the IFCT to insure that its funds are not used
for working capital purposes, the provision of which
is the province of the commercial banks. IFCT has
elaborate procedures and regulations which determine
whether a loan will be disbursed. Once the funds
have been disbursed, however, the IFCT seems to have
few sanctions at its disposal in the event proceeds
are not used exactly as intended. It can call in
the loan, of course, but this is a drastic step which
can be employed only very occasionally. The IFCT
does have a follow-up division, but beyond occasional visits to the plant site there is little it
can do in case of deviations from the loan agreement.
Nevertheless, there appears to be little justification for the IFCT to grant loans below the lowest
alternative market rate. The lowest rate for bank
accommodation is currently 10 per cent per annum (except for certain loans given for foreign trade) and
there is little a priori reason for IFCT to make industrial loans at 9 per cent. The effect is not
only to provide a subsidy (so far mainly borne by the
taxpayers) but also to give an incentive to large,
well-established undertakings to seek subsidized
funds when they could perfectly well pay the market
rate and still prosper. Equalizing the maximum IFCT

rate with the minimum banking rate would also eliminate much of the banking circle's resentment against
"unfair competition" of the IFCT.

In any event, if IFCT is ever to raise funds
through issue of its own securities to private investors, it will have to offer at least one or perhaps two basic points above the rate payable on time
deposits. It would hardly be possible, however, for
IFCT to operate if it were to pay 9 per cent and earn
no more than that on its loans. But liberalizing its
operating provisions and increasing the interest
charges is not likely to make a major difference to
the scale of financing done by the IFCT in the future.
To the extent that the borrowers tend to be, increasingly, the bigger and better established firms, there
is the danger that a portion of IFCT finance will
merely change the pattern of supply of lendable funds
rather than increase its volume.

Ultimately, the IFCT must look to equity finance
as a way out of its impasse. By financing enterprise
on an equity participation basis, the IFCT (or some
related sister institution) could, in principle at
least, obtain a return which would appear attractive
to some investors willing to take risks. By selling
its holdings from time to time and by revolving its
portfolio, the Corporation could replenish its funds
without recourse to the fisc. IFCT is aware of these
possibilities and is exploring them. Whether the
exploration of equity financing should be entrusted
to the IFCT as it is presently organized, or whether
this function should be given to some other entity,
is a separate question. IFCT has the powers to undertake the activities required or contemplated in the
equity market. The question is whether its name or
reputation has not been associated for too long with
a certain kind of financing and with a certain approach which might prove to be a psychological obstacle to its undertaking drastically different functions.

On the other hand, IFCT has acquired a good deal
of managerial acumen, technical expertise, and valuable experience. It pioneered and continues to

pioneer in project evaluation and in loan appraisal
based on the success of the project rather than on
the status of the borrower. It leads in accepting
collateral other than land (even though it suffers,
together with other lenders, from lack of firm legal
provisions in the Thai civil code for chattel mort-
gate) and in assigning to that collateral a reasonable ratio with respect to the amount of loan.
IFCT's loss experience has also been quite good. As
of September 1967, only three loans to the aggregate
amount of 1.2 million baht were overdue for more than
six months.

LIFE INSURANCE COMPANIES

In most of the developed countries and in quite
a number of the developing ones, life insurance institutions are among the most important financial
intermediaries. Even in the Far East, where the insurance habit and the formation of contractual savings
institutions has lagged behind, say, Latin America,
life insurance companies account for a substantial
proportion of the financial assets of households in
the Philippines and in Japan. As shown in Tables
8.9 and 8.10, however, Thailand ranks well near the
bottom of the list of Far Eastern countries in this
respect. Table 8.9 refers to a period for which
relevant and comparable data were available. Life
insurance is measured by net premiums. In Table 8.10
selected indicators for several countries are compiled
for 1960 and 1965 which suggest that life insurance
in Thailand has remained a minor component of the financial markets.

Life insurance in Thailand is of minor importance as an outlet for household financial savings
and of even lesser importance as a provider of long-
term capital funds. Indeed, judged by quantitative
criteria alone, there would have been little point
in devoting considerable research effort to life insurance in Thailand were it not for the fact that
life insurance has demonstrated its importance in
financial intermediation elsewhere and that, even in
Thailand, it is capable of a not insignificant contribution to capital formation.

TABLE 8.9

"Saving" Through Life Insurance, Selected
Far East Countries, 1955-1959

Country	Life Insurance as % of Gross Household Saving	Gross Household Saving as % of Disposable Income
Malaya	7.6	11.0
Japan	10.3	17.3
South Korea	0.6	8.6
Philippines	14.7	9.7
India	3.1	6.3
Thailand (1960)	0.5	12.3

Source: Based on United Nations, _Economic Bulletin_
for Asia and the Far East, Vol. XIII, No. 3
(Bangkok, 1962), pp. 9-12.

The advantages of life insurance as a financial
intermediary have often been cited and discussed,
and there is no need to repeat them at length here.
In brief, the contractual character of life insurance
claims and assets makes it possible to provide long-
term funds to deficit saving units and to enhance
both the flow and the composition of household savings.[7]

Thus the very fact that, in Thailand, life insurance currently plays such a small part in financing
capital formation and in mobilizing voluntary saving,
warrants a study of these institutions, first, in
order to determine some of the reasons for their lag-
gard performance to date, and, second, to gauge their
likely contribution in the future.

No attempt will be made to give a full analysis
of the life insurance industry in Thailand. Instead,
certain salient features of life insurance in the
Kingdom will be discussed, particularly as they bear
on the problems of financing economic development.[8]

TABLE 8.10

Life Insurance in Thailand, the United States,
and Three Developing Asian Nations,
1960 and 1965, Selected Indicators

Indicator	U.S.		Taiwan		Philippines		Thailand		Korea	
	1960	1965	1960	1965	1960	1965	1960	1965	1960	1965
GNP per capita ($)	2,810	3,500	147	225	149	161	100	124	83	102
Cost of Living Index	100	107	100	112	100	126	100	107	100	204
Sum Insured/GNP	1.41	1.60	.016	.037	.18	.20	.044	.063	.046	.083
Life Insurance Assets GNP	.24	.23	.0025	.0074			.0072	.0061	.002	.005
Life Insurance Assets Commercial Bank Deposits	.65	.58	.026	.032			.063	.033	.034	.082
Premiums/GNP	.024	.024	.024				.0015	.0023	.0017	.0028

Sources: International Monetary Fund, International Financial Statistics 1967 (Washington, D.C., 1968); U.S. Institute of Life Insurance, Life Insurance Fact Book 1967 (New York, 1968); Government of Thailand, Report on Insurance Business in Thailand (Bangkok, 1965); Central Bank of China, Taiwan Financial Statistics Monthly (Taipei: May, 1967); Bank of Korea, Economic Statistics Yearbook, 1965 (Seoul, 1966).

Casualty insurance, which accounts for some 40 per
cent of total corporate insurance assets in Thailand,
will not be discussed in this chapter, inasmuch as
casualty insurance is regarded more in the nature of
a business service than financial intermediation.

Life insurance companies operating in Thailand
have had a checkered career. Business on any significant scale did not start until the early 1950's,
but the public's acceptance of the newly available
services was uneven and, on occasion, rudely shaken
by disturbances within the industry. The greatest
of these shocks to public confidence occurred in
1964, when one of the largest of the life insurance
companies then in existence failed and was liquidated.
But even prior to this there were both events and
rumors which put into question not only the veracity
of the agents and the competence of the managers but
the integrity of the corporate owners as well. Of
the twelve companies operating in 1967, only three
or four are considered to be at all sound and three
of these account for 60 per cent of total life insurance assets of some 500 million baht. Many of the
smaller companies are undercapitalized, are operated
by owner-managers whose main interests often lie
elsewhere, and/or are little more than devices to obtain cheap working capital for businesses unrelated
to the insurance operations.

This state of affairs emerged largely as a consequence of the fact that from 1949 until 1967 the
life insurance industry in Thailand was only very
loosely regulated, if at all. The industry was subject to an administrative set of rules called "Conditions Governing Life Insurance" with vaguely defined
legal powers which stipulated a minimum paid-in capital, a deposit with the Insurance Comptroller, and
annual financial reports which were seldom audited.
The right to inspect the companies was hardly ever
exercised.

Yet, as seen from Table 8.11, life insurance
companies did increase the scale of their operations
between 1960 and 1966 in terms of the number of offices outside the metropolitan area, the number of

TABLE 8.11

Life Insurance Companies in Thailand: Growth
of Offices, Agents, and Home Office Staff,
1960 and 1966

Company	Offices Up-country 1960	1966	Agents 1960	1966	Staff 1960	1966
Southeast	13	18	496	494	173	301
Thai Prasit	11	11	690	1,126		612
Ocean	10	58		2,974	44	48
Muang Thai	14	20	114	249	17	52
Ayudhya Oriental	15	15			55	33
Siam Life	0	0	521	2,726	23	40
Thai Life	5	10	120	180	28	2
Thai Sreshthakich	0	0			2	
International American Insurance Association			314	1,299	25	79
China Underwriters		9	30	104	5	11
Total[a]	68	141	2,285	9,152	372	1,178

[a]Based on incomplete information.

Source: Compiled from information provided by the life insurance companies.

324

agents, and the quantity of staff. At the same time,
other data suggest that the intercompany competitive
effort was not paralleled by enhanced efficiency.
Thus, quadrupling of the number of agents between
1960 and 1966 led to slightly more than doubling of
the premiums in the same period. Similarly, the
tripling of the office staff increased the number of
policyholders by a factor of two. The expansion of
facilities has not, as yet, been able to capitalize
on the economies of scale which are inherent in a
financial business.

Net premiums are those paid in, less amounts
paid out to reinsurers. Amount insured is a less
significant index of growth because of the rather
high rate of lapsation and surrender prevailing in
Thailand. It is uncertain to what extent the increased number of policyholders represents an increase in the number of separate households covered,
or an increase in the number of persons insured within the households. The reserve fund figure is particularly unreliable in Thailand because until 1967
the life insurance companies were permitted to set
aside 65 per cent of their gross earnings even though
their operating expenses averaged over 40 per cent.

The three factors of the inefficiency of most
life insurance companies, the lack of public confidence in the business, and the loose character of
supervision were jointly responsible for holding back
the industry to a very minor role in Thai financial
markets.

If the record of the life insurance industry in
attracting household savings was a poor one, its performance on the supply side of the schedule of investible funds was even less impressive. In Table
8.12 the distribution of industry assets is given
for 1961 and 1965. Although the exactness of the
percentages may be open to doubt, the orders of magnitude are probably not far from the mark. An analysis of these assets reveals that very little of
household savings is being channeled by Thai life
insurance companies into long-term financing of industry. The portfolio of stocks and shares represents

mainly the holdings of stocks in companies in which
the insurance business is a subsidiary or an adjunct.
There is very little portfolio investment in equities, and very few, if any, of the stocks are purchased through the stock market. Between 1961 and
1965 the most pronounced change in the composition
of life insurance assets took place in real estate
investments, and there is reason to believe that the
16 per cent shown for 1965 substantially understates
the investment in buildings. The supervisory agencies frown on investment in real estate, in general,
and severely restrict it in the case of foreign-
controlled companies. There are two such companies
operating in Thailand, one of which is the largest
in the industry. Both in 1961 and in 1965 the greatest proportion of total assets was in policy loans.
These loans are granted to policyholders on demand,
mainly to provide for consumption needs and occasionally to forestall lapsation. They represent a contingent claim on the disposable funds of the Thai
life insurance companies. The decrease in the relative size of this type of asset is to be welcomed,
as it provides management with greater latitude in
the use of its funds.

Policy loans yield 8 per cent per annum, which
is above the estimated 5 per cent return on all assets. This is a very low rate of return in a country
where commercial bank deposits yield up to 7 per cent
and the average cost of bank loans exceeds 12 per
cent.

Loans other than policy loans may appear at
first to include loans to industry and perhaps also
term loans. In fact, however, many of these are
short-term warehouse loans given against merchandise
collateral at rates of interest ranging between 3
and 4 per cent per month. Allegedly, they also include loans made to influential persons without security but at a high rate of interest, and the decline
in the relative importance of "other loans" is said
to reflect the growing concern of the life insurance
companies with the unsecured nature of some of these
assets. For comparison purposes, Table 8.13 gives
the distribution of the assets of U.S. life insurance

companies. It must be borne in mind that most U.S.
insurance companies are limited by state laws as to
the proportion of equities in their total portfolios.
The proportion of equities is much higher in the
United Kingdom.

TABLE 8.12

Life Insurance Companies in Thailand:
Per Cent Distribution of Assets,
1961 and 1965

Asset	Per Cent Distribution	
	1961	1965
Government bonds	4.9	6.2
Policy loans	29.6	23.2
Other loans	19.9	11.9
Other investments	0.7	1.6
Stocks and shares	7.4	5.4
Cash in hand	1.0	0.5
Cash in banks	6.6	11.3
Accts. receivable, etc.	4.4	8.3
Sundry debtors	8.9	8.3
Buildings	6.2	15.9
Equipment	5.5	2.8
Head office A/C	4.4	4.7
	100.0	100.0

Details may not add up to total because of rounding.

Source: Ministry of Economic Affairs, Royal Government of Thailand, Report of the Insurance
Division, 1961 and 1965 (Bangkok: 1963 and
1967). Data for 1965 modified in the light
of information supplied by companies.

In spite of the rather dismal record, there are
reasons to beliefe that the life insurance industry
in Thailand faces a brighter future and that its importance as a collector of household savings and as
a purveyor of industrial finance could be enhanced
substantially. These reasons are of two kinds. First,

there are forces which are not confined to Thailand but which augur well for the future of life insurance, and, second, there are special circumstances in the Kingdom which tend to accentuate these forces.

TABLE 8.13

Percentage Distribution of Assets of U.S. Life Insurance Companies, 1961 and 1965

Asset	Percentage Distribution	
	1961	1965
U.S. government bonds	4.9	3.2
Foreign government securities	.3	.6
State, provincial, and local securities	4.0	3.4
Railroad bonds	2.8	2.1
Public utility bonds	13.4	10.7
Industrial bonds	22.6	24.2
Stocks	4.9	5.7
Mortgages	34.9	37.8
Real estate	3.2	3.0
Policy loans	4.5	4.8
Miscellaneous	4.5	4.5
	100.0	100.0

Source: Institute of Life Insurance, 1967 Life Insurance Fact Book (New York, 1968), p. 63.

In most of the developing countries, mortality rates can be expected to fall more precipitously than in those countries which have already achieved a high level of medical care and public health. The rates of growth of insurance purchases are bound to be higher in countries which start from a low base and where income, urbanization, and educational trends all point to a greater interest in life insurance in the future. Whether alone or in conjunction with the spread of other contractual forms of savings, life insurance must benefit from the growth of social security schemes which, in the Far Eastern countries,

lag considerably behind those of Europe and Latin
America.

In Thailand, moreover, the mortality tables currently used already overstate existing mortality
rates, and there is relatively less competition for
household savings in the Kingdom than in many of the
surrounding countries. The past managerial record is
capable of rapid and substantial improvement, and the
supervisory authorities have finally awakened to the
need for a more vigorous regulation of the industry.

At the time of writing the detailed provisions
of the Insurance Act of 1967 were still awaiting
interpretation by ministerial decrees. The act does,
however, stiffen capital and deposit requirements and,
in addition, imposes control over premium rates,
agent commissions, the allocation of premiums to reserves, and the composition of assets. Most importantly, the act institutionalizes a system of periodic inspection and audit of the activities of the life
insurance companies.

Most importantly, the predominant form of life
insurance policy in Thailand is the endowment type.
Seventy-eight per cent of policies in force are of
the endowment type, and they account for 65 per cent
of the sum insured. These policies are issued for
a period of from 10 to 20 years. This type of policy
enables the insurance companies to assume the intermediation role much more confidently. Not only is
the management of funds easier under the known schedules of liabilities prevailing under endowment policies, but such policies contain a greater proportion
of saving than do term insurance policies.

The emphasis on endowment policies--with their
accumulation of savings over the life of the policy
rather than, as is the case with term insurance, over
the last few years of the policy--is at least in part
due to the reluctance of Thai insurance executives to
sell policies on the basis that families are protected
and safeguarded against the risk of death. These aspects are the ones usually emphasized in the United
States and the United Kingdom. In Southeast Asia it

is considered bad form to mention the possibility of
death to the prospective purchaser of an insurance
policy; instead, savings aspects of a policy are
stressed (the Chinese word for life insurance trans-
lates as "man-long-life").

One recent development in the operations of Thai
life insurance companies merits attention. In addition to the competitive struggle to establish offices
in provincial cities, which raised the number of such
offices from 68 in 1961 to 141 in 1965, there have
been attempts to sell life insurance directly to rural households.

One reason why life insurance is believed to be
capable of increasing the ratio of voluntary saving
to disposable income of households is that unlike
commercial banks, for example, life insurance companies can aggressively seek savings, can approach
potential savers directly, and can "sell" the concept
of periodic and contractual savings to those hitherto
consuming most of their money income.

One company, in particular, has been quite successful in selling life insurance policies to farmers
and others generally regarded as being a poor market,
and it now sells three-fourths of its policies in the
countryside. In 1965 it collected 47 million baht in
premium, the highest amount in Thailand, and about
nine times its volume of 1960. The company issues
small policies which require only about 20 to 30
baht in monthly premium payments. Although the program is still in its experimental stage, is subject
to high lapsation rates, and is rather expensive to
run, the company is satisfied with its progress to
date and its potential for the future.

Granted that the Thai life insurance business
is capable of accelerated growth in the future, what
is its potential within, say, ten to fifteen years?
If premium payments of between 4 and 5 per cent of
disposable income are considered to be the maximum
that a household would be willing to put into insurance, the number of policies in force could quadruple
or quintuple. At present, the average annual premium

payments are about 475 baht, with 13,000 baht as the
mean value of the sum insured. Inasmuch as the best
prospects for expansion of the life insurance market
lie among the lower income groups, some 1,500,000
households could pay a maximum of 300 baht a year so
as not to exceed the 4 or 5 per cent stipulated. Increases in income over time will increase the number
of eligible households, but insurance cannot be expected to be the only outlet for incremental savings.
In the United States the ratio of premiums to disposable personal income (which is lower than household income) is about 4 per cent. To the extent that
the growth in life insurance assets is increasingly
directed into long-term financing, at the end of,
say, ten years the Thai life insurance industry could
provide between 100 and 200 million baht annually to
the capital market. Even this modest contribution
to the flow of investible funds cannot be taken for
granted. To achieve it, the life insurance business
will have to overcome a number of shortcomings and
obstacles, some of which lie within the industry itself (and have to do with management and the integrity
of both owners and agents) and some of which have to
do with the legal and institutional setting within
which the life insurance business operates in Thailand.
Of these latter obstacles, perhaps the most serious
is tax treatment, which appears to discriminate in
favor of commercial bank deposits. Life insurance
companies pay a business tax of 2.5 per cent on premiums, while commercial banks do not pay taxes on deposits. In a number of countries premium payments
are exempt from the individual income tax, and in
yet others contractual savers receive, in addition,
a cash bonus (i.e., Germany). Exemption of premiums
from individual income has been suggested for Thailand.

It is not likely, therefore, that even a great
increase in the industry's efficiency and appeal will
produce major additions to the flow of investible
funds in the foreseeable future. In a number of developing countries the importance of life insurance
in the capital markets derives not so much from voluntary purchases of life insurance by households as
it does from the tie-in of insurance with various

pension and provident fund schemes and, particularly, from the compulsory character of much of the insurance protection sold.[9]

Given the circumstances prevailing in Thailand, the introduction of compulsory elements into contractual savings is not likely to advance very far in the near future. Elements of compulsion do exist, however, with respect to provident funds (see the next section).

EMPLOYEE BENEFIT FUNDS

The various kinds of employee funds under which a stated sum of money is periodically set aside to provide benefits to an employee upon his retirement, death, or resignation are, throughout most of the world, among the fastest-growing vehicles for financial savings of households. Even so, it was something of a surprise to discover that this holds true as well for Thailand, a country where contractual forms of savings are in their infancy, where a social security system is well-nigh nonexistent, and where there are relatively few large-scale employee organizations.[10] Yet, at the end of 1966, the liabilities of the various provident and pension funds operating in Thailand aggregated at least 1,410 million baht, and the available data indicate a compound annual rate of growth of more than 10 per cent.

There is absolutely no information available on employee benefit funds in the private sector. Data on those in the public sector are held in widely scattered departments and have never before been collated or aggregated. The information given in this section is the first known attempt to present reasonably comprehensive data on this subject.[11]

As shown in Table 8.14, the employee benefit funds in Thailand are predominantly provident funds, pension funds accounting for less than 30 of the 124 funds whose existence could be ascertained. A provident fund is one where benefits are cumulated over a number of years and paid out to the employee on his termination of employment. It differs from a pension

fund mainly in that the benefits paid out cannot exceed the accumulation in the fund, whereas the aggregate of annuities paid a retiring employee until he
dies cannot exceed the accumulation under a pension
scheme.

TABLE 8.14

Employee Benefit Funds[a] in Thailand:
Liabilities, 1960-1966
(million baht)

Type of Fund	Amount of Liabilities			
	1960	1964	1965	1966
Provident funds, government	335	492	551	615
Provident funds, state enterprises	268	407	463	524
Provident funds, private	52	114	135	163
Pension funds, state enterprises	15	46	52	56
Pension funds, private	19	39	44	51
Total	689	1,098	1,245	1,409

[a]Does not include nonfunded government pension payments which amounted to 143 million baht in 1960,
242 million in 1964, 273 million in 1965, and 296
million in 1966.

In terms of total liabilities, the most important benefit funds are the Official Provident Funds
of the government, with 615 million baht. These are
followed by the provident and pension funds of the
various state enterprises (the State Railway Fund
accounting for some 326 million baht of the 600 million in this category) and the numerous funds in the
private sector totaling, at the end of 1966, less
than 120 million baht in liabilities. In addition
to its provident fund, the Thai Government does maintain a pension scheme, but the latter is not funded,
does not require any contribution from the civil
servant, and is financed out of current revenues. In
1966 the payment of pensions out of the regular budget amounted to nearly 300 million baht. Most of the
pension schemes run by the state enterprises are

similarly unfunded, but almost every one of the pension schemes administered by large corporations is a self-insured, funded scheme of the type which predominate in the United States and the United Kingdom.

Even more surprising than the discovery that employee benefit funds are quite significant mobilizers of saving in Thailand is the finding that the bulk of the household savings which flow into these funds is of a compulsory nature. Two-thirds of the funds deduct a fixed proportion of the employee's salary every month. The government's Official Provident Fund was established in 1950. In 1967, 4 per cent of a civil servant's salary was deducted each month and deposited in the fund. The contribution of the government consists of interest payments of 5 per cent.

For some unexplained reason these interest contributions are not shown explicitly in the accounts of the Official Provident Fund. They are deducted from the fund's balance, however, when the employee retires and collects his benefits in lump sum. Under the pension plan, the employee is given an option of a lump sum payment or an annuity payment. Retirement, hence, pension entitlement, is contingent upon the completion of a minimum of 10 years of service. Under provident fund provisions, however, the civil servant is entitled to receive his accumulation whenever he leaves the government employ.

The provident funds of state enterprises ("mixed" corporations controlled by the government but managed outside the civil service system; they run the public utilities and monopolies in Thailand) and private companies pay accumulated benefits upon retirement, death, or resignation of the employee; but, unlike the Official Provident Fund, they match the employee's salary deduction in addition to the interest on the cumulative balance. Typically, the monthly salary deduction is 5 per cent of salary, but the matching contribution is frequently calibrated so as to provide an incentive to the employee to stay on the job longer. Conversely, in the event an employee quits before a minimum number of years (usually 10) on the job, his benefits will be less than the full accumulation

of salary deductions and matching contributions plus
interest.   Interest is usually fixed arbitrarily.
The company contribution is often graduated by the
length of service so as to provide an additional in-
ducement to longer employment.

Pension plans of private corporations (only one
funded plan is operated by state enterprise) are financed in a variety of ways, none of which bear any
relation to actuarial expectations.   These include
the setting up of a special fund out of capital and
annual appropriations, allocation of a share of profits, and so on.   Typically, pension rights are accumulated after a minimum of 25 years with the company.

There is little doubt that employee benefit funds
will grow in the future, although the rate of growth
is not certain.   In the public sector, the increase
in the number of civil servants and the expected increase in their average compensation is bound to increase the total liabilities quite sharply in the
near future.   The pay increase for civil servants
has been long delayed.   Moreover, the 1967 revision
of the provisions governing the administration of the
Official Provident Funds had the effect of substantially increasing the average monthly payroll deduction.   Prior to 1967, the scale of deductions ranged
from 1 to 4 per cent of salaries rather than, as at
present, 4 per cent across the board.   In the private
sector, the formation of funds is still in its initial stages and the aggregate of liabilities may be
expected to grow pari passu with the adoption of employee benefit funds by other businesses and the
further expansion of those firms which already operate such funds.   In the period 1964-1967 only about
one-third of the labor force (in establishments with
more than 10 workers) in the metropolitan area is
covered by employee benefit funds.   Even so, it is
unlikely that, under the conditions prevailing in the
country, the flow of financial saving through employee benefit funds will exceed 200 million baht annually over the next few years.

Between 1964 and 1967 the annual increase in
total liabilities has been about 200 million baht.

However, a substantial proportion of this increase,
about 40 per cent, represents employee contributions,
only a small fraction of which would become financial
savings of households were these contributions replaced by salary increases. On the other hand, the
data collected understate the scope of employee benefit funds. Thus, in addition to those funds whose
existence is not known, there are provident funds of
local and municipal employees, which, however, are
quite small.

But this modest forecast could be revised upward
quite substantially were the conditions under which
employee benefit funds operate to change. At the
present time the funds are confined to larger employers who alone have the resources, financial and
managerial, to administer funds which are not insured, which have no actuarial provisions for outpay-
ments, and where the assets are frequently comingled
with those of the operating company. To a large extent the employee benefit funds, particularly those
in the private sector, represent an effort of the
sponsor to reduce costly turnover of personnel and,
if need be, to pay to that end out of the company
profit or capital. A large spurt in the liabilities
of provident and pension funds could come about only
through their institutionalization; i.e., through
some form of social insurance or through another device which ties in the contractual and compulsory
elements of the funds to life insurance operations.
Proposals for a fairly comprehensive social insurance scheme have been debated in Thailand since at
least 1954. A 1965 proposal would provide benefits
in case of sickness, maternity, death, and permanent
disability, but none for old age. Medical care would
be provided free. The scheme is to be financed by
employee, employer, and government contributions and
is to be administered by a bureau under the Ministry
of the Interior.[12]

Neither of these schemes is likely to become
operative in the near future. The most immediate
and most direct steps which could be taken to increase the flow of household savings to employee
benefit funds are those which provide tax benefits

and/or remove disincentives. At present employee
contributions are not exempt and benefits are taxed
at graduated income tax rates when received in lump
sum. Employers can deduct actual payments but not
annual contributions. In a country where large-scale
units are only beginning to form and where the labor
force is young both in chronological age and in time
of employment, annual contributions are much larger
than annual benefit payments.

Employee benefit funds can be expected to contribute to long-term finance to an extent even greater than life insurance. Their payments are more
predictable and their receipts more stable than those
of life insurance companies. Yet, in Thailand, the
employee benefit funds perform rather poorly as financial intermediaries. The largest of them, the
Official Provident Fund, simply holds its balances
at the Treasury, where they earn no interest and
where there are no provisions whatsoever for their
investment. In the past, these balances were occasionally employed to make special purpose loans to
other government departments and, in some cases, to
individuals. This policy was discontinued.

Inasmuch as current Treasury balances are rather
large relative to budget deficits, there seems little
reason why the balances belonging to the Official
Provident Fund could not be more productively employed. A number of suggestions and proposals have
been informally advanced to that end. The simplest
of these would be to use Official Provident Fund
balances to purchase government securities. Even
though the interest return on such an investment
would equal the cost to the government, the government, to the extent it needs to borrow, would save
on its total interest bill. Other suggestions include
support of the IFCT and the support of new financial
institutions.

In Malaya the entire official provident fund is
held in government securities. In the Philippines,
only 9 per cent of the official fund is held in government securities, an additional 15 per cent is held
in corporate securities, 18 per cent in personal loans,
and so on.[13]

Table 8.15 shows the asset distribution of employee benefit funds in Thailand, other than the Official Provident Fund, for four recent years. While the portfolios are quite diversified, only a small fraction of the resources of these funds find their way to the capital market. The one item which may connote the provision of long-term capital to the market, "shares in other companies," more likely than not, represents the purchase of the stock of parent or related companies. About the only item which can be said to represent genuine provision of capital to industry at large is the minuscule amount held in the Thai Investment Fund (TIF), a mutual investment fund with a portfolio consisting of stocks of corporations listed on the Bangkok Stock Exchange. As far as is known, only one of the 124 employee benefit funds in operation includes units of the TIF among its assets. Yet the provision of risk capital to industry at large may well be the most rewarding and the most productive use of the growing resources of the employee benefit funds.

THE STOCK MARKET

The market for corporate securities in Thailand consists of three segments: the Bangkok Stock Exchange, the mutual investment companies, and "independent" security dealers. It is a narrow and thin market without any official supervision and regulation, with little reliable information available to the public at large, and with a limited appeal.

The Bangkok Stock Exchange opened in July 1963 with six members and five corporations listed on its board. The number of members has increased to over 40, and the number of corporations whose securities are traded approximates 30. The corporate sector in Thailand is not treated separately in national income accounts nor is there any precise information available on its size and composition. Since 1956 the Department of Commercial Registration has been publishing figures on new registrations, but the total up to that time has never been compiled. From published and other information it would appear that

TABLE 8.15

Employee Benefit Funds in Private and State Enterprises,
Asset Distribution, 1960-1966
(million baht)

Asset	1960		1964		1965		1966	
	Amount	%	Amount	%	Amount	%	Amount	%
Cash	3,623	1.02	4,409	.73	1,261	.18	3,109	.39
Government bonds	124,772	35.15	285,734	47.13	322,929	46.54	351,374	45.15
Fixed bank deposits	119,983	33.80	166,170	27.41	165,390	23.83	181,910	22.86
Other bank deposits	31,278	8.81	14,189	2.34	15,577	2.24	20,638	2.59
Shares in other companies	12,000	3.38	-	-	26,475	3.81	50,000	6.28
Shares in own stock	-	-	-	-	12,500	1.80	12,500	1.57
Loans to employees	19,628	5.53	28,881	4.76	33,884	4.88	38,751	4.87
Loans to owners	743	.21	1,564	.26	1,682	.24	4,283	.54
Thai investment fund	-	-	10	.0016	60	.0086	191	.0239
Premium savings certificates	-	-	30	.0049	33	.0047	41	.0051
Land and equipment	-	-	2,072	.34	2,072	.30	2,072	.25
Sundary accounts	-	-	141	.02	131	.0188	140	.0175
Not specified	42,906	12.09	103,072	17.00	111,907	16.13	130,866	16.44
Total	354,933	100	606,272	100	693,901	100	795,875	100

there are at least 4,000 corporations (limited companies) in Thailand with an average paid-in capital of one million baht.

One of the member-brokers does about 80 per cent of the Stock Exchange business, and several of the members are nominees of the listed corporations. About one-fourth of the members are domiciled abroad. A resident member pays a 5,000 baht membership fee and undertakes to do a minimum of 300,000 baht of business annually. The great attraction of membership is that transactions among members are exempt from the brokerage fee of 1.25 per cent which the public pays both on the sale and on the purchase of 1.25 per cent which the public pays both on the sale and on the purchase of a listed security. Thus a member can collect a commission of 3 per cent on a given transaction on the exchange without paying any fees himself.

It is estimated that of the less than 1 million shares traded annually, more than 50 per cent are traded among the members themselves.

Of the approximately forty securities listed, only about one-half appear to be traded at all, and among these only very few can be said to be truly available for "at market" orders. The number of buyers has exceeded the number of sellers ever since the opening of the Bangkok Stock Exchange, and the listing of a stock at a given price is no guarantee that that stock is, in fact, available, let alone at the listed price.

The thinness of the market is brought out in Table 8.16. In 1966, the most popular stock was traded only 66 days, and the amount of stock traded was less than 2 per cent of the total stock issued. Nor is it clear that the trend in trading is upward even though the total volume of shares has increased considerably from the 70,000 traded in 1962. The increase in trading volume seems to have been due principally to the addition of other securities to the board.

TABLE 8.16

Trading Activity, 1964-1966, Corporations Listed on
Bangkok Stock Exchange

Corporation and Date of Incorporation	Number of Days Traded			Shares Traded as % of Shares Issued		
	1964	1965	1966	1964	1965	1966
Bangkok Investment Co., Ltd. (1961)	16	21	19	5.9	9.4	7.77
Commercial Credit Corporation, Ltd. (1964)		2	11		3.75	17.85
Construction Material Marketing Company, Ltd. (1962)	20	25	28	1.74	2.92	1.2
Concrete Products & Aggregate Company, Ltd. (1952)	38	25	23	4.58	1.95	5.06
Dumex Limited (1959)	4	7	13	0.56	0.58	1.5
Industrial Finance Corporation of Thailand (1959)			1		.001	
Jolaprathan Cement Company, Ltd. (1956)	7	5	1	0.26	1.09	.06
Kamasuta Corporation, Ltd. (1952)	3	17	14	0.67	4.68	3.72
National Enterprise Co., Ltd. (1963)		11	27		11.02	11.55
North Star Company, Ltd. (1956)	2	3	9	0.67	5.93	11.82
Sumsuk Company, Ltd. (1953)		5	2		0.07	2.42
Siam Cement Company, Ltd. (1931)	41	55	66	0.88	0.96	1.48
Siam Fibre Cement Co., Ltd. (1938)	30	48	21	0.61	1.19	.98
Siam Industrial Credit Co., Ltd. (1966)			16			6.38
Thai Danu Bank (1945)	1	1	2	0.05	0.78	0.12
Bangkok Drying & Silo Co., Ltd. (1963)	8	3	2	8.25	2.46	0.5

Source: Compiled from information provided by the Bangkok Stock Exchange and from annual statements of listed corporations.

In brief, the Bangkok Stock Exchange is more in the nature of a private club than a truly national market. This, together with the lack of any official control over its activities, causes some of the large issuers to bypass its facilities and to limit its importance in the process of financial intermediation.[14]

It would seem that in order to gain a greater degree of acceptance and popularity it would be useful for the Bangkok Stock Exchange to bind itself by a limited number of regulations, perhaps administered by the Bank of Thailand, which would assure those who prefer to stay outside the Exchange that such practices as "cash sales," "insider trading," and "rigging of the market" will be either prevented or severely punished. While there is no hard evidence that such abuses have ever taken place on the Bangkok Stock Exchange, a number of institutional and private investors have expressed some uneasiness and foreboding. Several have cited instances of manipulation which allegedly took place.

Of the three mutual investment companies operating in Thailand, only one, TIF, makes available information, however sketchy, relating to its performance. The Thai Investment Fund, managed by an American venture corporation, is the only one of these funds whose modus operandi comes close to that of a U.S. investment company or a British unit trust. It is an open-ended investment company which began its operations in 1963 and whose units are quoted on the Bangkok Stock Exchange. The other two, the National Mutual Fund and the Bangkok Mutual Fund, appear to be related by managerial and other ties. No record of their operations was available, and indeed it is not clear whether the National Fund ever operated at all, at least in public. In spite of their names, these two funds appear to be primarily devices to garner individual savings into contractual plans, the return on which exceeds that available at the commercial banks, the leverage gain accruing to the managers. Initial capital was 5 million baht. Units are sold in minimum denominations of 1,000 baht. In addition to brokerage fees, a 3 per cent management fee is charged to purchasers.

TABLE 8.17

Thai Investment Fund: Selected Operational Indicators

Indicator	Amount				
	1963	1964	1965	1966	1967[a]
Number of units sold	73,490	119,015	154,990	189,364	243,616
Number of units redeemed	--	49,012	72,947	116,425	166,635
Number of units outstanding	73,490	70,003	82,043	72,939	76,981
Number of unit holders	5	32	67	101	146
Average holding per unit holder	14,698	2,188	1,225	722	527

[a]Three quarters only.

Source: Compiled from data made available by the Thai Investment Fund.

343

Table 8.17 indicates that the number of units
outstanding have remained fairly constant because of
a rather high rate of redemptions. The number of
accounts was, in 1967, less than 150, which, though
a considerable increase from the initial five, is
still very low given the fact that TIF has been in
operation for several years and the return on its
money invested has been in excess of 20 per cent per
annum. This high rate of return, however, has been due
chiefly to the high level of realized capital gains,
with the return from dividends and interest below
that available from fixed deposits at commercial
banks. It would seem that TIF's appeal was chiefly
to a limited group of investors who through their
contacts, knowledge, and sophistication were able to
take advantage of capital appreciation of the fund's
assets. The managers of the fund find it much easier
to sell units to foreigners than to the Thais but
do not appear to have made a major effort to expand
their market substantially.

The last segment of the Thai stock market includes at least one major commercial bank and a few
independent dealers in securities who have no direct
connection with the Stock Exchange. Moreover, a number of large corporations, often subsidiaries or af-
filiates of major foreign corporations, prefer to
distribute their securities to the public outside
the Stock Exchange, either via direct-mail selling
or through the underwriting and marketing facilities
of some other intermediary.

In 1969, two leading Thai commercial banks, the
Bangkok Bank, Ltd. and the Thai Farmers Bank, combined
with U.S. and Philippine institutions to form the
Thai Investment and Securities Company (TISCO) and
Bangkok First Investment and Trust, Ltd. (BIFT).
TISCO includes, besides the Thai Farmers Bank, the
Bankers Trust of New York and the Bancom Development
Corporation of Manila. BIFT is a joint venture of
the Bangkok Bank and the First National City Bank of
New York. Both BIFT and TISCO have done some under-
writing, mainly of corporate debentures.

NOTES

1.   See, for example, Sidney E. Rolfe, Capital
Markets in Atlantic Economic Relationships
(Boulogne-sur-Seine, France: The Atlantic Institute,
1967).

2.   There is a vast literature making the case
for the improvement of capital market institutions
and instruments in developing countries; see Edward
Nevin, Capital Funds in Underdeveloped Countries
(London: St. Martin's Press, 1961), particularly
Chapters 4 and 5 and the sources cited therein.

3.   This section and the statistical data relating thereto are based on information from the
Government Savings Bank and from other sources, published or not, which were available. For additional
details see Government Savings Bank, Annual Report,
1963, 1964, and 1965 (Bangkok); The Savings Bank Act,
Royal Decrees and Ministerial Regulations (Bangkok,
1965); R. Amatayakul and K. A. Pandid, "Financial
Institutions in Thailand," IMF Staff Papers (December,
1961); Henry Houston, "Report of the UN Adviser on
the Government Savings Bank" (Bangkok, 1964) (Mimeo.);
and Direk Raibin, "Savings and Statistics" (M.A.
thesis, National Institute of Development Administration, Bangkok, 1965). (Mimeo; in Thai.)

4.   Kingdom of Thailand, Industrial Finance
Corporation of Thailand Act (1959), Section II.

5.   See Chamlong Tohtone, "Practice and Problems
of IFCT," Bangkok Bank Monthly Review (February, 1964),
p. 48.

6.   The bulk of the statistical information given
in this section has been obtained from the records,
published and unpublished, of the IFCT. Additional
information was obtained from interviews and other
sources, some of which are indicated.

7.   For a convenient summary of the advantages
of life insurance for capital markets and economic
growth in general, see: United Nations, ECAFE,

Economic Bulletin for Asia and the Far East, XIII,
3 (Bangkok, 1962); and Organization for Economic
Cooperation and Development, Capital Markets Study,
General Report (Paris, 1967).

8. Very little is available in readily access-
ible form about life insurance in Thailand. The very
few printed works on Thai financial structure contain
only very brief paragraphs on life insurance. The
annual report of the Insurance Commissioner of Thailand includes some statistical information which is
several years out of date, not always reliable, and
which requires considerable processing before it can
be used at all. There is rumored to exist an industry
study of life insurance published around 1964 or
1965; but if such a study does indeed exist, it remains
extremely well hidden. Authoritative representatives
of life insurance companies deny its existence. There
is a 1959 report on life insurance in Thailand prepared for the Technical Assistance Program of the
United Nations which deals mainly with the administrative and managerial practices of Thai life insurance
companies. The report remains on the restricted list.
The data and information given in the text have been
culled from a variety of sources, written and verbal,
but the bulk of the data was derived from a study of
life insurance business in Thailand conducted by
Richard Sandler in 1967 under the supervision of the
writer. This study included an extensive series of
interviews with most of the life insurance companies
operating in Thailand and an analysis of the responses
to a comprehensive questionnaire submitted as part of
these series of interviews. For a variety of reasons
Mr. Sandler's study cannot be said to be fully comprehensive, nor are the data entirely reliable, but its
findings do represent the best available intelligence
on the subject.

9. See United Nations, ECAFE, Economic Bulletin
for Asia and the Far East, op. cit., pp. 5-10.

10. A developed social security system could be
considered to be competitive with contractual saving,
although a recent comprehensive study concluded that
this need not be so; see Organization for Economic

Cooperation and Development, Capital Market Study,
General Report, op. cit., p. 13.

11.   Data were obtained by Richard Sandler and
Sommode Phasee. They derive from a series of interviews, from a mail questionnaire covering over 200
establishments, and from other sources. For a variety of reasons, the results are incomplete and subject to the usual caution about reliability.

12.   "Social Insurance Planning in Thailand,"
unpublished report prepared by the Ministry of the
Interior, Social Security Division (Bangkok, 1965).

13.   Franco Reviglio, "Social Security: A Means
of Savings Mobilization for Economic Development,"
IMF Staff Papers (July, 1967), pp. 353-355.

14.   For a recent discussion of the role of
stock exchange in the process of capital formation
see David William, "The Growth of Capital and Securities Markets," Finance and Development (Washington:
International Monetary Fund, September, 1966).

CHAPTER **9** FINANCIAL MARKETS
IN THAILAND--
CONCLUSIONS AND
RECOMMENDATIONS

SUMMARY OF EMPIRICAL FINDINGS

The financial structure of Thailand is basically
a by-product of the country's economic history. It
was formed, and is still being formed, by the forces
which have shaped the Thai economy. Unlike a number
of other pre-industrial countries where more or less
deliberate attempts were made to structure financial
institutions so as to influence the path of development,[1] the Thai financial nexus, for the most part,
mirrors the economic past. Even the establishment
of the central bank came about not as a fully con-
scious effort to coordinate and manage the financial
affairs of the Kingdom but as a response to the political and financial pressures of Japanese occupation authorities.

The organized money market in Thailand is dominated by the commercial banks. The role of foreign
banks in Thailand has steadily diminished with the
development of the country's economy, and at present
the bulk of deposits and earning assets is in the
hands of the 16 locally chartered banks. Very few,
if any, of these banks originated as institutions of
credit. In most cases they were started as appen-
dages to export operations, remittance shops, or other
businesses. Even now, most Thai bankers are heavily
involved in a number of busines ventures, and the
banking business may not necessarily be the most important.

Every Thai commercial bank has at least one field marshal, general, or member of the royal family on its board, and the political muscle of the Thai banks is an important aspect of the financial nexus.

Partly for this reason and partly because of its traditions, the central bank's control over commercial banks is exercised primarily through moral suasion. The Bank of Thailand is loathe to use the control instruments which, in law, it has possessed since the passage of the Commercial Banking Act of 1962.

The commercial banks, though they account for over 50 per cent of all financial liabilities recorded as being in the hands of the public, still finance only about one-fifth of private capital formation. In the Thai second six-year plan, less than 10 per cent of all private-sector finance was expected to come from the financial institutions. Clearly, much of the financing of business enterprise, not to mention rural households and consumption needs, comes from outside the organized financial nexus.

The commercial banks do not appear to push their lending operations to the full limits of their capacity, actual or potential, to obtain additional funds. It would appear that this reluctance to maximize long-run banking profits is due in part to the oligopolistic position of these banks, in part to their unwillingness to abandon the lucrative and well-trodden path of trade accommodation, and in part, too, to the lack of experience and personnel to venture into untried and risky areas of term credit and manufacturer's credit.

The central bank, the Bank of Thailand, has an excellent record of maintaining price stability in a quite rapidly growing economy, but it has only recently recognized its responsibility for providing, or at least guiding, developmental finance, particularly in offering certain lines of rediscounting. Its debt management policies, in particular, have helped the commercial banks to maintain a degree of

underutilization of capacity in the face of an allegedly high level of demand for funds. By enabling
the commercial banks to hold a large fraction of their
reserves in the form of high-interest-yielding, tax-
free bonds, the central bank countervailed any tendency which may have developed among the commercial
banks to compete by offering lower terms for accommodation or by entering new lines of activity.

The relatively dense network of commercial bank
branches in Thailand is a potentially valuable developmental resource, but it is used, to a large extent, as a device for transferring savings from the
countryside to the Bangkok headquarters. These savings, however, are not utilized to the full; and to
the extent that they are utilized, they are not directed into those channels which appear to have high
developmental priority.

There appears to be some confusion in official
circles as to whether debt management should be employed primarily as a budgetary instrument or whether
it should be designed as a device to create a bill
and intermediate credit market. The Treasury accum-
ulates cash balances at the same time it issues bonds
and bills. Often the size of these balances is close
to the amounts borrowed annually. There is no attempt, as yet, to tailor government issues to the
needs of various markets, and up to 1969 there was
only one type of bond issued by the Treasury, thus
making it necessary to attach to the entire issue
terms which would make it acceptable only to the marginal, most reluctant buyer. The market for bills
is also rather limited in terms of variety of offerings, and there seems to be a regression in the former tendency to create a secondary market in tap
bills.

The capital market is both less efficient and
less sophisticated than the money market. Its institutions suffer from an inability to obtain lendable
funds from households, primarily because of their
commitment to lend funds below the market rate. The
provision of long-term finance is further limited by
the absence of noncontractual capital and by lack of

flexibility as to the terms at which capital is made available.

There are very few public institutions within the Thai capital market. There is the Government Savings Bank which channels household savings into the government budget, but the annual flow of these savings is overshadowed by those accruing to the commercial banks in the form of fixed deposits. The Bank for Agriculture and Agricultural Cooperatives was set up only in 1967 and has yet to make its mark, but its predecessor, the Bank for Cooperatives, played but a very minor role in financing rural households.

The Industrial Finance Corporation of Thailand did not account for more than a fraction of 1 per cent of total private capital formation in 1967. The Small Loan Industry Fund and the Housing and Welfare Bank are either very recent or very insignificant. Life insurance companies do not, as yet, do long-term financing, and the various pension and provident funds also have not entered those markets. The Bangkok Stock Exchange was set up in 1963 by a group of foreign entrepreneurs, and it is neither recognized nor regulated by the Thai authorities. It operates in a narrow and thin market, and perhaps only one or two listed corporations are traded daily.

The unorganized urban financial market has many layers and encompasses a great variety of borrowers and lenders (many of whom are also active in the organized markets), and it accounts for at least one-fifth of the annual capital requirements of Thai business enterprises. This proportion is even higher when urban centers other than the metropolitan areas of Bangkok and Thonburi are considered and when initial capital needs are included. The unorganized markets, even more than the organized, tend to favor the trader and the speculator over the manufacturer. The volume of business done in the unorganized markets is heavily weighted with trade credit, which is of little use to the nascent manufacturing enterprise. Most of the finance provided by the unorganized markets (and this is true also for the organized markets) is on a contractual basis, which, with its

heavy and often immediate interest obligations inter-
dicts many a potential manufacturing enterprise.
There is a striking paucity of equity finance.

Less than 5 per cent of total annual financing
of agricultural households is handled by the organized
financial institutions in the countryside. Much of
the financing provided outside these institutions,
at best, maintains the value of the assets of the
farmer, but it is not concerned with increasing the
value of his assets and, hence, does not expand the
income and saving of the rural householder.

Contrary to the views held by some, unorganized
financial markets in a country such as Thailand play
an important role in urban as well as rural areas.
They are still relatively more important in the countryside, however, and they remain the predominant
vehicle of finance for rural households.

In Thailand, over 80 per cent of the initial
capital requirements of business enterprise come from
an entrepreneur's "own" resources, and less than 7
per cent is obtained in the organized financial market. Even for ongoing, annual requirements, more
than 20 per cent of capital requirements come from
outside the institutions of the organized markets.
(As was emphasized in Chapter 7, these percentages
are illustrative; and though they reflect the orders
of magnitude, they cannot claim to be exact figures.)
Savers prefer to transfer resources to investors outside the purview of official scrutiny and control because of the opportunity to exact higher interest
rates than those obtainable from the organized financial intermediaries and because of a desire to keep
the extent and the source of savings hidden from
authorities. Despite the higher cost of borrowing,
investors find the unorganized markets attractive for
a number of reasons. These include speed and simpli-
city of transactions, more flexible collateral requirements, and a strong predilection for keeping loan
dealings confidential.

There is some evidence to suggest that there exists a penumbra of the commercial banking system in

Thailand which diverts funds available to the organized markets into the unorganized markets and which, at the same time, makes the cost of borrowing higher. The sample survey of urban credit in the unorganized markets also suggests that much of the moneylending activity is performed under the guise of "friends and relatives."

The level of interest rates in both the organized and the unorganized markets is high (especially in the latter), and the rates are almost certainly higher than they would be if either of these markets were truly competitive. This high level of interest rates--about 25 per cent is the modal annual rate payable by a legitimate entrepreneur of moderate size--militates against long-range undertakings and in favor of quick pay-off schemes.

Other terms and conditions of loans (other than the rate of interest) tend to inhibit the financing of manufacturing enterprises, particularly those enterprises which are locally owned and have only modest initial resources. The emphasis is on land as a collateral and on the status of the borrower rather than on the prospects of the enterprise. These practices, together with various other legal impediments, all tend to favor the trader and the speculator and discriminate against the small or moderate-size would-be manufacturer.

The rotating credit society is known throughout the underdeveloped world as a consumption-serving, rural-based, face-to-face grouping, but in Thailand it is primarily an urban institution of the unorganized market which, surprisingly, finances business as well. In fact, some 5 per cent of the annual financial needs of Thai business are financed from this source, and approximately 30 per cent of all business undertakings, concentrated among small and medium-size firms, resort to this medium of finance.

These empirical findings point out the aspects of the structure of the Thai financial markets which are of crucial importance to the country's developmental strategy. There is some evidence that

agricultural saving has been in excess of investment
in the agricultural sector, implying a net transfer
of resources out of agriculture.[2] An important component of the intersectoral financial transfer has
been an increase in the profits of the trading community which is concentrated in the metropolitan
Bangkok-Thonburi area. During the period 1961-1965,
more than one-third of the increase in agricultural
output was exported, and agriculture contributed
three-fourths of the country's total export earning
in that period. During this same period the industrial sector's average propensity to save rose from
0.133 in 1961, to 0.147 in 1962, to 0.164 in 1963,
to 0.184 in 1964. A significant factor in this rising
saving propensity, it appears, is a high marginal
savings ratio among traders engaged in exporting agricultural commodities. There has been a positive correlation between savings and exports, and the key to
this relationship may lie in the export traders' high
marginal savings ratio. In open, dualistic economies,
and ones where there is a considerable degree of
income inequality, an increase in agricultural output
leads to a sharp increase in disposable incomes of
port traders as larger volumes of exports move through
the ports. Even though these traders save an increasing proportion of their income increments, the investment of these savings takes place largely outside the
agricultural sector.[3] But the trading community in
Thailand is composed of exporters and importers, many
of whom are both. It is a tightly knit community
which is simultaneously deeply involved in banking,
insurance, warehousing, and other activities. Accumulated savings are translated into investment in trade,
service enterprise, and import-substitution manufacturing much more readily than into agriculture or
export-promotion industry.

DEVELOPMENT STRATEGY AND THE STRUCTURE
OF FINANCIAL MARKETS

In Chapter 1, a three-pronged conceptual framework was presented which is capable of yielding broad
guidelines as to the ways and means of structuring
the financial market. The three prongs are those of

economic efficiency, developmental priorities, and
extension of the scope of the organized markets. The
broad guidelines for Thailand were three:

1. The cost of long-term capital should be
lowered and spread between the reward to the saver
and the cost to investor narrowed.[4]

2. The flow of capital to the small and medium-
sized manufacturer should be increased, particularly
when his output has a world market. Such a flow
should be increased both absolutely and relatively
to the volume of financing of trade, construction,
and speculative activities.

3. Competitive institutions and instruments
should be set up in the organized markets which are
able to attract lenders and entrepreneurs hitherto
confined to the unorganized markets.

These three broad guidelines provide a convenient device for grouping the suggestions and recommendations for modification of the Thai financial
markets. Most of these suggestions and recommendations were made in the preceding chapters, and most
of them are minor in nature in keeping with the
"piecemeal engineering" approach indicated at the
close of Chapter 1. Inasmuch as the guidelines themselves are interrelated, there can be no clean-cut
distinction between a specific suggestion designed,
say, to improve the economic efficiency of the particular financial market and one designed to increase
the scope of the organized markets. The allocation
of a given suggestion to one of the three categories
implied by these broad guidelines will thus be largely arbitrary and determined by a judgment as to the
direction of the primary impact of such suggestion,
when implemented.

SUGGESTIONS FOR INCREASING THE EFFICIENCY
OF THE FINANCIAL MARKETS

The suggestions made in Chapter 3 for bringing
branches of the commercial banks into agricultural

credit are designed primarily to expand the scope of
the organized market in financing rural households.
But they also contain some recommendations which are
meant to enhance the efficiency of these markets.
By posting a fixed spread between the rediscounting
rate and the maximum lending rate, the commercial
banks could increase their profits by lowering their
operational costs, by stretching their overhead over
a larger number of loans, and, finally, by better
control over the purpose of loans so as to minimize
losses from nonrepayment.

The efficiency of commercial bank operations
could be increased by greater emphasis on the purpose
of the loan rather than on the status of the borrower.
A banking self-insurance scheme would attract more
depositors. It is also possible that commercial bank
lending could benefit from simplifications of mortgage registrations and, particularly, from some device which would result in splitting deeds to large
parcels of property into components adequate to cover
a single loan. Some consideration could also be
given to the extension of nonlending functions of banks
by allowing them, say, to administer trusts and estates
on a comingled basis. (Some of these trusts are not
legal in Thailand.)

The central bank could also improve the effi
ciency of the banking system by streamlining its rediscounting procedures and allowing the commercial
banks to assume exclusive responsibility for credit
risks. It would also seem desirable to abolish the
present quota system which determines the ceiling on
the amount of rediscounting done by a single bank.

But perhaps the greatest single contribution to
efficiency of the financial markets which could be
made by the central bank lies in the area of debt
management. By tailoring the various types of securities to the various segments of the market, the
Bank of Thailand could not only reduce interest costs
to the Treasury but also contribute to the reduction
of the interest costs charged by the commercial banks.
To improve the efficiency of the institutions of the
capital market, a series of suggestions were made in

Chapter 8. These included the abandonment by the
Government Savings Bank of marginal functions such
as selling life insurance, the assumption by the
IFCT of exchange risk and the simplification of its
procedure for importing machinery, as well as the
possibility of transferring a portion of idle Official
Provident Fund balances to the IFCT.

SUGGESTIONS FOR CHANNELING RESOURCES
INTO DEVELOPMENT PRIORITIES

The developmental priorities range from channeling resources away from trade and speculative construction toward the provision of medium and long-
term capital to industry, in general, and export-
oriented manufacturing in particular. The primary
responsibility for channeling funds into developmental priorities rests with the Bank of Thailand.
Specific suggestions include allowing commercial banks
a greater spread on paper rediscounted for small manufacturers, so as to provide these banks with greater
incentive to engage in this type of business. The
Bank of Thailand could also attempt to discourage
certain financial activities by removing the prefer-
ential treatment of exports and other trading transactions implicit in Section 10 of the 1962 Banking
Act and by helping to bring about a change in the
tax system in the direction of taxing speculative
property transfers. On the positive side, the Bank
of Thailand should insure the speedy implementation
of pending legislation which would allow lending
against chattel mortgage, thus making it easier to
lend against the security of machinery and equipment.
By periodic review of the licenses of branches of
commercial banks, the Bank of Thailand could exert
some influence on these banks to expand productive
activities in the areas they serve. Similarly, the
Bank of Thailand should be somewhat less rigid in
allowing agencies to be set up in the provinces whenever the record of the mother institution seems to
justify it.

In reforming its government debt management policy to orient the sale of government securities

toward different buyers, the Bank of Thailand could
give consideration to the issuance of a special bond,
of intermediate maturity, which could be made convertible into equity shares in either state enterprises or private undertakings.

In addition to the suggestion pertaining to the
Bank of Thailand, the commercial banks themselves,
through cooperation in the provinces with the IFCT,
perhaps on a share-the-risks arrangement, could contribute to a greater flow of finance toward developmental ends.

SUGGESTIONS FOR EXPANDING THE SCOPE OF ORGANIZED FINANCIAL MARKETS

Perhaps the most potentially productive of the
suggestions for expanding the scope of organized financial markets, and certainly the most detailed,
is one which aims at bringing the commercial banks
into the field of agricultural credit. In order to
induce the commercial banks to enter the difficult
business of granting supervised, productive loans to
groups of farmers, a two-pronged approach is adopted
of extending simultaneously a carrot and a stick.
The stick should take the form of an increase in the
legal reserve which the banks are required to hold
against their deposit liabilities, with the option
that the extra required reserves can be held in the
form of agricultural paper. The carrot should be a
generous rediscounting of this paper by the central
bank. Higher and growing income of farmers is the
best way to insure, in time, a market for manufacturing enterprise and enable that enterprise to grow in
size. Thailand's network of bank branches suggests
reliance on these rather than on artifically created
and sustained public institutions in the rural credit
field, whose record to date is rather poor. The public institutions should concentrate, rather, on the
provision of longer-term credit to the farmers and
on the costly and time consuming training of credit
supervisors.

The commercial banks should also be encouraged
to begin to engage in term lending, thus attracting

some of the would-be borrowers who are forced to seek funds elsewhere.

In the preceding chapters it is suggested, in several places, that the interest rate charged by a number of institutions is below the market rate, thus effectively depriving these institutions of access to household savings and making them dependent on budgetary and quasi-budgetary appropriations. This is true for the Bank for Agriculture and Agricultural Cooperatives, for the IFCT, and for LOSID.

By bringing the maximum lending rate at least to the level of the minimum rate charged by the commercial banks on similar types of accommodation, these institutions could hope to divert some funds from the unorganized market.

Other suggestions designed to encroach, directly and indirectly, on the unorganized markets are, briefly, greater emphasis on lottery bonds in Government Savings Bank operations, certain tax concessions for contribution to life insurance and provident funds, and a broad regulation of stock exchange operations.

DEVELOPMENT OF AN EQUITY MARKET

The preceding suggestions for improvement of the financial markets in Thailand are, with one or two exceptions, limited in scope and in probable impact. In particular, they do not address themselves to one glaring deficiency in the financial structure of Thailand, i.e., the almost complete lack of equity finance (other than that associated with the garnering of entrepreneurial "own" capital resources) in both the unorganized and the organized markets. Not only is equity financing likely to reduce the spread between the costs to the investor and the rewards to the saver; it is also quite possible that the predilection for enterprises with a short pay-off period is, in large measure, due to the inability of legitimate bueinsesmen to secure venture capital within the confines of the organized portion of the Thai financial markets.

The provision of funds to nascent enterprise
on the basis of participation in future profits, devoid of heavy annual contractual burden and with a
grace period equivalent to the period in which the
enterprise establishes itself and begins to make dis-
tributable earnings, would thus be consonant with
all three guidelines for improving the developmental
performance of financial markets in Thailand. But the
development of a market in equities goes beyond the
piecemeal reforms of financial institutions. Both
on the supply and on the demand side of such a market,
the developmental planner must contend with deeply
encrusted attitudes, beliefs, and prejudices which
are not likely to be changed overnight by changes in
legislations or administrative procedures. It would
seem that what is called for is a truly national effort, combining the resources of the private sector
and of the official agencies and mobilizing the skills,
talents, and opportunities right across the entire
spectrum of society.

Ideally, one would be tempted to suggest the
formation of an institution of the private sector,
but with official backing, which combines the functions
of a national unit trust and a development corporation. Such an institution would act on both sides of
the market for lendable funds. It would issue its
own securities (units) to the savers and it would
provide the proceeds to the investors. The securities offered to the savers would be redeemable at par,
either in perpetuity or for a stated number of years,
and would carry a rate of return which would vary according to the return realized by the enterprises held
in the portfolio of such a hybrid institution.[5] The
proceeds from the sale of the units would be used to
provide equity capital to both existing and nascent
enterprise, including, in Thailand, hopefully, also
the shares of state enterprises which the government
would make available.

An important part of the job of this institution
would be to actively seek out and promote the formation of manufacturing enterprise, using the lure of
provision of venture capital with a modicum of control
and supervision. Such a hybrid combining, say, the

roles of the Pakistini Unit Trust with that of the
Mexican Nacional Financiera appears quite suited to
the Thai setting, whether under the umbrella of the
Industrial Finance Corporation (already empowered
to engage in equity financing) or under some other
aegis.[6]

But, whatever the merits of such proposal, it is
not likely to be adopted. One of the principal reasons why it would not find favor with the authorities
is that it would not receive the necessary support
of some of the most powerful commercial banks who
prefer to exploit the opportunities in the capital
markets by themselves rather than work in tandem with
the smaller, poorer banks who, initially at least,
are not in a position to contribute either much capital or much expertise to a national enterprise of
the kind suggested in the preceding paragraphs. As
was mentioned at the end of Chapter 8, during 1969
a number of U.S. giant banks became intrigued by the
potentialities in Thailand. The joint ventures which
these banks set up in cooperation with the leading
Thai banks have as one avowed purpose the propagation
of equity financing. It is to early to judge whether
these joint ventures are as expression of a genuine
interest in equity portfolio investment or whether
they are, for the foreign participants, a means of
securing a useful foothold in a country where a commercial banking charter is both difficult to obtain
and quite valuable.

In any event, whatever the institutional framework which seeks to develop the supply of and the
demand for equity securities, it will have to be
backstopped by a broad range of reforms vigorously
pursued by the government. Even then the results
will be slow in coming and often disappointing.
Nevertheless, such reforms have to be formulated and
implemented.

On the supply side, the most important task is
to encourage the formation and propagation of public
corporations. Here, certain reforms of the tax system
may be helpful, particularly those provisions of the
tax code which discriminate in favor of bank deposits.

Thus, for example, dividends are taxable to the re-
cipients but interest on deposits is not. But perhaps more important than tax concessions would be
a throughgoing revision of the Companies Law and a
series of enactments which would have the effect of
increasing the supply of share offerings to the public. Most of the commercial banks, promoted companies (i.e., those which receive special tax and
other benefits upon approval from the Board of Investments), foreign concerns, joint ventures, and other
enterprises could be required to sell a portion of
their stock to the public at large.

On the demand side, a large-scale educational
effort would have to be supplemented by clear-cut
regulations designed to protect the small investor,
the minority stockholder, and the unwary. This implies a reform of the accounting practices, of reporting procedures, and of requirements for disclosure.
Whether by legislation or by moral suasion, life insurance companies, provident funds, the IFCT, and
other institutions will have to be induced to hold
increasing amounts of stocks.

Most importantly, some means must be found to
convince the stock issuers and stock purchasers that
the function of the capital market is to provide finance for long-lived assets designed to increase the
productive capacity of the enterprise over time.
Stock issues must not be allowed to procure working
capital, with dividends competing with high cost of
such capital in the money market. The Bank of Thailand or some other regulatory agency must assume responsibility for the health and the well-being of the
capital market in the Kingdom.

FINANCIAL STRUCTURE AND ECONOMIC GROWTH

The suggestions for modifying and reforming the
Thai financial structure have ranged from the detailed
and elaborate to those merely implied. They include
some rather pedestrian and practical suggestions as
well as some which may be considered rather vision-
ary. Some of these suggestions appear to be quite

feasible of prompt implementation, others may wait
for a long time, if not forever, before they see the
light of day.

The enactment of any specific suggestion depends
on many considerations of which an outside observer
is only dimly aware. It would therefore be superfluous to indicate which of the several proposals is
the most "important" or the least "costly" or the
most "productive." Some of the specific suggestions
for the improvement of the financial markets would
be of little avail in the absence of other reforms
in other spheres. Others would take a long time to
bear fruit, and yet others may be simple in principle
but in practice strenuously opposed.

But if the suggestions made are meant to be tentative, and if they are not presented in the context
of a rigorous cost-benefit analysis, what is their
significance for development planning? In part, the
answer to this question was given in Chapter 1. It
was argued there that the very success of the Thai
economy to date, together with the uncertainty regarding the optimal growth path of the economy in
the future, calls for a strategy of piecemeal social
engineering applied to the reform of its financial
markets. In addition, however, there are reasons
to believe that even a moderate degree of improvement
in financial institutions in Thailand may play a
significant role in helping that country to maintain
its growth rate.

In developing their criteria for evaluating
economic development potential, Adelman and Morris
have concluded that Thailand's highest probability
is in becoming a member of an "intermediate" group
rather than a "high potential" group, even though
the Kingdom was initially assigned a place in the
"high prospect" group.[7]

The preliminary classification of 73 underdeveloped non-Communist countries was made on the basis
of past performance. The top group, which included
Thailand, was composed of 16 countries showing, between 1950-1951 and 1963-1964, an average rate of

growth of per capita GNP of at least 2 per cent and which, in addition, ranked fairly high with respect to five of seven key indicators.[8]

Following the preliminary classification, the 73 countries were subjected to a discriminant analysis where the inputs included 22 indicators in addition to the initial seven. It was as a result of this extended analysis that Thailand was given a lower growth prognosis.

As was indicated in Chapter 1, a single discriminant function accounted for 97 per cent of the discriminable variance between the three groups, to wit:

D_1 = .71 F + 26K + .52M + .37L, where F stands for degree of improvement in financial institutions, K for degree of improvement in physical overhead capital, M for the degree of modernization of outlook, and L for the extent of leadership commitment to economic development.[9]

Without going into details of statistical analysis, the implication of the downgrading of Thailand development potential is that its ranking with respect to one or more of the four key variables has been low enough to affect its over-all standing, or, more precisely, the probability of its remaining in the high potential group.

As a matter of fact, with respect to the four variables which composed the D_1 function, Thailand was classified as follows, A+ being the largest possible classification and C- the lowest:

K	-	A-
F	-	A-
L	-	B
M	-	C

The variables K and F have been based on economic indicators, both statistical and judgmental, while variables L and M derive from political and social indicators.[10]   (See Table 9.1.)

TABLE 9.1

Level and Improvement of Effectiveness of Financial Institutions,
Selected Indices, Selected Countries, 1960 and 1966a

| | Level of Effectiveness | | | | Improvement of Effectiveness 1966-1960 | |
| | GFCF/GDP % | | M+QM/GDP % | | DD + TD/GDP % | 1966 RCPS / 1960 RCPS % |
Country	1960	1966	1960	1966		
Ceylon	15.0	13.7	29.4	33.6	2	1.45
Japan	31.2	31.4	87.7	83.9	30.6	2.50
Korea	11.2	20.2	11.6	15.4	5.7	1.98
Malaysia	12.3	17.3	33.7	35.1	8.1	2.55
Philippines	9.9	18.5	21.7	26.0	5.2	2.11
Taiwan	20.1	22.3	17.3	33.1	16.8	4.12
Thailand	14.9	22.2	22.7	30.8	8.9	2.25
Vietnama	7.9	8.6	21.8	36.0	10.5	2.96

aFor Vietnam, figures are for 1965, rather than for 1966.

GFCF – Gross Fixed Capital Formation   QM – Quasi-money
GDP – Gross Domestic Product   DD – Demand deposit
M   – Money   TD – Time deposit
RCPS – Claims on the Private Sector Deflated by Cost of Living Index.

Source: Calculated from data in International Monetary Fund, International Financial
Statistics (Washington: Statistics Division, IMF: June 1967, March 1968),
and Supplement to 1967-68, International Financial Statistics.

At first it would seem that the surest way to improve the prognosis of Thailand with respect to its development potential would be to improve its ranking in the L, and especially K, indicators. This may indeed be true. But there are several consider- ations which point to F as the variable, whose up- grading may be even more rewarding.

In the first place, the importance of F in the discriminant function D_1 is significantly greater than M or L.   This means that a slight improvement in F may have the same effect on the over-all prob- abilities as would a more substantial improvement in M or L.   In the second place, and perhaps more im- portantly, a slight amelioration in the rating of F (from A- to A+) appears to be easier to effect than a more substantial improvement in M and/or L, both of which depend on political and social attitudes and change rather slowly over time. Finally, some of the suggestions for improving the structure of the Thai financial markets (F) given on the preceding pages are certain to improve L and eventually to af- fect even M in the upward direction.[11]

The sense of the preceding argument is that to the extent that some of the suggested modifications of the Thai financial markets are put into practice, particularly those that improve the performance of the financial institutions in the provision of fi- nance to agriculture and industry, the likelihood of the Kingdom maintaining its high rate of growth will be enhanced.[12]

In terms of the conceptual framework developed in Chapter 1, without a reform of its financial struc- ture Thailand runs the danger of slowing down in its growth rate in the years to come. By reforming its financial markets along the lines indicated, it im- proves considerably its chances of becoming a member of the "high potential" group of developing nations.

NOTES

1. See, for example, Robert L. Bennett, The Financial Sector and Economic Development--The Mexican Case (Baltimore: The Johns Hopkins Press, 1965), especially p. 138.

2. See Alek A. Rozental, "A Note of the Sources and Uses of Funds in Thai Agriculture," Economic Development and Cultural Change (April, 1970).

3. "All these suggested relationships would not seem unreasonable in the Thai circumstances where an export boom can be expected to be associated with a shift of income distribution toward the trading community, leading to an investible surplus there which then, through the well-established channels of the so-called unorganized capital market, is made available to entrepreneurs seeking funds": International Bank for Reconstruction and Development, The Economic Situation in Thailand (Washington, D.C., April, 1966), p. 5. (Mimeo.)

4. The spread was taken as an index of efficiency. Ideally, the efficiency of a financial market (defined as its ability to provide an optimum investment mix; i.e., a capital-output ratio which is the best that can be obtained, given the "state of arts") will be maximized when the spread is zero.

The argument may be stated symbolically. If S measures the flow of lendable funds and $S = \phi (R_I R_S F)$ where R_I measures the "cost" to the investor, R_S measures the "rewards" to the saver, and F denotes the financial structure, the function of F is to maximize the capital-output ratio "a," then:

$$\frac{\partial a}{\partial F} = \phi ' (R_I R_S F)$$

$$\frac{\partial a}{\partial F} = 0 \quad \text{and} \quad \frac{\partial^2 a}{\partial F^2} < 0$$

This implies $\dfrac{\partial R_S}{\partial F} > 0$ and $\dfrac{\partial R_I}{\partial F} < 0$

and $R_I - R_S = \min.$

5. The experience of TIF (see Chapter 8) suggests that without substantial government support and propaganda, without redemption features and other supporting legislation, the market for units of a private mutual fund will be a limited one. On the other hand, the experience of the Government Savings Bank with its lottery bonds shows that claims with a low contractual return but high potential pay-off are very attractive.

6. The Nacional Financiera was established in 1933 with "the fundamental objective of mobilization and reintegration into the economy of real property expropriated by the government and for the purpose of aiding the existing credit institutions in the channeling of investment capital into creation and expansion of industrial enterprises and to develop a national market in stocks and bonds": see Marcello Aquinal y Mayo, "The Nacional Financiera, S.A. of Mexico" (circa 1955). (Mimeo.) In mid-1961 Nacional Financiera owned stock in 60 industrial enterprises, and in 13 of these it was the majority stockholder. At the end of 1959, its financing accounted for some 8 per cent of Mexico's GNP; see Robert L. Bennett, op. cit., pp. 54-55. The Nacional Financiera provides equity finance to enterprises but does not collect household savings in form of equity units, i.e., its "participation certificates" promise a fixed return. The Pakistani Unit Trust, on the other hand, issues units to the public with variable return but does not itself invest the proceeds in new undertakings, nor does it seem to promote new ventures but acts primarily as an official support to the stock market. In 1966, however, an Investment Corporation of Pakistan was established which is to act as a development corporation: Information obtained from official pamphlets published by the Unit Trust and the ICP. It should be stressed that both the Nacional Financiera and Pakistani Unit Trust are government-sponsored institutions.

7. Irma Adelman and Cynthia Taft Morris, "Performance Criteria for Evaluating Economic Development Potential: An Operational Approach, Quarterly Journal of Economics (May, 1968), p. 275;

Thailand's probability of membership in the high potential group was found to be .21, in the intermediate group .73, and in the low-potential group .05.

8. The seven indicators were (1) change in degree of industrialization since 1950; (2-6) improvement since 1950 in agricultural productivity, physical overhead capital, effectiveness of financial institutions, the tax system, the rate of investment; and (7) rate of additions to the stock of human resources: ibid., p. 261.

9. This function was given in a slightly different (normalized) form in Chapter 1 so as to bring out the relative importance of the four variables, i.e., $D_1 = 127F + 65K + 108M + 72L$.

10. A description of the 41 indicators, which include the 29 indicators referred to previously, is given in Irma Adelman and Cynthia Morris, Society, Politics and Economic Development (Baltimore: Johns Hopkins Press, 1967). This description was supplemented by information obtained from personal communications with the authors. A rating of B with respect to "extent of leadership commitment to economic development" was given to countries in which "some government leaders evidenced a definite commitment to economic development (during the period 1957-1962) as indicated by the practice of some form of national development planning. However, it was typical of the countries in this category that the activity of the agencies involved in central guidance of the economy were poorly coordinated and that government attempts to alter institutional arrangements unfavorable to economic growth were infrequent or poorly sustained": ibid., p. 80. With respect to "degree of modification of outlook," a rating of C was given to "countries in which the outlook of the educated urban sector was partially but not significantly modernized and on which programs of modernization, if they existed, gained relatively little support among either the urban or the rural population": ibid., p. 56. With respect to K--"degree of improvement in physical overhead capital"--countries classified

A- are countries that have shown either an average annual rate of increase of 10 per cent or more in miles of paved roads or an average annual rate of increase of more than 7 per cent in miles of paved roads, plus an average annual rate of increase of net ton-kilometers carried by rail of more than 7 per cent: ibid., p. 112.

The final category is "countries that have demonstrated a marked improvement in the effectiveness of their financial institutions as indicated . . . by either an increase of more than five percentage points in the ratio of time and demand deposits to GNP or more than a fivefold increase in the real value of private domestic liabilities to the banking system": ibid., p. 122. Thailand received a ranking of A- in this category but a lower ranking, B, with respect to "level of effectiveness of financial institutions."

For an up-to-date reconstruction of the elements of both level and "degree of improvement" of F on a comparative basis, see Table 9.1, and note the positions of Japan and Taiwan vis-à-vis Thailand.

11. Some of the arguments for allocating F rather than M or L apply equally well to K, except that F is relatively more of a determinant than K.

12. Provision of medium-term and long-term capital to agriculture and industry was deemed by Adelman and Morris to be an important judgmental indicator of the level of performance of financial institutions in the 73 countries studied.

ABOUT THE AUTHOR

Alek A. Rozental has had several years of field experience in the developing countries of Asia. After five years as an economic adviser with the U.S. missions in Laos, Vietnam, and India, he directed a research team in Thailand on behalf of the Center for Development Planning of the National Planning Association. He is currently economic and financial consultant to the Republic of China's Council of International Economic Cooperation and Development, under the auspices of the United Nations Development Programme.

Dr. Rozental has taught at the Universities of Minnesota and Saint Louis and has lectured at several universities in the Far East. He has contributed numerous articles to leading professional journals and is the co-author and editor of <u>Studies in Vietnamese Economy</u> (Saigon, 1964).

Dr. Rozental did undergraduate work in economics at the University of London and received a Ph.D. in economics from the University of Minnesota. In 1957-1958 he was the recipient of a Ford Foundation postdoctoral fellowship in International Relations.

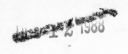